THE RISE OF THE KU KLUX KLAN

THE RISE OF THE KU KLUX KLAN

Right-Wing Movements and National Politics

Rory McVeigh

Social Movements, Protest, and Contention
Volume 32

University of Minnesota Press
Minneapolis • London

Published by the University of Minnesota Press
111 Third Avenue South, Suite 290
Minneapolis, MN 55401-2520
http://www.upress.umn.edu

Library of Congress Cataloging-in-Publication Data

McVeigh, Rory.
The rise of the Ku Klux Klan : right-wing movements and national politics / Rory McVeigh.
    p.   cm. — (Social movements, protest, and contention ; v. 32)
Includes bibliographical references and index.
ISBN 978-0-8166-5619-6 (hardcover : alk. paper) —
ISBN 978-0-8166-5620-2 (pbk. : alk. paper)
    1. Ku Klux Klan (1915–)—History—20th century.   2. Right-wing extremists—United States—History—20th century.   3. Social movements—United States—History—20th century.   4. Racism—United States—History—20th century.   5. United States—Race relations—Political aspects—History—20th century.   6. United States—Politics and government—1913–1921.   7. United States—Politics and government—1921–1923.   8. United States—Politics and government—1923–1929.   9. Political culture—United States—History—20th century.   I. Title.
  HS2330.K63M38 2009
  322.4'20973—dc22

2008052973

Contents

1. The Klan as a National Movement   1

2. The Rebirth of a Klan Nation, 1915–1924   19

3. Power Devaluation   32

4. Responding to Economic Change: Redefining Markets
    along Cultural Lines   49

5. National Politics and Mobilizing "100 Percent American" Voters   86

6. Fights over Schools and Booze   112

7. How to Recruit a Klansman   139

8. Klan Activism across the Country   167

9. The Klan's Last Gasp: Campaigning to Keep a Catholic
    out of the White House, 1925–1928   180

Conclusion: Right-Wing Movements, Yesterday and Today   196

Acknowledgments   203

Notes   205

Works Cited   221

Index   231

1

The Klan as a National Movement

The people are disgusted to exasperation with hollow shams. They have lost interest in parties without character, courage or program. Politics must be born again. The people require justice instead of expediency. They scorn administrations controlled by predatory interests.
—*Fiery Cross*, August 17, 1923

On July 4, 1923, thousands of men, women, and children flocked to Malfalfa Park on the outskirts of Kokomo, Indiana, for a day filled with food, games, entertainment, fireworks, and stirring patriotic speeches. No one knows for certain how many people were in attendance that day. Estimates made by various newspapers within the state range from 10,000 people to upward of 200,000. One thing is clear—the crowd was unusually large for a Fourth of July celebration. Those in attendance had fought their way through the worst traffic jam in Kokomo's history.[1] They came from every corner of the state, while many others descended on the small central Indiana city from neighboring states of Ohio, Illinois, Michigan, and Kentucky. Some even ventured from as far away as Atlanta, Georgia. This was no ordinary Fourth of July celebration. The people were assembled to celebrate the nation's independence, but they had other things to celebrate as well. Representatives from each of Indiana's ninety-two counties were on hand to receive official charters from the national headquarters of a fledgling organization that had enjoyed phenomenal growth within the state over the past two years. These were the men and women of the Ku Klux Klan.

Signifying the importance of the occasion, the Klan's national leader, Imperial Wizard Hiram Wesley Evans, was on hand to speak to the assembled

1

Klansmen and Klanswomen. Taking note of the rapid growth of the Indiana Klan, Evans began,

> Pure, progressive, American principles take a great stride forward in Indiana this Independence Day and it is very fitting that the Klans of Indiana should have selected July Fourth for the reception of their official charters and the establishment of their state organization. Having emerged from a provisional status and become fully operative units of the Invisible Empire, the Klans in this great realm will approach the stupendous task which lies before them with even greater enthusiasm and zeal than in the past.[2]

During the celebration, D. C. Stephenson was appointed as the Grand Dragon of Indiana and was also given control of operations in twenty-three states of the Klan's northern realm.[3] This was no small honor for Stephenson because by 1923 the Klan was expanding rapidly throughout the nation and was growing particularly strong in Indiana, Ohio, Pennsylvania, Illinois, and in several other western and midwestern states that were now under his control.

After a brief introduction from the Imperial Wizard, Stephenson also addressed the crowd, communicating his vision of the Klan's role in politics in a lengthy speech titled "Back to the Constitution." Stephenson hailed the wisdom and foresight of the nation's founding fathers and railed against alleged perversions in contemporary politics that threatened to destroy the republic that the founders had created. He characterized the United States as an exceptional nation that was blessed in the eyes of God. America's exceptionalism, according to the newly appointed Grand Dragon, was rooted in an Anglo-Saxon inheritance of pride and patriotism and an "irresistible urge toward self-determination."[4]

The festivities in Kokomo continued on into the evening with a parade down Main Street. Robert Coughlan, a writer who grew up in Kokomo, recalled,

> There were thirty bands; but as usual in Klan parades there was no music, only the sound of drums. They rolled the slow, heavy tempo of the march from the far north end of town to Foster Park, a low meadow bordering Wildcat Creek where the Klan had put up a twenty-five-foot "fiery cross." There were three hundred mounted Klansmen interspersed in companies among the fifty thousand hooded men, women, and children on foot. The marchers moved in good order, and the measured tread of their feet, timed to the rumbling of the drums and accented by the off-beat clatter

of the horses' hoofs, filled the night with an overpowering sound. Many of the marchers carried flaming torches, whose light threw grotesque shadows up and down Main Street.[5]

Understandably, Coughlan viewed the events of the day—the throngs of sheeted and hooded men and women overflowing Malfalfa Park, the solemn procession on Main Street, and the torching of a giant cross—as ominous. As a Catholic in Kokomo, he and his family were in the minority and Klan members during that time period tended to see Catholicism at the root of many societal problems. The Klan of the 1920s claimed to be a "one-hundred percent American" organization and promised to unite white, native-born Protestants in a common cause. Catholicism, Klan leaders claimed, was incompatible with American democracy. In Indiana, and elsewhere, Catholic merchants were frequently subjected to Klan-sponsored boycotts and other forms of harassment.[6] Perhaps surprisingly, the Klan often flourished in towns such as Kokomo where Catholics, the Klansmen's nemeses, were so few in number that they did not pose any serious threat to the established social, economic, or political order within the community.

Indeed, the Klan faced little opposition in Kokomo. Coughlan claimed that "literally" one-half of Kokomo's adult males were members of the Ku Klux Klan. His claim appears to be only slightly exaggerated. Klan documents uncovered in 1925 by a correspondent for the *New York Times* include membership figures for eighty-nine of Indiana's ninety-two counties.[7] According to these documents 3,998 men were members of the Klan in Howard County, of which Kokomo is the county seat. In other words, approximately 28 percent of adult native-born white males in the county were members of the Ku Klux Klan. A chapter of the Women's Ku Klux Klan (WKKK) was also located in Kokomo at the time, but membership figures are unavailable for the women's organization. According to Kathleen Blee, membership for women's chapters rivaled those of the men's organization in many Indiana communities.[8]

The Klan's support in Kokomo certainly extended beyond that provided by its dues-paying members. Klansmen and Klanswomen could operate freely within the community, trusting that most residents in the town were at least sympathetic to the organization and its goals. Coughlan notes, for example, that many Klan members did not even bother to conceal their identities in public. Merchants openly courted Klan patronage, with "TWK" (Trade with a Klansman) signs posted on their establishments.[9] Few county residents were excluded by the way in which the Klan used race, religion, and nativity to construct the boundaries of the organization. Data from the U.S. census indicate that only 2.1 percent of Howard County residents were black and 97.1 percent were native-born. Only 13.6 percent of religious adherents in the county were Catholic.[10] In this favorable context, Klan-endorsed political candidates were swept into local offices in 1924.[11]

Beyond Kokomo

How did the Ku Klux Klan take control of a small Indiana city? To answer that question, it is tempting to zoom in on Kokomo to ascertain what local problems, events, and issues stimulated the organization's growth. However, the lesson to be learned from Kokomo is that a bird's-eye view, rather than a microscopic view, will be the most useful in understanding the growth of the Ku Klux Klan in the early 1920s. Why would an organization promoting the supremacy of native-born, white Protestants be so successful in a community where blacks, immigrants, and Catholics were few in number and posed no realistic threat to the dominate order? Why was the Klan able to generate similar levels of support in hundreds of other cities across the nation, some of which were similar to Kokomo in many respects, while others were dissimilar? Could it be that Klan members were responding to national, rather than exclusively local, concerns?

When D. C. Stephenson addressed the crowd in Kokomo he used the opportunity to discuss national issues. For example, in a lengthy discussion of "currency and credit" the Grand Dragon argued that

> The constitution must be vitalized to compel common economic justice with respect to currency and credit. Otherwise, in another fifty years, this nation will be experiencing all the agonies of class conflict that can end only in economic chaos and political revolution. More and more will the great middle class be wiped out. Already the tendency is dangerously toward an unproductive dividend-clipping aristocracy of wealth, with every billion that it gains through manipulations of money and monopolization of credit adding by inverse ratio to the numbers whose unjust impoverishment becomes a menace to the nation.[12]

Later in the speech, Stephenson discussed the long- and short-term costs of the recent world war, and argued that

> The solvency of the world, the sanctity and security, nay, the very existence of civilization are involved in this problem. If its solution were in the keeping of men like the founders they would outlaw war; they would

permit no secret diplomacy; they would publish to the world the full truth respecting concessions and every related economic cause of war; they would provide in the constitution that this nation should never engage in war, except to repel invasion, unless, through a referendum, the sovereign people themselves had determined the fateful issue.[13]

Notably, in his speech Stephenson refrained from discussing any local threats posed by blacks, Catholics, or immigrants. Perhaps that should be expected, given that he spoke on Independence Day and addressed a large audience. Many people in the crowd were not, themselves, locals. Yet (as will be demonstrated in later chapters), Klan leaders' diagnoses of contemporary national problems should have been warmly received by many individuals who joined the Klan. Scholars who have studied the movement have not fully appreciated the ways in which changes in the structure of American society in the early 1900s contributed to the phenomenal growth of the Ku Klux Klan.

Explaining the extraordinary popularity of the 1920s Klan has challenged historians, sociologists, and other social scientists for many decades. In fact, one sociologist, John Moffat Mecklin, attempted to wrap his hands around the puzzle in a book published in 1924, at a time when the movement was still gaining strength. In his book, *The Ku Klux Klan: A Study of the American Mind,* Mecklin seems at a loss to account for the Klan's appeal. For example, referring to the state of Oregon, he wrote,

> Here is a state composed of eighty-five percent native Americans. It has no race problem. It is predominantly Protestant in faith, the Catholics forming but eight percent of the population. It is not torn by industrial conflict. It is not threatened by radicalism in any form. It has progressive laws, an admirable educational system, less than two-percent illiteracy. Yet this typical American state has been completely overrun and, for a time at least, politically dominated by a secret oath-bound organization preaching religious bigotry and racial animosity and seeking primarily its own political aggrandizement.[14]

In the end, Mecklin characterized the Klan as an example of middle-class hysteria.[15]

Klan leaders seemed to recognize that the growth of their organization baffled many outsiders. In fact, an article in the Klan's national newspaper, the *Imperial Night-Hawk,* sought to explain why the Klan thrived in locations where the movement's enemies (Catholics, immigrants, and blacks) seemed to pose no real threat to the majority group's interests. The Klan writer instructed,

First, it should be remembered that the Klan is a national organization and deals with nation-wide problems, as well as local conditions. . . . Since every community should be vitally interested in the public welfare of the nation as a whole, and each one has special conditions with which the Klan deals, it cannot be truthfully stated of any place that there is no need of an organization that has to do with national problems and seeks to improve national as well as local conditions. Most of our problems are of national scope and directly concern every community in America.[16]

What were these national issues that the Klan promised to address? Did the movement really build its support through its capacity to offer solutions for pressing national-level problems? Of course, it would be unwise to rely upon the Klan's propaganda to gain an objective understanding of the movement's appeal. Klan leaders had few qualms about stretching the facts or, perhaps more accurately, running roughshod over the facts if it served their interests. Doing so helped them both to bring in new members and to line their pockets with money from membership dues and the sale of Klan robes and other paraphernalia. However, close (but skeptical) attention to the Klan leaders' rhetoric—their "framing" of societal problems—may offer important clues about the organization's successes and its failures.

Early scholarly studies of the movement tended to ignore the Klan leaders' own interpretations of their organization and its goals, and instead assumed that the response to the movement from members and supporters represented some sort of collective psychological phenomenon. Recent research on the 1920s Klan has cleared up many misconceptions about the organization and has dramatically improved our understanding of the "Invisible Empire." Kathleen Blee, for example, wrote an outstanding book about the Women's Ku Klux Klan in Indiana, reconstructing the movement through intensive in-depth interviews with surviving members of the organization. Nancy MacLean's fascinating study of a Klan chapter in Athens, Georgia, draws attention to the centrality of populist themes in the movement's discourse. Her work also shows how the Klan's adherence to republican ideology was especially attractive to middle-class Americans during that moment in history. Other excellent studies have highlighted the Klan's affinity with the progressive movement of the era. The Klan's pursuit of populist and progressive goals, however, was interwoven with its appeals to white supremacy, and with its xenophobia and religious bigotry.[17]

Although the fog surrounding the Klan's appeal in the 1920s is beginning to clear, many important questions remain unanswered. Most research on the movement has been based on case studies of Klan activity in a single community or in a single region of the country. Yet Klan leaders claimed to be a national organization concerned with national issues. Although such claims should be treated with some skepticism, they merit thorough investigation. Why did the movement grow so rapidly in the early 1920s? What was it about this moment in history that allowed the Klan to recruit so many members in so many different locations? Are there discernible geographic patterns in the movement's recruiting successes and failures? The Klan's role in politics, particularly its role in national politics, has received little attention from scholars. With millions of followers spread across the nation, the Ku Klux Klan certainly had the potential to be a major player in national politics. Although some scholars have examined the Klan at the national level, this work, while informative and often fascinating, is largely descriptive and does not provide a theoretical framework that can be used to account for the uneven geographic diffusion of Klan mobilization in the 1920s.

I show how macro-level changes in the structure of American society facilitated the growth of the Klan in some locales, but not in others. I argue that the Klan can best be understood as a response to devaluation in the economic, political, and status-based "purchasing power" of the movement's constituents, and I extend the analysis to shed light on the Klan's attempts to influence national political outcomes. I find that many of the conditions that contributed to the Klan's recruiting successes imposed severe constraints on the movement's capacity to influence national politics and these conditions contributed to the movement's rapid decline.

Beyond the Case of the Ku Klux Klan

By 1924, the Klan could boast of having more members nationwide than the American Federation of Labor.[18] Nevertheless, most Americans (including many academics) have little or no knowledge of the size and scope of the organization in the 1920s and would be surprised to learn that the movement enjoyed stronger support in northern states such as Indiana, Ohio, and Illinois than it did in the states of the Deep South. This book will promote a deeper understanding of the rise and fall of the Ku Klux Klan by calling attention to the way in which movement leaders articulated grievances that were national in scope. The rise of the Ku Klux Klan coincided with significant changes in the structure of social relations in the United States, and Klan leaders developed interpretations of these changes that were designed to attract members and adherents to their organization.

Acquiring a deeper understanding of the Ku Klux Klan is important in its own right, but I also use this fascinating historical case to develop theoretical insights that can be applied more generally. The book should be of particular interest to social scientists who study social movements and collective action. The Klan took only a few years to recruit millions of dues-paying members, yet this important movement simply cannot be explained with the theoretical tools most commonly used by social movement scholars. Some scholars have argued that right-wing mobilization represents a reactive response to a social group's declining status. Movement participants, from this perspective, long for a return to the days in which their group was held in high esteem and such longings and desires bring them together to promote the superiority of their group's culture, values, and lifestyle. These arguments typically overlook important economic and political incentives for right-wing mobilization and tend to characterize movement participants as irrational or misguided. While I do not hold that right-wing movement participants always act rationally, and I certainly do not condone their action, I do argue that right-wing movements often provide individuals with an effective vehicle for preserving status-based interests as well as political and economic interests.

The most widely utilized theories of social movements, resource mobilization theory and political opportunity theory, also miss the mark because these theories were developed with a different type of social movement in mind. They were designed to explain how relatively powerless groups are able to engage in collective contention to bring about social change. The theories were not intended to explain how, and under what conditions, social movements emerge among members of relatively advantaged groups that organize to preserve, restore, and expand their collective privileges. Although many of the concepts developed by contemporary social movement scholars are valuable in understanding a case such as the Ku Klux Klan, the underlying logic regarding causal processes must be altered substantially. A central goal of this book, therefore, is to present and apply a theory of social movement action—the "power-devaluation model"—that is specifically designed to analyze right-wing mobilization.

The case of the Ku Klux Klan can also be used to generate new insights related to racial and ethnic conflict and maintenance of racial and ethnic inequality. Ethnic competition theory predicts that conflict is most likely to occur when ethnically distinct groups are coming into close contact and are competing over jobs or other scarce resources.[19] Along these same lines, it has often been shown that intergroup conflict represents a majority group's response to a threat posed by members of a minority group.[20] Yet, as noted above, the Klan often thrived in homogeneous locales where Klan members would have been relatively insulated from localized threats and competition. For the most part, Klan leaders advocated white separatism rather than open conflict with out-group members.

Mary Jackman argues that scholars miss out on much of the action when they focus on intergroup conflict rather than analyzing ways in which dominant groups seek to minimize conflict while maintaining advantages over subordinate groups. Indeed, John Gaventa argues that conflict is a sign that a dominant group is losing its capacity to control subordinates through less visible dimensions of power.[21] In the 1920s Klan leaders presented white privilege as natural and preordained, and they appealed to constituents by interpreting social change through the lens of white (and Protestant) supremacy. As George Lipsitz points out,

> Race is a cultural construct, but one with sinister structural causes and consequences. Conscious and deliberate actions have institutionalized group identity in the United States, not just through the dissemination of cultural stories, but also through systematic efforts from colonial times to the present to create economic advantages through possessive investment in whiteness for European Americans.[22]

Leaders of the Klan frequently claimed that blacks, Catholics, and immigrants had no reason to fear the law-abiding men and women of the Ku Klux Klan. At the same time, they sought to mobilize millions of Americans to preserve a wide range of privileges reserved for native-born, white Protestants.

The book should also interest anyone in the general public who cares about politics, race relations, and contemporary social problems. Developing a theory of right-wing activism is much more than an interesting intellectual exercise. Social theory not only provides us with a means of gaining a deeper understanding of the case under study—in this case the 1920s Klan—but it can also be invaluable in making sense of similar events, cases, and processes in contemporary settings. Indeed, social theory can help us to predict the future, and when good theory motivates social policy it can contribute to a better society.

In the 1920s millions of American men and women donned sheets and hoods and marched through towns such as Kokomo, Indiana. They participated in massive rallies, parades, and countless meetings. They involved themselves in charity work and community service, but they also intimidated, threatened, and at times inflicted violence on African Americans, Catholics, Jews, and immigrants. In some locations, they captured the machinery of state and local government. Although the 1920s Klan collapsed soon after it reached its peak in 1924, anyone who is familiar with contemporary world events will recognize that we have yet to find effective ways of dealing with and containing organized racism and bigotry.

Episodes of racial and ethnic conflict continue to emerge in Europe, and in nations outside of Europe, as immigration streams bring different groups into contact, often leading to competition over jobs, housing, and other limited resources. Recently, white racists rampaged across beaches in Australia, using modern technology to coordinate attacks on local Muslim citizens and immigrants. In the United States, vigilante groups patrol the border between the United States and Mexico and political representatives compete for votes by taking tough stands on immigration. At the same time, a wide variety of racist groups continue to find a niche in the American social fabric—many of them taking advantage of the Internet to spread their messages of white supremacy and white separatism.[23] An analysis of the 1920s Klan, therefore, should illuminate an important and fascinating case in American history. Perhaps more important, the analysis should generate new insights into more general problems faced in the modern world that involve conflicts rooted in racial, ethnic, religious, and class identities.

Geographic Diffusion of Klan Activism

My primary aim in this book is to investigate the Ku Klux Klan of the 1920s as a national movement. Rich case studies of local Klan chapters provide deep insight into the movement and the ways in which it was able to generate support in local settings. Yet by relying solely on case studies to understand the Klan, we risk creating a situation similar to that described in the fable about the blind men and the elephant. Each observer comes away with a different understanding of the whole based on an examination of a single part. The Klan in Athens, Georgia, for example, may have been qualitatively different from the Klan in Oakland, California, or from the Klanswomen of Indiana.[24] Although each local chapter was different, they all claimed allegiance to the same national movement, and narratives constructed by national leaders imposed constraints on the extent to which local leaders could innovate when attempting to build and maintain support.

By examining the way in which national Klan leaders defined their movement, and by paying close attention to structural transformations taking place in the United States in the early 1900s, it should be possible to identify conditions that allowed the Klan to thrive in some locations but not in others. My analysis, therefore, does not contradict the insights that have been gained through case studies but instead aims to situate local Klan activity within a broader context. I rely heavily upon the Klan's national publication, the *Imperial Night-Hawk,* to gain access to the way in which national leaders constructed narratives that were designed to generate support for their movement. The *Imperial Night-Hawk* was published weekly and distributed to all Klan chapters throughout the country during a time period, 1923 to 1924, when the movement was at its peak. Articles in the *Imperial Night-Hawk* outlined the goals of the movement and also conveyed the Klan's stances on a wide variety of issues. The publication also provided information about activities and progress of Klan chapters across the country and therefore provides a means of systematically assessing geographic variation in the movement's strength.

Although it will never be possible to construct a perfect measure of Klan strength, the content of the *Imperial Night-Hawk* does provide a unique opportunity to examine geographical variation in the movement's activities in the early 1920s. The first article published in the inaugural issue, "The Purpose of This Publication," announced that the central mission of the *Imperial Night-Hawk* was to "keep Klansmen informed of activities at the Imperial Palace in their behalf and of the progress and advancement of the Knights of the Ku Klux Klan throughout the nation."[25] Subsequent issues, published weekly, delivered on this promise. Each issue provided information on a wide range of Klan activities and events taking place all over the country. The editors frequently reminded readers that they should send information about local events to the Imperial Palace in Atlanta, so that the information could be published in the Klan's national magazine. In some cases, local Klan events were covered in depth but in many other cases short descriptions of events were published in the Klan Komment column or mentioned in articles interspersed throughout the pages of the magazine. Almost invariably, the descriptions of Klan activity include information about the geographic location. In some cases the articles only mention the state in which the activity took place, but in the vast majority of cases the town or city is also identified.

Because the *Imperial Night-Hawk* fulfilled its mission to keep readers informed about Klan events taking place throughout the country, systematic coding of the magazine's content can provide a valuable measure of state-level variation in Klan activity. Although the measure does not represent an exhaustive list of all Klan activity that occurred in the early 1920s, it does give us a precise count of Klan events and activities that were mentioned in the movement's national publication. Given the publication's mission—to keep members informed about Klan activity taking place throughout the nation—this measure should closely approximate state-level differences in the total amount of Klan-sponsored activity that took place in the early 1920s.

To construct a measure of Klan activism, each article of the *Imperial Night-Hawk* was read and content-coded by two different coders. A total of eighty issues, published from March 28, 1923, to November 19, 1924, are included.[26] Almost all issues are eight pages in length, but some contain a few additional pages. Because my research assistants were coding for manifest rather than latent content, there were few intercoder discrepancies. I was able to resolve each of the discrepancies that did occur. I opted for a broad and inclusive definition of Klan activism. Any type of Klan activity mentioned in the publication was recorded and counted, but only if the geographic location of the activity was specified. For example, a statement claiming that Klan membership has been growing rapidly in the United States would not be counted because it does not specify a state or town. If an article noted that membership had been growing rapidly in Howell, Michigan, on the other hand, that would be counted as an event and included in the total number of events listed for the state of Michigan.[27] If the same event or activity is mentioned in more than one article, or several times within the same article, it is only counted once.

The events recorded in my data reflect a wide range of activity. In many cases, they represent references to initiation ceremonies, marches, parades, rallies, meetings, charitable acts, and cross burnings. The magazine also includes lists of donations made by Klan members to a special fund intended to offer support for the wife and children of a Klansman who was killed while marching in Carnegie, Pennsylvania. I counted these as events as long as the geographic location of the contributor was specified and as long as it was clear that the contributors were Klan members. I include these donations because they represent a form of Klan activity (charitable acts) and also indicate that Klan members were present and active in the location of the contributor. References to actions or activities of Klan opponents were not counted if the article does not also indicate that Klan members were present at the same location. For example, if an article mentions that a speaker in Boston publicly condemned the Klan, no Klan event would be recorded because the article does not refer to Klan activity in Boston. However, if the article reports that Klansmen were attacked by an unruly mob in South Bend, Indiana, an event would be recorded because Klansmen were engaged in activity in South Bend when they came under attack.[28]

Certainly some of the events recorded in my data were more important than others in terms of the number of people involved and the impact that they had on their communities. Yet a record of all Klan-related activity mentioned in the *Imperial Night-Hawk* reflects state-level differences in the total volume of Klan activism and also reveals how broadly the movement diffused in the early 1920s. In fact, the data show that the *Imperial Night-Hawk* reported a total of 2,669 events or activities in 1,285 different towns and cities. The broad geographic diffusion of the movement is particularly impressive in light of the short time span involved. The Klan was confined to two southern states until 1920, but within a few years it had established at least a minimal presence in more than 1,000 communities throughout the nation.

The data also reveal that the Klan was able to establish a presence in both rural and urban locations. According to the U.S. census, in 1920 there were a total of 144 cities in the United States with a population larger than 50,000. At least one Klan event was reported for 101 of those cities (70.1 percent). Most of the forty-three cities with a population above 50,000 and without reported Klan activity are located in the industrial core region of the country (see Table 1). In addition, in all but nine of these cases, residents of white and native-born parentage represented the numerical minority.

Although the Klan was able to establish a presence in most major cities, it is noteworthy that the majority of events occurred in smaller towns and cities. In fact, of the 2,669 events recorded in my data only 668 (25 percent) occurred in cities with a population greater than 50,000 (see Table 2). The state of Texas leads the pack, with 216 events recorded, with these events occurring in 112 different towns or cities. These figures certainly reflect a high volume of Klan activity in the state, but may also reflect the close tie between the Texas Klan and the movement's national headquarters because the Imperial Wizard, Hiram Evans, hailed from the Lone Star State. Consistent with other scholarly work on the Klan, the data also show that the movement had a particularly strong presence in Pennsylvania, Indiana, and Illinois. Georgia, not surprisingly, is also high on the list with the majority of activity taking place in the city of Atlanta where the Klan's national headquarters were located. Alabama Klansmen and Klanswomen were also active. However, my data show that in spite of the southern roots of the original Ku Klux Klan, southern location is not strongly related to Klan activity in the 1920s. Relatively little activity, for example, is reported for the states of North Carolina and Virginia.

With the exceptions of New Jersey and Pennsylvania, very little Klan activity is reported in northeastern states. And in both of these states, the majority of recorded events took place outside of the major cities. Thirty-one events are recorded for the state of New York, but it is important to keep in mind that New York was the most populous state in the nation in 1920. Only one event, a cross burning, was reported for New York City, and approximately 75 percent of events in New York State occurred in towns with

Table 1. Cities with over 50,000 inhabitants in 1920 with no reported Klan activity

City and state	Population	White and of native parentage (%)	City and state	Population	White and of native parentage (%)
Albany, N.Y.	113,344	49.6	New Britain, Conn.	59,316	18.8
Allentown, Penn.	73,502	70.7	New Haven, Conn.	162,537	27.3
Augusta, Ga.	52,548	51.2	Niagara Falls, N.Y.	50,760	26.6
Bayonne, N.J.	76,754	18.9	Passaic, N.J.	63,841	13.8
Boston, Mass.	748,060	24.3	Pawtucket, R.I.	64,248	23.0
Brockton, Mass.	66,254	37.2	Portsmouth, Va.	54,387	49.2
Cambridge, Mass.	109,694	26.5	Providence, R.I.	237,595	26.8
Camden, N.J.	116,309	48.4	Richmond, Va.	171,667	60.0
Canton, Ohio	87,091	61.8	Salt Lake City, Utah	118,110	47.6
Chester, Penn.	58,030	44.2	Schenectady, N.Y.	88,723	49.5
East Orange, N.J.	50,710	54.1	Scranton, Penn.	137,783	35.4
Elizabeth, N.J.	95,783	27.0	Sioux City, Iowa	71,227	54.4
Gary, Ind.	55,378	29.8	Somerville, Mass.	93,091	34.7
Hoboken, N.J.	68,166	21.2	Springfield, Mass.	129,614	37.8
Holyoke, Mass.	60,203	18.3	Toledo, Ohio	243,164	51.0
Jersey City, N.J.	208,103	29.2	Troy, N.Y.	72,013	45.9
Lawrence, Mass.	94,270	13.1	Utica, N.Y.	94,156	35.8
Lowell, Mass.	112,759	21.9	Waterbury, Conn.	91,715	24.1
Lynn, Mass.	99,148	34.4	Wheeling, W.Va.	56,208	60.6
Macon, Ga.	52,995	52.7	Wilkes Barre, Penn.	73,833	38.9
Manchester, N.H.	78,384	24.0	Yonkers, N.Y.	100,170	30.0
New Bedford, Mass.	121,217	16.6			

Source: U.S. Department of Commerce, *Statistical Abstracts,* 1924. Population and Principal Cities, no. 38.

less than 50,000 population. Only forty events are recorded for the six New England states of Vermont, Rhode Island, New Hampshire, Connecticut, Massachusetts, and Maine. North Dakota and South Dakota are the only states with no reported Klan activity. Farmer-Labor Party activism, rather than Klan activism, was a force to be reckoned with in these states and also, particularly, in the state of Minnesota.[29]

Table 2. Number of Klan events reported in the *Imperial Night-Hawk*

State	Total events	Events in large cities with population over 50,000 (%)	Number of towns/cities with at least one event	Larger cities with Klan events (number of events)
Texas	216	52 (24.1)	112	Dallas (23); El Paso (7); Fort Worth (12); Houston (4); San Antonio (6)
Pennsylvania	213	48 (22.5)	118	Altoona (17); Bethlehem (4); Erie (1); Harrisburg (5); Johnstown (1); Lancaster (1); Philadelphia (3); Pittsburg (15); Reading (1)
Indiana	168	43 (25.6)	72	Evansville (5); Fort Wayne (6); Indianapolis (16); South Bend (4); Terre Haute (12)
Illinois	158	49 (31.0)	76	Chicago (31); East St. Louis (3); Peoria (4); Rockford (5); Springfield (6)
Georgia	127	90 (70.9)	23	Atlanta (89); Savannah (1)
Alabama	126	31 (24.6)	52	Birmingham (27); Mobile (4)
Kansas	121	21 (17.4)	65	Kansas City (1); Topeka (13); Wichita (7)
Oklahoma	102	17 (16.7)	57	Oklahoma City (9); Tulsa (8)
Ohio	96	36 (37.5)	40	Akron (4); Cincinnati (4); Cleveland (1); Columbus (10); Springfield (11); Youngstown (6)
Missouri	96	32 (33.3)	47	Kansas City (15); St. Joseph (9); St. Louis (8)
California	89	25 (28.1)	45	Berkeley (1); Long Beach (1); Los Angeles (9); Oakland (7); Sacramento (3); San Diego (3); San Francisco (1)
Arkansas	85	19 (22.0)	46	Little Rock (19)
Michigan	83	23 (27.7)	37	Detroit (9); Flint (2); Grand Rapids (2); Lansing (8); Saginaw (2)
New Jersey	81	11 (13.5)	35	Atlantic City (2); Newark (3); Paterson (1); Trenton (5)

Table 2. Number of Klan events reported in the *Imperial Night-Hawk* (continued)

State	Total events	Events in large cities with population over 50,000 (%)	Number of towns/cities with at least one event	Larger cities with Klan events (number of events)
Iowa	71	19 (26.8)	38	Davenport (1); Des Moines (18)
West Virginia	70	3 (4.3)	37	Huntington (3)
Louisiana	67	8 (11.9)	34	New Orleans (8)
Tennessee	64	25 (39.1)	24	Chattanooga (19); Knoxville (1); Memphis (4); Nashville (1)
Mississippi	58	0 (0)	37	—
Washington	55	18 (32.7)	24	Seattle (15); Spokane (2); Tacoma (1)
Kentucky	50	6 (12.0)	28	Covington (1); Louisville (5)
Oregon	49	15 (30.6)	24	Portland (15)
Maryland	38	6 (15.8)	22	Baltimore (6)
South Carolina	37	7 (18.9)	16	Charleston (7)
Colorado	34	6 (17.6)	20	Denver (6)
Florida	33	6 (18.2)	18	Jacksonville (3); Tampa (3)
Arizona	31	0 (0)	13	—
New York	31	8 (25.8)	14	Binghamton (3); Buffalo (2); New York City (1); Rochester (1); Syracuse (1)
Virginia	29	3 (10.3)	17	Norfolk (1); Roanoke (2)

Delaware	23	7 (30.4)	9	Wilmington (7)
North Carolina	22	0 (0)	11	—
Minnesota	20	5 (25)	7	Duluth (1); Minneapolis (4)
Wisconsin	19	10 (52.6)	6	Milwaukee (9); Racine (1)
Nebraska	16	7 (43.8)	7	Lincoln (4); Omaha (3)
Montana	15	0 (0)	13	—
Wyoming	15	0 (0)	7	—
Massachusetts	13	5 (38.5)	8	Fall River (1); Haverhill (1)
Maine	12	3 (25.0)	5	Portland (3)
Connecticut	10	4 (40.0)	4	Bridgeport (3); Hartford (1)
Idaho	10	0 (0)	9	—
New Mexico	7	0 (0)	3	—
Nevada	2	0 (0)	1	—
New Hampshire	2	0 (0)	2	—
Rhode Island	2	0 (0)	1	—
Utah	2	0 (0)	0	—
Vermont	1	0 (0)	1	—
North Dakota	0	0 (0)	0	—
South Dakota	0	0 (0)	0	—

When examining the specific towns and cities in which Klan activity occurred, the diversity of locations, both in terms of geography and in terms of population size, is striking. The Klan was active in Indianapolis, Indiana, but also had a presence in Logtown, Mississippi. Klan activity occurred in Modesto, California, but also in Columbus, Ohio. Because the Klan established a presence in so many different communities and in so many different types of communities, it is risky to draw general conclusions about the movement based on case studies of a single Klan chapter in a single location. The Klan in Modesto, for example, was certainly different in many respects from the Klan of Indianapolis. Authors of several case studies of the movement that have been published in recent years have wisely refrained from making sweeping generalizations based on only a single case.[30] The deep insights generated in these studies have been extraordinarily valuable to me as I have attempted to study the Klan as a national movement. By analyzing the diffusion of the Klan throughout the nation as a whole, it should be possible to understand how the Klan was able to build a mass movement within only a few years' time. In spite of the diversity of the towns and cities in which the Klan mobilized, there are discernible patterns in my data. Some states were especially hospitable to Klan activism while the movement struggled to establish a foothold in many other states. The power-devaluation model can be used as a tool to reveal these patterns and to explain state-level variation in Klan activism.

2

The Rebirth of a Klan Nation, 1915–1924

Under the direction of Imperial Wizard Dr. H. W. Evans the Knights of the Ku Klux Klan is now financially able to combat the assaults of its enemies, is in a position to permit the Klansmen of the nation to enjoy the fruits of national economies and has also ample funds available for vigorous membership extension campaigns through the United States.
—Imperial Night-Hawk, August 22, 1923

Approximately forty years after the original Ku Klux Klan disbanded, a new Klan rose from the ashes in 1915. The founder of the second Ku Klux Klan, Colonel William Joseph Simmons, envisioned the Klan as the ultimate fraternal lodge. Simmons was the son of a rural Alabama physician. In his younger years he had spent time as a farmer, a circuit-riding preacher, and a lecturer in southern history at Lanier University.[1] He eventually threw himself into organizational work for several different fraternal organizations. Although a veteran of the Spanish American War, the title of "Colonel" was bestowed upon him by the Woodmen of the World.[2] In addition to the Woodmen, Simmons did organizational work for the Freemasons, the Knights of Pythias, and the Odd Fellows.

Early in 1915 Simmons designed the organizational framework for the new Ku Klux Klan. Obtaining a copy of the 1867 Reconstruction Klan Prescript, he designed the rituals and hierarchy of offices for the new organization, closely patterning it after the original Prescript. Simmons reserved the top position of Imperial Wizard for himself. When he was finished, the self-appointed Wizard had produced a "highly classified" fifty-four-page pamphlet, which he named the *Kloran*. While he would swear members to secrecy regarding the *Kloran*'s contents, Simmons had the document copyrighted in 1917 and placed two copies with the Library of Congress.[3]

Although the Imperial Wizard claimed that divine inspiration led to his decision to revive the Klan, his real inspiration was more down-to-earth. Simmons intended to capitalize on renewed interest in the Reconstruction-era Klan that resulted from two events that were beyond his control. In 1915 the rape and murder of fourteen-year-old Mary Phagan in Marietta, Georgia, sparked public outrage when the girl's body was discovered in the basement of the pencil factory where she worked. Leo Frank, her Jewish employer, was arrested and convicted of the crime. Georgia's governor commuted Frank's death sentence to life in prison in response to pressure from civil liberties groups. On August 16, 1915, an angry mob took Frank from his Georgia prison and lynched him. Referring to the Frank incident, former Populist leader and U.S. congressman Thomas E. Watson called for a revival of the Ku Klux Klan. The Klan, Watson proposed, should be organized to restore home rule.[4]

Popular interest in a Klan revival was given an even stronger boost by the 1915 release of D. W. Griffith's groundbreaking film *The Birth of a Nation*. No previous film release could compare to Griffith's epic in terms of its technological sophistication or in terms of its box-office success. It was the controversial storyline, however, that stimulated the initial growth of the Klan. The movie was adapted from Thomas Dixon's novel *The Clansman*. The Reconstruction-era Klan played a prominent role in both the book and the movie, being cast as valiant defenders of the South's culture and political institutions, as well as guardians of the purity of white womanhood. The film climaxed with a dramatic and drawn-out scene in which Klansmen on horseback rode to rescue Flora Cameron from Gus, a lust-crazed black assailant. Flora's character was clearly intended to symbolize innocence and purity of white southern women, and the film played on deeply entrenched fears and stereotypes regarding black men's animalistic cravings for white women. In the film, the Klansmen got their man, unceremoniously dumping Gus's dead body in the street in front of the local sheriff's office. According to historian Kenneth Jackson, in movie theaters throughout the nation the chase scene prompted whoops and wild cheers from the audience and, on one occasion, gunfire, as an overly enthusiastic moviegoer shot up the screen.[5]

Ever the opportunist, Colonel Simmons strategically placed advertisements for his new organization in Atlanta newspapers, alongside promos for showings of *The Birth of a Nation*. He solicited new members by billing the Ku Klux Klan as a "HIGH CLASS ORDER FOR MEN OF INTELLIGENCE AND CHARACTER."[6] Simmons made use of his fraternal ties to recruit new members and, drawing upon the skills that he crafted as a circuit-riding preacher, used fiery religious oratory in public-speaking engagements to motivate audience members to join his new organization. Simmons initially had limited success, enlisting approximately 2,000 members in the first five years.[7] In spite of the uproar surrounding the Leo Frank case and the continued interest in *The Birth of a Nation,* the Klan struggled to survive for several years. By early 1920 the movement was still confined to the states of Georgia and Alabama and was facing severe financial problems.[8]

The Movement Takes Off

The organization's fortunes shifted dramatically in 1920 when Simmons acquired the services of professional organizers Edward Young Clarke and Elizabeth Tyler. Clarke and Tyler's *Southern Publicity Association* became the Propagation Department of the Ku Klux Klan. The Propagation Department sent recruiters, Kleagles, into the field working on commission. It kept 80 percent of all fees collected from new members (initiation fees were $10), paying commissions and other expenses out of its 80 percent share. The remaining 20 percent went to National Headquarters in Atlanta.[9] Newly appointed Kleagles dispersed from the home base in Atlanta, promoting "100 percent Americanism." Over 200 Kleagles were in the field by the summer of 1921.[10] Kleagles were instructed to identify issues of concern within communities and then offer the Klan as a solution to those concerns.[11] Klan recruiters gave particular attention to Protestant ministers and to members of fraternal organizations. To the clergymen, Kleagles offered free membership, complimentary subscriptions to Klan publications, and the promise to actively promote the supremacy of Protestant Christianity. Embossed invitations to join the order were mailed to Masonic groups, patriotic societies, and other fraternal orders.[12]

The Klan's recruiting efforts were remarkably successful. During the first eighteen months that Clarke and Tyler directed recruitment, the organization expanded into the South, beyond the borders of Georgia and Alabama, as well as into the Southwest, the Midwest, and the West Coast. In a 1921 report to Colonel Simmons, Clarke claimed that the Klan had gained 48,000 members in only three months, adding, "In all my years of experience in organization work I have never seen anything equal to the clamor throughout the nation for the Klan."[13]

Recruitment received an unintended boost from a three-week exposé of the Klan that ran in the *New York World* in September 1921. Eighteen other major newspapers across the nation picked up the *World*'s coverage of the Klan. The newspaper estimated that the organization had 500,000 members in forty-five states. The primary purpose of the exposé, however, was to call attention to the Klan's darker side. The paper documented 152 separate incidents of alleged Klan violence.[14] Partly in response to the *World*'s exposé, Colonel Simmons was called to testify before a concerned congressional committee.

In retrospect, the congressional hearing may have been Simmons's finest hour. The Imperial Wizard testified before Congress, assuring those assembled that the Klan neither endorsed nor participated in violence of any sort. Simmons reasoned,

> If the Knights of the Ku Klux Klan has been a lawless organization, as has been charged, it would not have shown the remarkable growth it has, for in the Klan is as fine a body of representative citizens as there is in the

Figure 1. The Klan's founder, Colonel William Joseph Simmons, at the House Committee investigation of the Ku Klux Klan in 1922. National Photo Company Collection. Library of Congress.

United States. In each community where there is a Klan will be found members from the leading citizens, men who stand at the forefront in their cities. These men would not stand for lawlessness.[15]

To counter charges that the Klan was essentially a money-making scheme to enrich its leaders, Simmons claimed that surplus revenue was being invested in worthy causes, such as the expansion of Lanier University. When questioned about the organization's secretive nature, he reminded the committee that the *Kloran* containing the organization's oath and ritual was on public record with the Library of Congress.[16]

Simmons also denied that his organization was organized to promote religious intolerance and to intimidate blacks: "If the Klan is to secure members on an anti–Roman Catholic, anti-Jew, and anti-Negro appeal, we do not want such members."[17] Simmons discussed at length his boyhood experiences playing with black children and his efforts as an adult to educate and assist blacks in any way that he could. Simmons, who claimed to be gravely ill during the hearings, summoned up all of his evangelical zeal in his closing statement. Addressing the movement's opponents, he declared,

> You are ignorant of the principles as were those who were ignorant of the character and work of the Christ. I can not better express myself than by saying to you who are persecutors of the Klan and myself, "Father forgive you, for you know not what you do," and "Father forgive them for they know not what they do."[18]

Congress did not pursue any further investigation and the Klan benefited immensely from the free publicity granted by the congressional hearing and the *New York World*. Most Americans, particularly outside of the South, were only vaguely aware of the movement's existence until the *World* and the congressional hearings brought it to their attention. Within the next four months, more than 200 additional chapters were founded and total membership rose to nearly one million.[19]

The Changing of the Guard

Although the Klan continued to grow under Simmons's reign, the organization lacked direction and a sense of purpose. Several state-level leaders within the organization felt that the Klan was not realizing its potential as a political force. Publicity concerning Simmons's drunken escapades and his alleged misappropriation of Klan funds also caused concern among the Klan faithful. Simmons's behavior was particularly troubling because the Klan presented itself as a staunch defender of prohibition and of

Christian morality. Revelations of boozing and sexual impropriety of the Propagation Department's Clarke and Tyler also damaged the organization's credibility.[20]

In November 1922, several disgruntled Klan leaders initiated a coup. Among them were Hiram Wesley Evans and D. C. Stephenson. At the first annual national convention of the Klan (Klonvocation) in Atlanta, the insurgents duped Simmons into accepting an exalted but meaningless position. Evans, a Texas dentist, was named as the new Imperial Wizard.[21] Like his co-conspirator Stephenson, Evans was determined to turn the Klan into a potent political force. Internal factionalism continued to plague the organization, however. After Simmons realized that he had been maneuvered into irrelevance, he attempted to reclaim the Imperial Palace in Atlanta, taking possession by force when Evans was out of town in April 1923. A lengthy legal battle ensued. In the end, it was determined that Evans would retain the position of Imperial Wizard, but the copyrights to the ritual, re-

Figure 2. House Committee investigation of the Ku Klux Klan, 1922. National Photo Company Collection. Library of Congress.

galia, and signs of the Klan were granted to Simmons. Simmons eventually accepted $146,000 in compensation and, with that resolved, he was officially banished from the Klan in January 1924.[22]

The infighting was costly, as some members left the movement either because of the bad publicity surrounding the legal battle or because they were faithful to Simmons.[23] Nevertheless, new members greatly outnumbered defectors.[24] The organization continued to expand into previously uncharted territory, and the base of the movement's support shifted from the southern to the midwestern states. The Klan's assets also rose sharply after Evans assumed the leadership. According to the Klan's *Imperial Night-Hawk,* total assets for the organization rose from $403,171 in July 1922 to $1,088,473 in July 1923. In addition to publishing the financial statement, a Klan writer added that "the Klan's finances are in splendid condition and that the gain made in membership and financial strength during the past year had broken all previous records."[25]

With both membership and assets growing, Evans could focus on his political agenda. An important part of his plan involved enlisting the aid of women, who, with their newly won voting privileges, could contribute to the movement's political clout. In another legal battle with Simmons, Evans secured the exclusive rights to organize women's chapters and founded the Women's Ku Klux Klan (WKKK) in 1923.[26] The WKKK was billed as "a Protestant Women's Organization which is for, by, and of women."[27] The WKKK contributed mightily to the overall strength of the movement. The charter membership numbered roughly 125,000, with membership doubling to 250,000 within the fist four months. The WKKK continued to grow, leading one critic of the Klan to claim that at least three million women had joined the order.[28]

The Klan in Politics

Across the nation, Klansmen and Klanswomen sought to elect "100 percent Americans" to political office. Early successes in Texas, Georgia, and Oregon encouraged the organization's national leadership. In 1922 Earle B. Mayfield of Texas became the first member of the Ku Klux Klan to be elected to the U.S. Senate. After defeating ex-governor and anti-Klan candidate Jim Ferguson in the Democratic primary, he went on to defeat Republican challenger George Peddy in the general election. The defeated Ferguson charged that in Dallas "the Ku Klux Klan is in the saddle. It has elected nearly all the county officials, and the law, therefore, can be violated with impunity."[29]

In 1922 the Georgia Klan elected several of its members and favorite candidates to local offices, including Klansman Walter A. Sims, who was elected mayor of Atlanta. Sims defeated James G. Woodward, who openly opposed the Klan in his campaign. The Klan also broke through at the state level in Georgia, helping to remove Gov. Thomas W. Hardwick from office after he demanded that the Klansmen remove their masks in public and refrain from violence. The Klan threw its support behind former state attorney general Clifford Walker. After winning the election, Walker appeared at the National Convention of the Klan in Atlanta, promising the assembled members that if the organization got into any trouble he would not report it to the press or to the electorate, but would instead come to talk directly with the Klan's leaders.[30]

The Klan's political success was not confined to the South. Beginning in 1922, the movement came to dominate Oregon politics. When the Klan's Republican candidate for governor lost in the primaries, the organization threw its support behind Democrat Walter Pierce in the general election. Pierce openly courted the Klan vote by declaring that he was "100 percent American" and by promoting the Klan's political agenda, which included the backing of a compulsory education bill, keeping "aliens" out of control of public affairs, and denying land ownership to aliens. With the Klan's backing, Pierce won the election as a Democrat, in spite of the fact that registered Republicans outnumbered Democrats in Oregon by more than two to one.[31] In the following year, a slate of Klansmen and Klan-supported candidates were ushered into local offices in Portland. Fred L. Gifford, the Grand Dragon of the Oregon Klan, positioned himself at the head of a political machine that dominated Portland politics for several years.[32]

The Klan also made waves in Oklahoma. In 1923 the movement played a central role in the successful impeachment of the governor, Jack Walton. Walton had run as a farmer-labor candidate, with the backing of the Socialist party. After alienating many of his own supporters, Walton became embroiled in a war with the Ku Klux Klan. By 1923 the Klan had helped elect several of its own members to the Oklahoma state legislature.[33] Throughout the state, Klan posses fought with union organizers and members of the Industrial Workers of the World (I.W.W. or the "Wobblies"). The Klan announced that it would break up any attempts to form a farmer-labor union. Walton responded by declaring martial law over the entire state— an act that generated widespread resentment. At his impeachment hearing, Walton claimed that he was only guilty of fighting the hooded empire.[34]

The high point for the Klan came in 1924. Gearing up for local-, state-, and national-level campaigns, leaders of state organizations worked to get out the vote and to identify the "100 percent American" candidates for the electorate. In some cases, the Klan threw its support behind a candidate who would have most likely won without its assistance. In Maine, for example, the Republican Klan-supported governor won handily, but because Maine was heavily Republican his chances of winning were never in jeopardy.[35] In other states, candidates jumped on the Klan's bandwagon, hoping to increase their appeal.

Nowhere was the political dominance of the Klan more apparent than in Indiana. By 1924 D. C. Stephenson's star was shining even brighter than that of the Imperial Wizard's. As head of operations in twenty-three northern states, Stephenson was responsible for pumping thousands of dollars into the national organization, and was himself becoming a very wealthy man from his percentage of membership dues and the sales of Klan paraphernalia. Stephenson was not averse to flaunting his wealth and power, which made Evans and the national headquarters nervous. Stephenson's growing power, and his increasing tendency to butt heads with the national organization, eventually led to a rift between Stephenson and Hiram Evans.[36] Yet the Indiana Klan remained strong in the months leading up to the November elections. After the election, Stephenson was able to direct practically all the state's political activity from his office in Indianapolis, with Klansmen deeply entrenched in the state's legislature, judicial branch, and law enforcement offices.[37]

The Klan also made its presence felt in national politics. Hiram Evans appeared on the cover of *Time* magazine for his role in silencing opposition to the Klan at the Republican Party's National Convention in Cleveland. Two weeks later, at the Democratic Convention in New York City, the Klan was at the center of controversy. The Party was deeply divided over a proposed platform plank that condemned the Ku Klux Klan. After a very close vote, the Democrats chose not to condemn the Invisible Empire. The Klan's leadership flirted with candidates from both major parties and displayed some initial curiosity about Robert LaFollette, the fiery Wisconsin senator who bolted from the Republican Party to run for the presidency as a Progressive.[38]

Klan leaders certainly recognized that an organization with millions of members and adherents nationwide could potentially impact national politics. Yet in the end, the movement was publicly spurned by LaFollette and by the Democratic presidential nominee, John W. Davis. Only Republican Calvin Coolidge declined to condemn the organization. Nevertheless, in the aftermath of the 1924 elections the Klan's Imperial Wizard declared victory.

TIME

The Weekly News-Magazine

IMPERIAL WIZARD
"—not appointed by Almighty God"
(See Page 5)

VOL. III   NO. 25   JUNE 23, 1924

Figure 3. Imperial Wizard Hiram Wesley Evans is featured on the cover of
Time *magazine in the aftermath of the 1924 Republican National Convention.*
Reprinted through the courtesy of the editors of Time *magazine. Copyright*
2007 Time Inc.

We Klansmen may be pardoned for our just pride in the part we have played in the saving of our country from alien propaganda. . . . Those who sought office through combinations of un-American influences were hopelessly defeated.[39]

By the time that Evans spoke these words, however, his movement was in steep decline.

Attributes of Klan Members

Who were the men and women who fueled the growth of the Ku Klux Klan through their participation and membership fees? There is no simple answer to that question because the composition of local organizations could vary substantially from community to community. What's more, the socioeconomic status of Klan members, even within a single local chapter, often spanned a broad range. For example, among the members of the Athens, Georgia, Klan there were two lawyers, ten ministers, two physicians, and three pharmacists but also two plumbers, seven electricians, and five bakers.[40] The socioeconomic diversity of the Klan's membership is not surprising in light of the Klan's opportunistic recruiting strategy—a strategy that involved offering the Klan as a solution to whatever issues might be troubling residents of a particular community. To some extent, the Klan did try to be all things to all people—at least for people who were native-born, white, and Protestant. It would be a mistake, however, to assume that the Klan's membership roles were representative of all those who were eligible to join. The few membership lists that have been recovered indicate that two groups were underrepresented. As Goldberg notes, the Klan seemed to appeal to all groups except the elite and the industrial proletariat.[41]

Several researchers have drawn attention to the disproportionate representation of the middle class in the Klan's membership and to the ways in which movement members and leaders pursued goals that benefited middle-class interests.[42] However, it is important to note that the "middle-class" label is only useful in this case if the term refers to one's relationship to the means of production, rather than to some middle strata in a hierarchy of wealth and status. As noted above, Klan membership often displayed quite a bit of diversity in regard to the members' wealth and status. Based on what we know about the occupations of Klan members, however, the movement seems to have been especially appealing to small businessmen, merchants, and skilled manufacturing workers—the "old middle class"—as well as to a "new middle-class" of managers, professionals, and clerks.[43] The Klan recruited heavily from fraternal lodges such as the Masons and the

Odd Fellows—organizations composed primarily of small businessmen, professionals, and skilled manufacturing workers.

This is not to say, however, that the Klan did not draw some unskilled laborers into its ranks. It did. This fact, however, as will be discussed in more depth in later chapters, should not distract our attention from the ways in which the Klan's leaders strategically articulated grievances faced by many middle-class Americans. Articles in Klan newspapers would, at times, describe the attributes of the organization's members. For example, articles published in the Klan's Illinois publication, the *Dawn,* described the typical members as clergymen, attorneys, bankers, doctors, financiers, clerks, and artisans.[44] Of course, such claims could reflect the types of individuals that the Klan hoped to recruit rather than the ones they actually recruited. But as mentioned previously, the claims are generally supported by the limited data available on the occupations of Klan members.[45] Perhaps equally important, the fact that movement leaders described the organization as being primarily a middle-class movement, and articulated grievances shared by many middle-class Americans, is meaningful when trying to understand the sources of the movement's strength.

Hiram Evans offered a stinging critique of industrial capitalism that heaped scorn on both the capitalist and the industrial proletariat. At a time when conflict between industrialists and laborers was increasingly coming to define national politics, Klan leaders criticized the greed and excesses of both classes.[46] The Klansman's Creed called for a closer and more harmonious relationship between capital and labor. The Klan press was particularly hostile toward labor radicalism. Drawing upon republican ideals, the Klan portrayed the political pursuit of class-based interests as detrimental to the nation as a whole.[47] As one article in the *Imperial Night-Hawk* expressed it, "We must discourage, by stern and swift rebuke, all efforts to create a class consciousness among our people."[48] Klan leaders resisted the advances of both capitalists and industrial laborers and promoted policies that would disproportionately benefit their middle-class constituency.

Although I will argue that economic factors contributing to the Klan's growth have not been fully appreciated, it would be a mistake to over-emphasize or exaggerate economic motives for joining the Ku Klux Klan. The causes of the movement's growth are more complex. The economy was just one of many issues addressed by movement leaders as they attempted to enlist the participation and support of native-born, white Protestants across the nation. In fact, the Klan addressed such a broad range of issues that, at first glance, it may appear that there is no rhyme or reason to the movement's phenomenal growth. Indeed, it is tempting to simply assume, as did many early scholarly studies of the Klan, that the movement's growth can best be understood as some sort of collective psychological phenomena—an irrational response to social change. However, the sources of the Klan's emergence and growth can be revealed through a close examination of the ways in which changes in the structure of social relations in the early 1900s led to shifts in the way that Americans understood their world. Through trial and error, and with opportunistic motives, Klan leaders developed interpretations of local and national problems that struck a chord with many American citizens. With abundant organizational resources available to those who were adversely affected by structural change, and in a political context that provided them room to operate, a mass movement emerged—a movement that aimed to wrest political power from those who opposed its agenda. The power-devaluation model, a theory of right-wing social movement activism, will help to reveal what cannot be seen without structured investigation—the secrets behind the Klan's successes and failures in the early 1920s.

3

Power Devaluation

Those who think that the purpose and business of the Klan is to oppose and fight Negroes, Jews, Catholics and foreigners are sadly mistaken, and have no conception of its ideals and principles.
—*Imperial Night-Hawk,* April 2, 1924

A sociologist (as I like to tell my daughter—a huge Nancy Drew fan) is very much like a supersleuth. The sociologist's job entails solving mysteries when the solution to the mystery is not obvious to the casual observer who stumbles upon the scene of the crime. Like a good detective, the sociologist closely examines evidence and relies upon logic, both inductive and deductive, to think about how various strands of evidence can be pieced together to reveal a solution to an intriguing puzzle. Sociologists, like supersleuths, require a good theory to help them organize the empirical clues at their disposal. The emergence and growth of the Ku Klux Klan in the early part of the twentieth century is certainly an intriguing puzzle, but the most widely utilized theories of social-movement mobilization provide little guidance to anyone who wishes to crack the case. Researchers who developed these theories did not have right-wing movements in mind.

When I use the term "right-wing movement" I am referring to a social movement that acts on behalf of relatively advantaged groups with the goal of preserving, restoring, and expanding the rights and privileges of its members and constituents. These movements also attempt to deny similar rights and privileges to other groups in society. This operational definition distinguishes right-wing movements from progressive movements, such

as the American civil rights movement, which seek to secure new benefits, rights, and privileges for members of relatively disadvantaged or oppressed groups—rights and privileges that are already enjoyed by members
of dominant groups. This distinction is critical when it comes to identifying
the underlying causes of a movement's emergence and growth. To appreciate the significance of this distinction, however, it is necessary to briefly
consider the historical development of social movement theory.

Do Grievances Matter?

When studying a social movement, it seems natural to begin by considering the sources of discontent among those who participate. What are the
participants' grievances? How long have the grievances been in existence?
Are conditions improving or are they worsening? The importance of understanding collective grievances seems obvious, at first glance, because people
do not engage in collective protest unless they have something to protest
about. However, contemporary social-movement theory does not treat collective grievances as an important causal factor. At most, social-movement
theorists tend to view grievances as necessary but insufficient causes of collective action.

This was not always the case. Prior to the 1970s, scholars tended to
view a social movement as a reflexive response to changes in the structure
of society that generate new sources of discontent. Social protest, according
to this line of thinking, signals a temporary disruption in what is, under
normal circumstances, a smoothly functioning society that operates like a
complex system of interrelated parts. Smelser's collective-behavior theory,
for example, proposed that changes in the structure of society can produce
structural strain.[1] This strain generates anxiety and frustration among some
individuals and leads them to engage in protest. Mass society theorists argued that mass movements emerge when structural changes disconnect individuals from social bonds that would otherwise constrain deviant action.[2]
In general, scholars viewed social-movement activity as a form of deviance
with its root causes being similar to those that lead to crime and delinquency. As Gurr expressed it,

> One of the most pervasive assumptions of theories of crime and conflict
> is that both are rooted in social tensions that are manifest in a prevailing
> sense of individual anomie, alienation, or discontent. It is plausible to
> suppose that such states of mind will motivate some to join in collective
> action and others, depending on their needs and opportunities, to take
> more individualistic courses of action.[3]

Some of these early theorists viewed social-movement activism as a kind of disarticulated political rebellion.[4] Others, however, treated social protest as having more to do with individual psychological processes (e.g., a way that anxious or frustrated people let off steam) than with politics. McAdam used the term "classical theory" to refer to mass-society theory, collective-behavior theory, and theories of relative deprivation, which, he argued, have a common explanatory structure. Each theory explains social-movement mobilization as primarily an individual psychological response to stresses and strains produced by changes in the structure of society.[5]

Stinging critiques of these "classical" theories began to emerge in the early 1970s, and by the mid-1980s the classical perspective on social-movement mobilization had been almost completely abandoned. The critiques focused on the way in which classical theorists, either implicitly or explicitly, characterized social-movement participants as being irrational and disconnected from social ties.[6] McAdam argued, for example, that classical theorists' naïve assumptions about the openness of democratic political institutions led them to overlook the political motivations of social-movement participants.[7] After all, if individual and collective grievances can be satisfied by participating within established institutions, protest must be serving some nonpolitical function. McAdam, however, joined a growing chorus of voices arguing that social movement action represents a strategic form of political participation for those who are denied routine access to political power-holders and decisionmakers.[8]

As a new generation of scholars examined social-movement activism occurring around them—for example, the civil rights movement, the women's movement, student movements, the antiwar movement—it became apparent that social-movement participants are typically embedded in dense social networks and are not, as some classical theorists suggested, disconnected from social bonds. Oberschall coined the term "bloc recruitment," referring to the way in which social-movement organizers often recruit members and participants among groups of individuals already organized for some other purpose.[9] This strategy is much more effective than recruiting isolated individuals one by one and it capitalizes on in-group solidarity that often motivates individuals to contribute to the provision of a collective good rather than to free-ride on the efforts of others.[10] Now, a large body of research confirms the importance of social-network ties in drawing individuals into protest activities and campaigns.

Resource-mobilization theorists argue that social-movement mobilization should be viewed primarily as an organizational problem rather than as a form of deviance, delinquency, or disarticulated individualistic rebellion.[11]

These scholars note that social-movement activism, like political action that takes place within political institutions, requires an organizational infrastructure, resources, and effective leadership. Pointing out that many impoverished and oppressed groups never rise up and engage in collective action, resource-mobilization theorists argue that collective grievances are largely irrelevant when it comes to explaining the emergence of a social movement. What is relevant, according to the theory, is the infusion of new resources that make it possible for groups to take action to redress grievances that, in some cases, have been in existence for years, decades, and even centuries.

Growing concurrently with resource-mobilization theory, political-opportunity theory places emphasis on how the political context either inhibits or encourages social-movement mobilization. As is true of resource-mobilization theory, political-opportunity theory downplays the causal significance of collective grievances. In what is perhaps the strongest statement of this approach, Tarrow asserts,

> Even a cursory look at modern history shows that outbreaks of collective action cannot be derived from the level of deprivation that people suffer or from the disorganization of their societies; for these preconditions are more constant than the movements they supposedly cause. What varies widely from time to time, and from place to place, are political opportunities, and social movements are more closely related to the incentives they provide for collective action than to underlying social or economic structures.[12]

The logic of both resource-mobilization theory and political-opportunity theory is compelling. Poor and oppressed people face formidable obstacles when it comes to challenging the existing order. Unless new resources become available or the political context becomes less oppressive, collective action is unlikely to occur. Yet this logic fails when the goal is to explain social-movement action that emerges among relatively privileged actors who are not subjected to state repression and typically have ready access to organizational resources. This is not to say that organizational resources and political opportunities are irrelevant to right-wing mobilization. However, the timing of a right-wing movement's emergence should be less dependent on both. The key question, it seems, is what leads members of relatively privileged groups to utilize preexisting organizational resources and to exploit preexisting political opportunities in order to restore, preserve, or expand their preexisting privileges.

Should We Return to Classical Theory? Yes and No (but Mostly No!)

So how do we explain the emergence and growth of right-wing movements? Interestingly, the classical theories that have been subjected to so much criticism in recent decades have enjoyed a longer shelf life when applied to right-wing movements. Perhaps this is because scholars are less likely to object when participants in extreme conservative movements are characterized as irrational and marginalized. Researchers who have studied the Klan have pointed to social changes taking place in the early 1920s—such as industrialism, urbanism, immigration—as causes of structural strain. Actions initiated by the movement have often been described as futile responses to irreversible social forces that did not address the real causes of collective grievances, but were instead merely expressions of frustration, anomie, and dissonance.[13]

Lipset and Raab, for example, argue that millions of individuals joined the Klan in the 1920s because the movement offered a release for psychological tension that resulted from rapid changes in society. Moore argues that a breakdown in traditional institutions such as the church and the family created social atomization and led individuals to attempt to reestablish community cohesion through their participation in the Klan. Jackson argues that the Klan lacked a meaningful reason for its existence and relied upon emotion rather than reason. David Chalmers, author of what is perhaps the most widely read historical study of the movement, describes the Klan as a response to a breakdown of traditional social order embodied in the religious and moral values of small-town America.[14]

The earliest scholarly attempts to make sense of the 1920s Klan rest on similar assumptions, as scholars sought to explain the movement primarily in psychological terms. Sociologist John Moffat Mecklin, the Klan's contemporary, wrote that the movement was "essentially a defense mechanism against evils which are more often imaginary than real."[15] Richard Hofstadter saw the movement as a response to status anxiety. He characterized Klansmen as "gullible nativists," and argued,

> The Klan impulse was not really a response to direct personal relationships or face-to-face competition, but rather the result of a growing sense that the code by which rural and small-town Anglo-Saxon America had lived was being ignored and even flouted in the wicked cities, and especially by the "aliens" and the old religion and morality were being snickered at by the intellectuals.[16]

Although it may seem comforting to think of Klansmen and Klanswomen as being irrational, ignorant, and gullible, more recent studies of the

Klan largely contradict such characterizations. Interviews with surviving members of the organization and close scrutiny of historical documents and of recorded minutes of Klan meetings indicate that Klan members were, in many respects, quite ordinary.[17] Of course, Klan members were racists and religious bigots, but it is important to keep in mind that the bigoted views articulated by Klan members and leaders were broadly held by native-born, white Protestant Americans in the early 1920s. During this time period, even some of the nation's most renowned scientists were involved in the study of eugenics and claimed to have evidence of the inherent superiority of Anglo-Saxons. Similar themes were also pursued in the popular press. In a widely read book, *The Passing of the Great Race,* Madison Grant attributed the success and prosperity of the United States to the intellectual and physical superiority of the nation's Nordic colonizers.[18] The Klan members' nativist views and their views on race and religion are certainly relevant in any attempt to explain the movement's appeal. However, it is important to recognize that these beliefs, to a great extent, mirrored mainstream beliefs and values in society at large.

Recent analysis of the Klan has also debunked the notion that Klan members were at the margins of society or were disconnected from social bonds.[19] Indeed, the Klan's form of bloc recruitment, which targeted fraternal organizations and Protestant congregations, ensured that many of its members would be embedded in dense social networks and would be actively involved in community life. Individuals who are socially isolated are rarely drawn into sustained social-movement activism regardless of the ideological orientation of the social movement in question. The 1920s Klan was not an exception to this rule. Although the Klan members and leaders expressed concern about the breakdown of traditional institutions, the movement often thrived in locations that were the most insulated from such changes. Even Leonard Moore, who argues that the Klan's growth was stimulated by white Protestants' perceptions that community cohesion was in decline, argues that in local communities the Klan's success "resulted from widespread support for traditional moral values and law enforcement."[20]

In light of available evidence, it would be unwise to return to classical social-movement theory to explain the rise of the Klan. The criticisms leveled against this general theoretical approach seem just as valid when studying right-wing movements as they do when studying more progressive forms of social-movement mobilization. However, neither resource-mobilization theory nor political-opportunity theory will do the trick, because these theories beg the question of why the Klan mobilized in the first place. The lack of prior mobilization (before 1915) cannot be explained in terms of insufficient resources or limited political opportunities. To solve the puzzle it is necessary to reconsider the possibility that collective grievances can play an important causal role when it comes to explaining right-wing mobilization. The power-devaluation model specifies the role of grievances in right-wing mobilization but rejects assumptions made by classical theorists about the attributes and motives of movement participants. Grievances resulting from structural changes in society do not automatically lead to participation in a social movement, but they can alter the way in which people interpret their circumstances and they can generate new incentives for right-wing mobilization.

The Power-Devaluation Model

A theory of social movement mobilization must address questions related to the timing of a movement's emergence and growth. With progressive social movements it is often the case that collective grievances exist long before the emergence of collective action. In such cases, extant social-movement theory correctly focuses on time-variant factors, such as availability of organizational resources and political opportunities, as possible causal factors. A grievance-based explanation of the movement's emergence would be unsatisfying because it begs the question of why the movement did not emerge at some earlier historical moment when collective grievances were also present.

I have defined a right-wing movement as a social movement that acts to preserve, restore, or expand rights and privileges of a relatively advantaged societal group. Almost by definition, then, the grievances of a right-wing movement's constituents are time-variant. The fact that members of the group are acting within a social movement suggests that participants sense that their capacity to maintain privileges by acting within established institutions is being threatened. Under normal circumstances, members of privileged groups seek to maintain an advantaged position in ways that minimize conflict with the disadvantaged because open conflict tends to shine a light on social inequality and processes of exploitation and domination, which can lead dominated and exploited groups to demand a greater share of societal benefits.[21] When right-wing mobilization occurs, it is likely in response to a threat to established power relationships that is generating incentives to act outside of established institutions and within a social movement. To be analytically useful, however, the power-devaluation model must further specify threats to power relationships that contribute to right-wing mobilization.

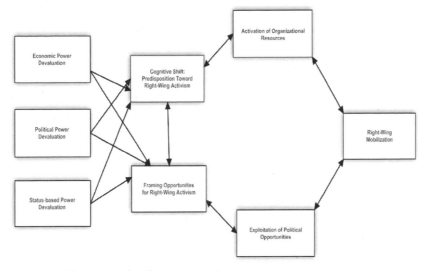

Figure 4. The power-devaluation model.

The power-devaluation model consists of three key components. The theory proposes that power devaluation, resulting from structural change, produces shifts in interpretive processes which, in turn, lead to activation of organizational resources and exploitation of political opportunities (see Figure 4). The model also includes feedback loops, representing movement mobilization as an ongoing process. As movements gain strength, they are likely to gain more resources and to produce changes in the political context. These changes also typically force movements to make adjustments in interpretive frames, as movement leaders seek to form alliances with other groups that will help the movement to gain power.

Power Devaluation (Economic, Political, and Status-Based)

To identify ways in which a threat to existing power relations can provide incentives for right-wing mobilization, it is useful to conceptualize three distinct markets of exchange based on economic relationships, political relationships, and status relationships. Changes in the structure of society can lead to devaluation in the "purchasing power" of various actors within these markets. When members of clearly identifiable groups appear to be disproportionately suffering from power devaluation, incentives for right-wing mobilization emerge. Although I view power devaluation as a social process, simple microeconomic logic is useful in determining when, where, and for whom power devaluation occurs. *Devaluation in actors' purchasing power within an exchange market results from a decline in the demand for what an actor offers in the exchange, and from an increase in the supply of others who offer the same thing in exchange.*

In an economic market, actors exchange labor, wages, goods, services, and money. Macro-level shifts in the structure of social relations can produce changes in both the demand for, and supply of, these basic exchange mediums. For example, mechanization of industry can reduce the demand for human labor while immigration can increase the supply of human labor. In both cases, the purchasing power of laborers within a preexisting labor pool undergoes devaluation. Similarly, power devaluation results when the demand for a particular service or commodity declines, or when there is an increase in the supply of the service or commodity in question.

In a democratic society, the political arena can also be viewed as an exchange market. Votes and monetary contributions are exchanged for representation and political patronage. As is true in an economic market, political "purchasing power" is affected by the demand for what an actor offers in exchange and the supply of others who offer the same thing in exchange. Macro-level structural changes can affect levels of supply and demand and can produce political power devaluation for some individuals and groups. Changes in factors such as fertility rates, migration, immigration, and economic cycles can affect the supply of voters and the supply of cash contributions in a political market. Electoral rules and regulations can also come into play. Extension of suffrage to a previously excluded group, for example, increases the overall supply of voters and leads to devaluation in the purchasing power of voters who were already in the electorate. Changes in rules governing elections can also affect the demand side. For example, if legislation was enacted calling for public funding of campaigns (and making private donations illegal), the demand for campaign contributions from private individuals or corporations would be eliminated, resulting in sharp devaluation in the political purchasing power of those who had previously used large campaign contributions to buy disproportionate attention from legislators and other political officials.

The metaphor of an exchange market is also useful when considering the role of status in right-wing mobilization. My thinking on this point is primarily influenced by Georg Simmel, but similar ideas can be found in the work of exchange theorists such as Blau and Emerson.[22] Much of Simmel's work calls attention to the ways in which individuals and groups seek to differentiate themselves from others in society. For example, Simmel notes the tendency for organizations to emphasize unity, while at the same time failing to resist inevitable movement toward factionalism. As Simmel expresses it, "It is as if each individual largely felt his own significance only by contrasting himself with others. As a matter of fact, where such a contrast does not exist, he may even artificially create it."[23]

Within a status market, individuals and groups offer certain behaviors, traits, cultural knowledge, and tastes in exchange for esteem from others. As is true in economic and political markets, one's purchasing power within a status market is determined by the demand for what an actor offers in exchange and the supply of other actors who offer the same thing. As Simmel notes in his discussion of fashion, an individual receives little recognition for simply adhering to widely shared norms and values.[24] Refraining from committing homicide is certainly a good practice, but it does not distinguish the individual or set her apart because most people, thankfully, exercise similar restraint. Instead, actors gain prestige and esteem by adhering to and displaying behaviors and traits that are simultaneously admired and relatively scarce. If these traits or behaviors become increasingly common, then the purchasing power of the actor displaying such behaviors or possessing such traits undergoes devaluation.

Simmel makes a similar point when he discusses how fashion is used by members of the upper classes to distinguish and separate themselves from the lower classes. When a trend-setting fashion is widely diffused and mimicked by those of various social strata, the fashion no longer serves its purpose. Members of the elite class will then seek out different means of distinguishing themselves from the masses. Macro-level changes that lead to an increase in the supply of individuals possessing a particular trait or behavior, therefore, can result in devaluation in status-based purchasing power. On the demand side, new cultural knowledge and behavioral practices can be imported into a given social system and used by some groups as a marker of status. Beisel, for example, describes how, in New York City in the early 1900s, the nouveaux riche consumed and displayed European artwork as a means of buying entry into elite social circles.[25] To the extent that such new cultural practices reduce the demand for preexisting status markers, devaluation results for those who previously derived status from such markers.

Multiple Sources of Devaluation

Although I have conceptualized three distinct markets, I emphasize that the markets should not be viewed as being completely independent of one another. As Max Weber pointed out long ago, processes related to status, class, and politics are distinct but also tend to be deeply intertwined.[26] Failing to recognize these interdependencies can lead to a flawed analysis. Incentives to support right-wing activism should be particularly strong when groups are experiencing power devaluation from multiple sources and in more than one market. Nicola Beisel's study of the antivice movement provides a noteworthy example.[27] She convincingly argues that many elite families supported the movement because they came to believe that their children's exposure to vice could bring shame upon the family. This public shame would have negative consequences in terms of their children's social capital and could lead to downward mobility in the class structure.

Status, as reflected in both cultural and social capital, certainly can affect one's purchasing power within economic and political markets of exchange.[28] As a general rule, power within each of the exchange markets that I have discussed is transferable to other markets. Economic power can be used to gain more political power and is often valuable in maintaining social esteem. Political power can be used to secure more wealth and income in an economic market. It is this transferability that makes simultaneous devaluation (power devaluation in more than one exchange market) important in stimulating right-wing activism. If an actor's purchasing power is only devaluating within one market, his power within other markets can be utilized to restore his devaluating purchasing power. When the actor is losing power within more than one market, however, there is a greater incentive to act outside of established institutions within a social movement. In such cases, the actor's capacity to maintain or restore power through institutionalized means is weakening.

I do not argue that every person who joins a right-wing movement is experiencing power devaluation. The circumstances described above, however, can contribute to the formation of a critical mass of activists who have particularly strong incentives to support right-wing activism. Once such a critical mass is formed, other supporters may be drawn into the organization for a wide variety of reasons (including social incentives—a point that will be addressed in depth in chapter 7). Social-movement organizations are typically diverse in terms of their members' level of commitment to the cause and in terms of their own ideologies and goals.[29] Yet, as discussed in the next section, individuals are unlikely to join an organization if that organization does not construct a rationale for its existence that at least appears credible in light of conditions that the potential supporter is able to observe within her or his community.

Interpretive Processes

I have identified conditions that produce economic, political, and status-based power devaluation. Macro-level shifts in the structure of social relations may be linked to changes in the supply of, and demand for, that which individuals offer in exchange. Devaluation in purchasing power within either exchange market can generate incentives to engage in right-wing activism, particularly when clearly identifiable groups are disproportionately bearing the brunt of devaluation. Power devaluation reduces a group's capacity to maintain its advantages within established institutions, and many individuals are likely to be open to any form of collective action that is oriented toward maintaining and/or restoring their power. Power devaluation by itself does not directly stimulate right-wing activism. It does, however, alter individuals' perceptions of their circumstances and provide opportunities to construct new interpretive frames that generate support for right-wing mobilization.

The insights of frame-alignment theorists are crucial here. In a path-breaking article published more than twenty years ago, David Snow and his colleagues, drawing on Goffman's frame-analytic perspective, emphasized the important role of cognition in social movement activism. The frame concept refers to schemata of interpretation that allow individuals to make sense of their social environment and the world at large.[30] Frame alignment refers to an active and ongoing process of making interpretive orientations offered by social movement organizations congruent with those held by individuals whose support the social-movement organization hopes to enlist. The key insight of the framing perspective on social movements is that individuals are unlikely to participate in collective action unless they first perceive that social change is both desirable and possible. McAdam makes a similar point, giving an important role to "cognitive liberation" in his political process model. As McAdam states,

> The important implication of this argument is that segments of society may very well submit to oppressive conditions unless that oppression is collectively defined as both unjust and subject to change. In the absence of these necessary attributions, oppressive conditions are likely, even in the face of increased resources, to go unchallenged.[31]

These general insights are crucial in the study of social movements. The framing perspective in social-movement research is a remedy for the way in which classical theories, and contemporary theories such as resource-mobilization theory and political-opportunity theory, have neglected micro-level mobilization processes. The framing perspective invites investigation into how members and leaders of social-movement organizations actively construct interpretive frames that encourage and inspire individuals to participate in collective action.

Power devaluation, as described above, can cause a shift in interpretive orientations and can lead many individuals to perceive that social change is indeed desirable. It is the time-variant nature of the collective grievances that is important in this regard. When individuals or members of a particular group have never possessed certain rights and privileges, it may not naturally occur to them that they deserve a claim to those rights and privileges. However, individuals and group members are more quickly disposed toward action when they are losing rights and privileges that they have previously enjoyed. Many of us may wish to own an expensive sports car, but we do not vigorously pursue the goal. An owner of a Ferrari, on the other hand, is quick to respond when his possession is threatened by thieves or by wind-blown shopping carts in the supermarket parking lot. Snow and his colleagues make a similar point when they discuss how collective action can be spurred by a "disruption of the quotidian," wherein groups respond to an event that "disrupts everyday subsistence and survival routines."[32]

Although power devaluation is likely to lead many individuals to desire social change—change that would preserve or restore their power—participation in a social movement requires more than desire. As the framing literature emphasizes, individuals must also perceive that social change is possible and that their participation in collective action will contribute to a successful outcome. Structural changes that lead to power devaluation, therefore, can generate a pool of individuals who are favorably predisposed toward right-wing mobilization. To capitalize on these conditions, leaders of an emergent movement must develop collective action frames that convince these same individuals that participation in the movement will not be wasted effort. Movement leaders and recruiters must demonstrate that they not only understand the problems of those they wish to recruit, but that they also have a solution. Along these lines, Snow and Benford point out that a successful collective-action frame includes diagnostic, prognostic, and motivational components.[33] To enlist support, movement leaders must diagnose the problems facing their constituents, propose a course of action that could address their grievances, and create a sense of both urgency and efficacy to encourage immediate action.[34]

These framing efforts must resonate strongly with those being targeted for recruitment.[35] A movement's diagnosis and prognosis need not be factually accurate to be effective.[36] The frames, however, must appear credible to those who are on the receiving end. Successful frames are those that speak directly to the source of the problems confronting potential members and supporters and also present a plausible course of action that could be taken to reverse power devaluation.

If power devaluation results from changes in the supply of, and demand for, that which actors offer in exchange, simple microeconomic logic implies a course of action that should be intuitively appealing to anyone experiencing power devaluation. An actor's purchasing power can be restored by (a) stimulating the demand for what the actor offers in exchange and/or (b) restricting the supply of competitors.

One strategic framing option that is available to those initiating right-wing mobilization is to activate cultural identities and offer these identities as alternative bases of exchange. Activation of cultural identities can add a motivational component to the frame. But it can also be useful in developing the frame's prognosis. Cultural appeals may be used to stimulate demand for what the movement's constituents offer in exchange. In this way, the movement seeks to enlist support from those who share a cultural bond. Such appeals can promote solidarity and a common consciousness among those who are experiencing power devaluation, but they may also gain support and sympathy from individuals who share the cultural bond but are not experiencing power devaluation in an economic, political, or status-based market. Cultural attacks can also be used to restrict the supply of competitors. Arguments for strict restrictions on immigration, for example, can be made on both cultural and economic grounds. Regardless of which grounds are used in the argument, enactment of strict restrictions limits the supply of individuals entering the country.

As is true in most social movements, organizers and recruiters for right-wing movements must foster a strong sense of collective identity. This process typically involves identifying group boundaries—that is, specifying which social groups the movement represents and which social groups it opposes. Individuals are unlikely to participate in a movement unless they view themselves as being a member of a clearly identifiable group represented by the movement.[37] The task of mobilizing right-wing activism, therefore, would be considerably more difficult if power devaluation was randomly distributed across members of all social groups. That is rarely the case, however. More often than not, the population experiencing power devaluation overlaps substantially with cultural boundaries, making cultural identity an effective tool for any movement seeking to reverse power devaluation.[38] The slogan "buy American," for example, encourages consumers to disregard quality and price of commodities and instead purchase American-made goods out of a sense of patriotism and civic duty.

Organizational Resources and Political Opportunities

I have argued that the emergence of right-wing social movements such as the Ku Klux Klan cannot be explained by either resource mobilization theory or by political opportunity theory. Each of these theories takes collective grievances as a starting point and seeks to explain how, rather than why, collective action emerges. Resource-mobilization theory treats collective action as an organizational problem and draws attention to how qualitative and quantitative changes in organizational resources available to a group can stimulate collective action. Political-opportunity theory gives attention to how changes in the political context can contribute to collective action primarily by influencing people's perceptions of the likelihood of succeeding if they were to engage in collective action. No matter how aggrieved people may be, if they sense that the political climate dooms them to failure they are unlikely to mobilize.

When we are considering collective action that is undertaken by relatively powerless and oppressed groups, both of these theories make good sense. In such cases, the why of collective action is not problematic. Members of the group are deprived of benefits enjoyed by others in society, and they are treated unjustly by legal and political authorities. It is often safe to assume that many members of the relatively powerless group desire social change, but require an organizational infrastructure and a favorable shift in the political context to make change happen. When considering right-wing mobilization, however, the why of collective action may not be obvious. More important, it is likely that time variant grievances, rather than an infusion of new organizational resources or a favorable shift in the political context, provide the initial impetus for action. Indeed, the reactive or defensive nature of right-wing action suggests that resources available to the movement's constituents are declining rather than increasing, and political circumstances are becoming less favorable rather than more favorable. These groups are, after all, oriented toward restoring and preserving preexisting benefits and privileges. Rather than capitalizing on new resources and new political opportunities to expand their rights and privileges, they are reacting to a new threat to their capacity to maintain an advantaged position.

This is not to say, however, that resources and political opportunities are irrelevant to right-wing mobilization. Indeed, it is difficult to imagine sustained collective action taking place when resources are lacking or where the political context is so oppressive that a movement does not have some room to breathe. Although neither resources nor political opportunities trigger right-wing mobilization, each plays an important role in determining the movement's growth and trajectory. According to my theory, power devaluation leads to a shift in interpretive processes, which can lead those who are experiencing power devaluation to activate preexisting organizational resources and exploit preexisting political opportunities in an effort to reverse devaluation.

Because right-wing movements act on behalf of relatively advantaged groups, the movement's constituents typically have access to organizational resources and they have some degree of access to those who hold political power. However, organizational resources and political opportunities should be treated as variables rather than as constants. Not all groups affected by power devaluation are equal in these regards, and these differences can determine whether or not collective grievances are transformed into sustained collective action. Sustained collective action, right-wing or otherwise, requires money, space, equipment, alternative media, and leadership.[39] The greater the availability of such resources, the more likely it should be that groups of individuals experiencing power devaluation will be able to attract large numbers of members and supporters and to sustain collective action.

Sustained collective action should also depend on the structure of political opportunities, defined by Tarrow as "consistent—but not necessarily formal or permanent—dimensions of the political environment that provide incentives for people to undertake collective action by affecting their expectations of success or failure."[40] Some of the primary forms of political opportunities that have been identified in the social movement literature have to do with popular access to the political system, instability of elite alignments, the presence of elite allies, and levels of state repression directed against the group.[41] Political opportunities vary over time and across space and, like organizational resources, can shape the trajectory and growth of right-wing mobilization. The more favorable the political context, the stronger the movement can grow.

Consequences of Right-Wing Movements

The logic of the power-devaluation model can be extended to analyze the consequences, as well as the causes, of right-wing mobilization. What determines whether or not a right-wing movement will influence the political process? To a great extent, this will depend on how successful the movement is in terms of recruiting members and supporters. Strength in numbers is clearly applicable when considering a movement's capacity to seize power by force, win power through electoral processes, or gain significant concessions from the state's representatives. All else constant, it is easier for a large and resourceful group to seize power than it is for a smaller and less resourceful group. Size also matters when it comes to influencing electoral outcomes or gaining concessions from state representatives. If a movement can deliver a large block of votes from its members and adherents, it is possible to elect candidates who will serve the movement's constituency. And if the movement is large and resourceful, any candidate seeking to maintain his or her power must consider the costs and benefits of granting concessions (or failing to grant concessions) to the movement.[42]

Even a strong and resourceful movement, however, must typically enlist support from allies if it is to seize power or if it is to win victories by influencing electoral processes.[43] The movement's core constituency may be of sufficient size to demand attention, but not large enough to overcome all other groups contending for power. Indeed, a right-wing movement typically generates a backlash, and the threat that it poses to those who are outside of the movement can promote unified opposition. In addition to organizational strength and the size of its membership base, therefore, the impact that the movement has on political processes will depend on its capacity to forge alliances with other groups. The movement's capacity to form such alliances is to some degree predetermined by the nature of power devaluation and the interpretive processes that gave life to the movement in the first place.

Right-wing movements draw upon cultural identities as a remedy for power devaluation, using cultural appeals to stimulate the demand for what their constituents offer in exchange and using cultural attacks to restrict the supply of competitors. In a sense, the movement is drawing new battle lines, promoting in-group solidarity on one front to overcome losses suffered by core constituents on another front. Once these battle lines are drawn it is hard to turn back, even when doing so would be necessary to form alliances needed to secure political victories. Framing strategies that are effective in recruiting members and supporters may limit a movement's capacity to forge alliances that are needed to secure political victories.

I apply the power-devaluation model in the remaining chapters of this book. I begin by considering how economic power devaluation contributed to the growth of the Klan. I identify important sources of economic power devaluation that affected many individuals who were drawn to the Klan in the early 1920s. I also show how Klan leaders responded to economic power devaluation as they developed collective action frames that were designed to attract members and adherents.

4

Responding to Economic Change:
Redefining Markets along Cultural Lines

*Klansmen should be taught that it is their sacred duty as Klansmen to al-
ways favor a Klansman in the commercial world, whether it be in buying,
selling, advertising, employment, political, social, or in any way wherein
a Klansman is affected.*
— *Imperial Night-Hawk*, November 7, 1923

According to the power-devaluation model discussed in the previous chapter, macro-level shifts in the structure of social relations can result in economic, political, and status-based power devaluation for subsets of the
population. This devaluation can provide incentives to support right-wing
mobilization. It alters the way in which individuals understand their circumstances and creates new framing opportunities for those who wish to
organize collective action. In this chapter I begin by identifying primary
sources of economic power devaluation that affected many of those who
were drawn to the Klan in the early 1920s, and I discuss how the Klan constructed interpretive frames that should have resonated strongly with those
whom the movement sought to recruit. I rely primarily upon the Klan's
publications, especially its national publication, the *Imperial Night-Hawk*,
to identify the major themes that the movement addressed within its framing efforts. The Klansmen's words, expressed in these periodicals, also provide a window into the way in which Klan leaders diagnosed the problems
confronting the movement's constituents.

Although I believe that scholars have not fully appreciated the role that
economic conditions played in stimulating the Klan's growth, I also feel it

is important to avoid economic reductionism. The economy is just one of several factors relevant in understanding the emergence and growth of the Klan. It is noteworthy that movement leaders had more to say about race, religion, and nativity than they did about the economy. However, Klan leaders did discuss economic conditions, and the power-devaluation model will help to illuminate the way that economic grievances articulated by the movement were intertwined with cultural identities. Because racial, ethnic, religious, and gender boundaries overlapped substantially with economic-class positions and occupational boundaries in the 1920s, cultural conflicts were often simultaneously economic conflicts.

Although I reject assumptions made by classical social-movement theory about the irrationality of social-movement participants, I believe it is also important not to exaggerate the rationality and foresight of the movement's leaders and members. I am not arguing that Klan leaders convened to discuss economic policies and as a result devised a clear, consistent, and always coherent set of positions that, if implemented, would have solved the economic grievances confronting the movement's members and supporters. It would be more accurate to say that the movement leaders, through processes of trial and error, stumbled upon a way of talking about the economy that appealed to many native-born white Protestant Americans during this specific historical moment. The Klan practiced an opportunistic form of recruiting. As discussed in the opening chapter, the movement began to hit its stride when recruiters were instructed to go into the field and identify problems facing community members and then offer the Klan as a solution to those problems. Through this process, recruiters certainly would have learned that the economic livelihoods of many Americans were being threatened by macro-level shifts in economic arrangements. These economic conditions provided a framing opportunity for the movement's leaders and recruiters.

Klan leaders emphasized that they were not in favor of policies that would benefit any particular social class. Indeed, they consistently argued that class divisions were dangerous to American society and Americans should subordinate their class interests to promote the common interests of all native-born, white Protestants. The "Klansman's Creed" includes statements professing the movement's belief in "a closer relationship of capital and labor" and "the prevention of unwarranted strikes by foreign labor agitators."[1] Varying responses to the Klan's message should have had less to do with specific attributes of individuals and more to do with how economic life was organized in local communities.

Consolidation of Capitalism and the Deskilling of Labor

The decade of the 1920s is often described as a period of economic prosperity that preceded the Great Depression, but the prosperity of the 1920s was unevenly distributed. Economic hardships and uncertainties facing many Americans during this decade were described at length by Robert and Helen Lynd in the classic sociological study *Middletown: A Study of American Culture*.[2] We now know that "Middletown" was actually Muncie, Indiana. Like nearby Kokomo, Muncie was swarming with Klan members in the early 1920s. In fact, according to the Klan's membership lists for the state of Indiana, 27 percent of white, native-born males in Delaware County (of which Muncie is the county seat) were members of the Ku Klux Klan. As the Lynds describe it,

> Coming upon Middletown like a tornado, catching up many of these latent differences into a frenzy of activity, the Ku Klux Klan has emphasized, during its brief career in Middletown, potential factors of disintegration. Brought to town originally, it is said, by a few of the city's leading business men as a vigilante committee to hold an invisible whip over the corrupt Democratic political administration and generally "to clean up the town," its ranks were quickly thrown open under a professional organizer, and by 1923 some 3,500 of the local citizens are said to have joined. As the organization developed, the business men withdrew, and the Klan became largely a working class movement. Thus relieved of the issue that prompted its original entry into Middletown, the Klan, lacking a local issue, took over from the larger national organization a militant Protestantism with which it set about dividing the city; the racial issue, though secondary, was hardly less ardently proclaimed.[3]

Although the Lynds emphasized the working-class composition of the Klan's membership in Muncie, it is important to keep in mind that the authors defined "working-class status" in very broad terms. Working-class individuals were defined as those who "address their activities in getting a living primarily to things, utilizing material tools in the making of things and the performance of services."[4] This definition includes skilled workers and artisans—for example, members of the old middle class who engage in labor but also own the means of production (such as tools and small shops).

As the Lynds describe it, social relations in Muncie were increasingly circumscribed by social class during this time period. An intensification of class stratification was accompanied by rapid changes in the organization of work in the city. Women were beginning to enter the labor force at an unprecedented pace, with many of them going into manufacturing occupations. Manufacturing employment was itself undergoing dramatic change. In a very short time span, the apprentice–master craftsman system that had characterized manufacturing production in the city had largely given way to assembly-line production. As the superintendent of a Muncie machine shop expressed it, "Seventy-five percent of our force of 800 men can be taken from the farm or high school and trained in a week's time." Muncie's workers were vulnerable to the fluctuating labor demands. In fact, 62 percent of the working class males interviewed by the Lynds had lost time due to a layoff in the first six months of 1924.[5]

The Lynds chose to study Muncie, Indiana, because of its middle-of-the-road quality. Muncie, they believed, was a representative case in the study of contemporary American life. Although Muncie may not have been perfectly representative of American cities, the conditions described by the

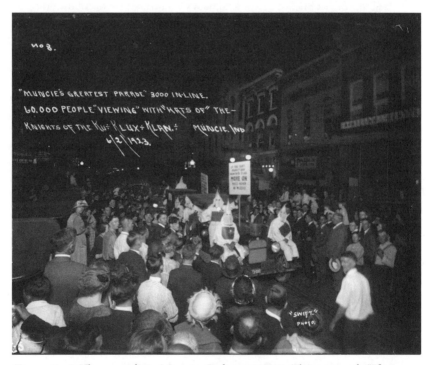

Figure 5. A Klan parade in Muncie, Indiana, 1923. The sign reads "If you can't respect our country's flag MOVE ON. You'll never be missed." W. A. Swift Collection. Courtesy of Ball State University. Copyright 2006. All rights reserved.

Lynds certainly extended beyond Muncie's city limits. In many communities throughout the nation, similar changes in manufacturing production were being implemented. Economic transitions in the early 1900s, of course, were rooted in ongoing processes of industrialization. The Industrial Revolution in the United States began, in earnest, in the aftermath of the American Civil War. It was not until the 1920s, however, that a majority of U.S. citizens resided in urban locations. As industrialization developed, economic and political power steadily accrued to the industrial elite. Along with prosperity generated by industrialization, many Americans also experienced negative consequences. As Link and McCormick describe it,

> When Americans of the early 1900s looked at their society, many sensed what a few articulated: the economic changes of the preceding generation had created profound social strains and widespread misery. Mothers worked for long hours in unsafe factories in exchange for fewer dollars than single people, let alone families, could survive on in decency.

Figure 6. Marching Klansmen attract a crowd of curious onlookers in Anderson, Indiana, 1922. W. A. Swift Collection. Courtesy of Ball State University. Copyright 2006. All rights reserved.

Twelve-year-old children labored there too; some of them fell down elevator shafts or lost their hands to the machines.[6]

Such conditions helped to give rise to the Progressive movement in the early 1900s. The banner of "progressivism" covered a wide variety of reform efforts initiated by numerous groups (often with contradictory goals). Progressives voiced their opposition to trusts, robber barons, big-money interests, and protective tariffs that sheltered manufacturing interests while raising prices for farmers and middle-class consumers. Progressives also opposed urban political machines. Middle- and upper-class reformers were critical of the machines because of the high real estate taxes that they imposed, their alleged corrupt practices, and the special attention that they paid to poor and working-class immigrants who often formed the base of the bosses' electoral support.[7]

Industrialization was also accompanied by the growth of organized labor. Total union membership increased from less than 500,000 just before the turn of the century to approximately 5,000,000 by 1920. Labor strengthened its position during World War I, as President Wilson granted several concessions in order to promote national unity during wartime. Labor exercised its growing muscles in the late 1910s and early 1920s with a series of strikes. As the war came to an end, however, capitalists intensified efforts to undermine the strength of labor through an open-shop drive combined with paternalistic practices. Workers were encouraged to express their grievances through company unions. Company unions had enrolled about 1.5 million workers by 1928, while membership in the American Federation of Labor plummeted during the 1920s.[8] Welfare capitalism of the 1920s was promoted by industrialists and by many in the Republican Party as a way to promote general prosperity that would benefit both employers and employees.

Organized labor was an impediment to capitalists' profits because the unions stood in the way of the rationalization of manufacturing production.[9] Much of the unions' bargaining power came from skilled manufacturing workers' ability to maintain control over the production process. A monopoly over the skills required for production gave workers some autonomy and allowed them to pace their work and control levels of output.[10] A booming wartime economy allowed employers to profit without aggressively pursuing wage reductions for employees.[11] However, the increased production levels during the war (and in the years before the United States entered the war) also provided a justification for consolidating industry and implementing more efficient production methods.[12]

During the wartime economic expansion, with labor in short supply, unions focused primarily on bargaining for higher wages rather than resisting rationalization.[13] A sharp postwar recession, however, provided additional incentives for capitalists to reduce worker autonomy in the workplace. Technological advances, particularly increased capacity to harness electricity in manufacturing production, facilitated the process. Phenomenal growth in the auto industry also provided a clear example of how the high-speed assembly line could dramatically increase productivity while simultaneously stripping control of the production process from the worker.

Changes in the organization of work sharply increased productivity in manufacturing production during the years in which the Klan was gaining strength. Although skilled labor still had a role to play in industrial production, industrialists increasingly relied upon unskilled labor in the pursuit of profit. Skilled laborers and small-scale manufacturers became increasingly vulnerable due to a declining demand for skilled labor and because small producers were at a competitive disadvantage due to the increasing efficiency and higher volumes of output in large factories employing unskilled labor. According to U.S. census reports, the number of manufacturing establishments in the nation producing in excess of $1 million in products increased from 3,819 in 1914 to 10,583 in 1925. In 1914 these large establishments employed approximately 35 percent of manufacturing wage earners in the United States. By 1925, more than half of manufacturing wage earners (56.8 percent) were employed by establishments producing more than a million dollars worth of products annually.[14] The average number of workers per manufacturing establishment remained relatively constant in the early part of the century, but then increased substantially from 1914 to 1919 (see Figure 7). Value added to manufacture in the United States also increased sharply during this same time period (see Figure 8).

Increasing reliance on unskilled labor in manufacturing production held cultural, as well as economic, implications. Those who occupied positions as skilled workers or as small-scale manufacturers were, overwhelmingly, native-born white Protestant males whose ancestors had come to the United States from northern and western European nations. Structural changes in the early 1900s, however, meant that different actors would be available to fill unskilled manufacturing positions. Immigration was an important factor. Immigration rose steadily in the first decade of the twentieth century and remained high until the onset of World War I (see Figure 9). After a steep decline during the war years, immigration rates began to rise again in the early 1920s. Unlike earlier waves of immigration, the vast majority of individuals entering the country in the early 1900s came from

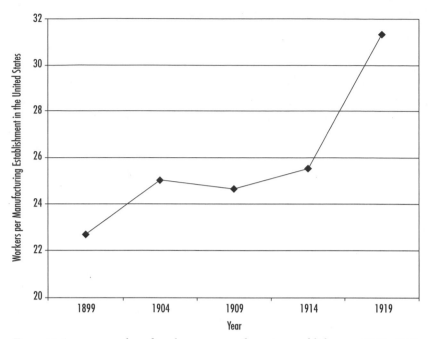

Figure 7. Average number of workers per manufacturing establishment, 1899–1919. U.S. Department of Commerce, Statistical Abstract of the United States, *1924.*

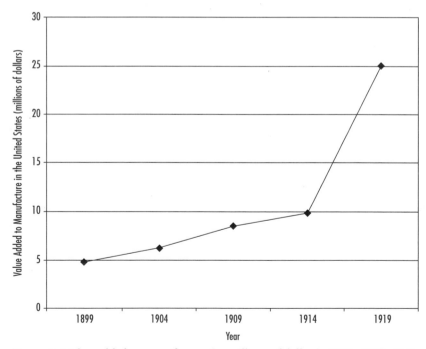

Figure 8. Value added to manufacture (in millions of dollars), 1899–1919. U.S. Department of Commerce, Statistical Abstract of the United States, *1924.*

central, eastern, and southern European nations. English was not their native tongue, and the immigrants tended to be Catholic or Jewish rather than Protestant. In the 1920s, the divide between skilled and unskilled labor overlapped substantially with ethnic and religious cleavages.

Immigration was not the only source of unskilled labor in the 1920s. Based on data from the U.S. census, the number of gainfully employed women in the United States increased from approximately 5.3 million in 1900 to 8.6 million in 1920. During this time period, the number of women in sales and clerical occupations increased by 390 percent. Although in manufacturing the change is less dramatic, women also increasingly entered manufacturing occupations. According to the census, the number of women entering into manual occupations (excluding mines and farms) increased from 1.48 million in 1900 to 2.05 million in 1920. The number of women listed as laborers (excluding mines and farm) increased by 45 percent. Among men, the number of laborers increased by 35 percent during the same period.

African American migration also provided a new source of unskilled labor in many urban locations. The Great Migration began around 1910 and

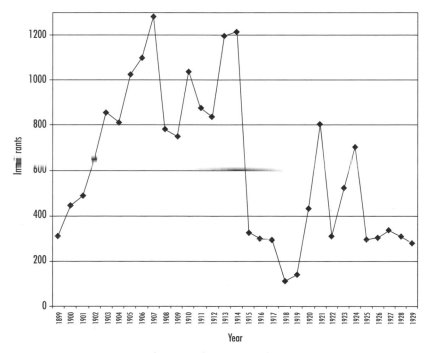

Figure 9. Immigration to the United States (in thousands), 1899–1929. U.S. Department of Commerce, Statistical Abstract of the United States, *1930.*

quickly accelerated. Between 1910 and 1930 the percent of southern-born blacks residing outside of the South rose from 5 percent to 13 percent.[15] In fact, more than five million blacks migrated out of the South from 1910 to 1919.[16] Census data indicate that the number of blacks living in northeastern states increased from 484,000 in 1910 to 1,147,000 in 1930. In north-central states, the black population increased from 543,000 to 1,262,000 during the same period. Although smaller in absolute numbers, the number of African Americans in western states more than doubled, rising from 51,000 to 120,000. While the Great Migration of African Americans has been well documented, it is important to keep in mind that the South also experienced substantial intraregional migration during this time period with African Americans moving from rural southern locales to southern cities. White southerners, also, migrated to nonsouthern states. And like African Americans, large numbers of white Americans migrated from rural to urban locations. According to census figures, approximately 48.7 percent of white Americans lived in an urban location in 1910. Twenty years later, almost 60 percent (59.3) resided in an urban location.

Changes in the organization of manufacturing production generated economic power devaluation for many native-born white Protestant Americans in the early 1900s. Skilled laborers experienced declining demand for their services as industrialists increasingly relied upon machinery and unskilled labor in the factories. Small-scale manufacturers also experienced devaluation resulting from an overall increase in the supply of goods being produced. Advances in modern transportation and the expansion of retail chain stores such as F. W. Woolworth, S. S. Kresge, and J. C. Penney also meant that goods produced in large cities and in distant locations were increasingly available for purchase in small towns throughout the nation. As a result, small-scale producers in midwestern, western, and southern towns increasingly found themselves in competition with large manufacturers in cities such as New York, Boston, Chicago, and Philadelphia. According to data from the U.S. Federal Trade Commission, there were only 257 retail chains in operation in 1910.[17] By 1920, that number had increased to 808, and only five years later, in 1925, there were 1,440 chains in operation.[18]

Just as skilled manufacturing workers were adversely affected by the consolidation of industrial capitalism, small merchants and shopkeepers also experienced economic power devaluation by virtue of the overall increase in supply of goods which could be purchased from a chain store or through a Sears, Roebuck and Co. catalog. Indeed, in many communities during the 1920s chain stores faced organized resistance. Historian Carl G. Ryant notes that Sears adopted the practice of shipping its goods in unmarked wrappers so that customers would not have to face the wrath of those who opposed retail chains.[19] The grievances against chain stores are nicely summarized by an operator of a foundry and machine shop in Shreveport, Louisiana:

> We have sought to portray the inequities attendant with short weights and inferior quality of merchandise sold by the chain store. We have attempted to bring to light the ruinous and devastating effect of sending the profits of business out of our local communities to a common center, Wall Street. We have appealed to the fathers and mothers—who entertain the fond hope of their children becoming prosperous business leaders— to awaken to a realization of the dangers of the chain stores' closing this door of opportunity. We have insisted that the payment of starvation wages, such as the chain-store system fosters, must be eradicated. . . . We have importuned those who labor to join in striking down the chain system in every form and character, before it enslaves the masses and holds them prisoners of an economic system which will destroy every vestige of individual initiative and personal incentive to progress.[20]

As this statement suggests, power devaluation could be widespread in many communities whose local economies had previously been driven by local production and where commodities had previously been marketed by local merchants. With profits flowing out of the community and toward large manufacturing centers and national corporations, local money supplies declined. Stagnating local economies could reduce consumer demand for goods and services as well as local employers' demand for labor.

Agricultural Depression

A severe agricultural depression in the early 1920s also produced power devaluation for many native-born white Protestant Americans. As was true of the industrial changes during this time period, changes in agricultural production were rooted in ongoing historical conflicts and struggles. By the late 1800s, fewer and fewer individuals could escape the impact that rich and powerful organizations had on their everyday lives. American farmers, in particular, were affected by the emergence of powerful corporations. Farmers relied upon the railroads to transport their goods to market, but resented the large profits falling to the railroad barons. They were also angered by the profits accruing to warehousers and speculators, believing that the rewards should go to the producers of goods, rather than to those with enough capital to hold them for speculation.[21] American farmers were also at the mercy of the seemingly mysterious forces that were responsible for the nation's money supply. Deflationary monetary policies hurt farmers by increasing the price of credit and by forcing down commodity prices.[22] Wall Street bankers came to symbolize farmers' increasing vulnerability to forces that were out of their direct control.

Although agrarian grievances lingered, many farmers reaped enormous profits in the 1910s. Agricultural exports increased dramatically during the decade (see Figure 10). The change is mainly due to increased exports to European nations whose populations were preoccupied with war. During this time period, many American farmers optimistically increased production levels and borrowed money to purchase new equipment to make farming more efficient. When the war came to an end, however, exports quickly plummeted, and the supply of agricultural commodities produced by American farmers substantially exceeded the demand.[23]

The problem was exacerbated by high tariffs. Protective tariffs had been relatively low during the years in which Woodrow Wilson, a Democrat, occupied the White House. When Republican Warren Harding assumed the presidency, high tariffs were reinstated with the Emergency Tariff Act of 1921 and the Fordney-McCumber Tariff Act of 1922. This contributed to

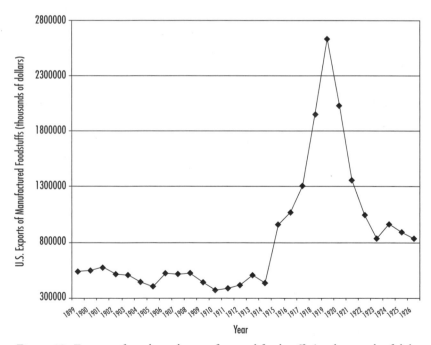

Figure 10. Exports of crude and manufactured foodstuffs (in thousands of dollars), 1899–1926. U.S. Department of Commerce, Statistical Abstract of the United States, 1926, Table 477.

economic grievances in America's heartland. The war had transformed the United States from a debtor to a creditor nation. The capacity of European nations to purchase American farm commodities hinged on their ability to sell products to the United States. Tariffs protecting American industry, therefore, impeded such sales. Many Americans residing outside of industrial centers resented the way in which tariffs benefited those who were linked to the industrial economy at the expense of those who were not. As can be seen, farmers' purchasing power rose to high levels in the years 1917 to 1919 before declining, after the war, to levels even lower than those of the early 1900s (see Figure 11). These conditions certainly helped fuel agrarian discontent in the early 1920s.

The agricultural depression did not affect all farmers equally. Those who produced crops for export were hit especially hard. During the war, for example, many hog farmers profited handsomely by exporting pork products to Europe. In 1918 hog prices were close to $18 per hundredweight. By 1923 prices had plummeted to $7.55 per hundredweight. Similarly, corn

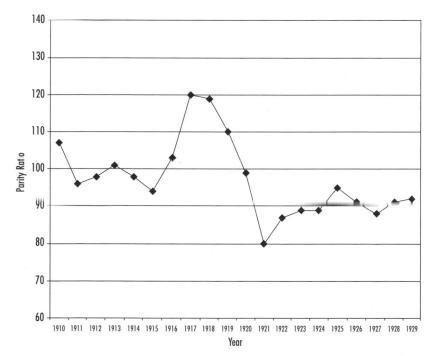

Figure 11. Ratio of prices received by farmers to prices paid, 1910–1929. U.S. Department of Commerce, Historical Statistics of the United States, Colonial Times to 1970.

(which many midwestern farmers grew to feed hogs) sold for approximately $1.50 per bushel in 1918 but dropped abruptly to $0.64 per bushel in 1920 and remained low in the early 1920s. Wheat farmers were also hit hard, with prices dropping from a high of $2.19 per bushel in 1919 to $0.93 per bushel in 1922. Cotton prices also peaked in 1919 at about $35 per pound, only to drop to about $17 per pound by 1921.

Changes in the agricultural economy in the early 1920s resulted in widespread power devaluation. Many American farmers bore the brunt of an abrupt drop in demand for agricultural commodities. Increases in protective tariffs further agitated long-standing resentments held by many Americans who paid higher prices for manufactured goods due to policies designed to protect the interests of large manufacturers located in a different region of the country. While farmers were directly affected by declining demand for farm commodities, the loss of farm income could have a devastating effect on an entire community where agricultural production drove the local economy. An overall decline in the supply of money in such a community meant that power devaluation would be experienced by merchants, shop owners, professionals, and individuals seeking employment.

The Klan's Framing of Economic Grievances

The 1920s Klan, in many respects, resembled European fascist movements that were emerging during the same time period. The organization employed a strategy combining electoral participation, violence, and intimidation as it sought to promote "100 percent Americanism," breaking down all class barriers. Like the Rexists in Belgium, the Klan was strongly anti-Communist, but also blamed big business for the impoverishment of small and medium sized family run businesses.[24] As was the case in 1924 Germany, where collapses in agricultural prices in some regions made rural communities susceptible to mobilization by the Nazi Party, devastating agricultural declines in the early 1920s made many American rural-dwellers receptive to the Klan's message.[25] And similar to the Italian case, where a socialist monopoly over employment opportunities and wage contracts pushed excluded groups toward fascism, the Klan acted against Socialists and other groups on the political left, and against the patronage systems typical of urban political machines in the United States.[26]

While many modern historians have overlooked connections between the 1920s Ku Klux Klan and rising European fascism, these comparisons were being made by contemporaries of the Klan, both by opponents of the movement and by Klan leaders who spoke admirably of European fascists.[27]

For example, one article in the Klan's *Imperial Night-Hawk* proclaims "the Facisti of Italy came into existence in a cloak of liberty, like a rainbow of promise, and was hailed by even the enlightened element of the world as a 'voice in the wilderness' of human freedom and religious tolerance." In another article, the *Night-Hawk* claimed that "Mussolini's battle in his home country to subdue communism and anarchy and halt Papal aggression was an entirely worthy cause."[28] Klan leaders of the 1920s saw their movement as playing a similar role.[29] According to Hiram Evans, the Klan intended to break down all barriers between classes to create a united America. He added that this required violence, at times, because of vigorous and organized resistance to this goal.[30]

Economic changes taking place in the United States generated incentives for many individuals to support right-wing mobilization. People who were adversely affected by these changes were not elite, yet they were also not poor and oppressed. For many, a relatively advantaged position was being undermined by decreasing demand for what they offered in economic exchange or from an increase in the supply of others who offered something similar in economic exchange. However, power devaluation does not automatically result in right-wing activism. For a social movement to emerge, interpretive frames must be constructed, and these frames must convince a critical mass of individuals that social change is both desirable and possible through collective action. These interpretive processes are vital when it comes to transforming collective discontent into collective action.

The Klan's leaders discussed a wide range of issues in public addresses and in the periodicals that they published. The power-devaluation model, combined with knowledge of the economic changes that were taking place in the early 1900s, can be used to show why the Klan's framing of economic problems struck a chord with many Americans in the early 1920s. The article below, penned by the Klan's national leader, Imperial Wizard Hiram Wesley Evans, nicely summarizes themes that were addressed elsewhere (albeit in a more fractionalized manner) in the Klan's literature. Here, the Klan's Imperial Wizard offers his analysis of economic transitions that were taking place in the early 1900s:

> Since the Lord said, "Six days shalt thou labor, and rest upon the seventh day," all the emphasis has been placed upon the latter part of that divine injunction. We have defied the Sabbath, when God intended and so arranged His universe, that the six days of labor should be all-important. The command from on high was to work, work, work, work, work,

work—and not by proxy, but with our own hands and hearts and feet. Otherwise it would not have been provided in nature's laws that health and happiness have no other source that is so invariably safe and sure.

This Nation has committed, or at least permitted, fundamental errors for which the curse of evil consequences may never entirely be obliterated. Slavery was instituted and the racial results of it will probably remain so long as the Republic has existence. Then, in response to the same un-Christian dread of creative work, more vaguely and yet more generally we established serventry [sic]. There followed logically, inevitably, the more modern and monstrous cheap labor idea. The steps have been: owner and slave, master and serving man, magnate and menial.

This is a national tendency which we cannot charge to immigration, old or new. In fact the old immigration is perhaps more guiltless than the native stock. But it is fundamentally related to our modern immigration problem.

Humanity has become a commodity. For mercenary motives, our importers of it want the most inferior grade. Industry desires cheap labor. Therefore, we have had this recent flood of 5 and 10-cent citizenship.

Take any map which shows the concentration of the South and Eastern European type of immigrant and you will see what has happened. Wherever manufacturing and mining and lumbering predominate, there the hordes of unskilled labor have overwhelmingly been assembled. In the last two decades it has reached the proportions of a deluge.

Do our overlords of industry realize what they are doing to America? Have they stopped to measure the national consequences of this cheap foreign labor idea? Is it the part of patriotism to import inferior mental and moral elements in such numbers as to lower our standards even below the danger point? Is profit more important than the sum total of American Citizenship?[31]

Evans's discussion of the economy reflects republican ideology and Jeffersonian ideals that were widely and deeply held by skilled laborers, farmers, and other middle-class Americans in the early 1900s.[32] Republican ideology stressed the importance of individual autonomy in sustaining democratic institutions. Individuals, according to this line of thought, must participate in the political process while considering what is in the best interest of the nation as a whole, rather than what is in the best interest of the individual voter. To do this, citizens must be free from coercion and, therefore, not dependent upon employers, spouses, religious authorities, or others who might limit their autonomy. Evans bemoans the commodification of human labor and notably places blame on the industrial elite—the "overlords of industry"—for prioritizing profit over republican virtue. The Klan's Imperial Wizard condemned slavery, arguing that the system reflected "un-Christian dread of creative work." In general, economic problems of the day, according to Evans's analysis, were rooted in the increasing reliance on unskilled labor in the pursuit of profit.

Although critical of industrial capitalists, Evans expressed no sympathy toward the proletariat. Indeed, as was common in Klan literature of the time, he conflates unskilled laborers and immigrants. Much of the article from which I have quoted above describes the recent wave of immigrants in very disparaging terms. For example, later in that article Evans writes,

> The present and recent flood of inferior foreigners has vastly increased our illiteracy, vitally lowered the health level and visibly menaced America by inheritable mental and moral deficiencies. Where among true Americans is the voice that would dare either to contradict or defend these evil conditions?[33]

The Klan's leader thus provides both an economic and a cultural argument for restricting immigration. The economic problem is that a steady flow of immigrants facilitates capitalists' efforts to rationalize manufacturing production, devaluing skilled labor in the process. At the same time, Evans characterizes immigrants as inherently inferior to the native stock.

Notably, Evans did allow for one important exception to the rule in terms of his condemnation of the use of unskilled labor. Referring to conditions in rural America he wrote,

> In this farm field exists the only legitimate and justifiable excuse for cheap labor, yet that class is moving irresistibly cityward to swell the slums and multiply immorality. For example, throughout the south the colored race, in numbers far beyond the statistical showing, is migrating to the North—not to its rural districts, but to its industrial centers.[34]

This argument could simultaneously satisfy two different constituencies. On the one hand, migration of blacks to urban centers was one factor facilitating the rationalization of manufacturing production and undermining the bargaining power of white laborers.[35] At the same time, many southern farm owners were facing severe labor shortages during this time period as blacks migrated toward the North and toward southern cities.[36] Stemming black migration would restrict the supply of unskilled labor in urban settings and would also maintain the demand for positions as agricultural laborers or sharecroppers, with the latter effect being desirable to Klan constituents in rural locales who exploited black labor.

Prognosis: Supply Restriction

The Klan's framing of economic conditions should have resonated strongly with many Americans in the early 1920s. Klan leaders spoke directly to grievances resulting from economic transitions and, just as important, they proposed a cure that would have seemed plausible to those in their targeted audience. As argued above, microeconomic logic should be intuitively appealing to anyone who is experiencing power devaluation. If power devaluation results from an increase in the supply of that which members of a particular group offer in economic exchange, then advocating courses of action that restrict the supply of competitors would seem like an effective means of reversing power devaluation. Klan leaders discussed economic conditions in a wide variety of ways. However, they consistently emphasized supply restrictions as a solution for economic problems.

Klan writers published numerous articles advocating immigration restriction. The general approach taken in these articles is similar to that illustrated in Hiram Evans's article. The Klan writers specify adverse economic consequences of immigration, but in order to expand their base of support, they also describe the immigrants in unflattering terms. By promoting ethnic and cultural solidarity, Klansmen could transform individual grievances into collective grievances. At the same time, appeals to cultural identities could be used to gain support among those who were not being directly affected by the economic consequences of immigration. For example, one Klansman writes,

> There are two great influences in this country opposed to checking this stream of European "riff-raff" and in favor of letting down the bars and flooding this country with the very scum of the earth. These influences are the Roman Catholic church and the big employers of pauper labor.[37]

Similar to Evans, the author points out industrialists' motive for supporting unrestricted immigration and, in the same sentence, also characterizes the immigrants as "scum" and "riff-raff."

The Klan's literature focuses primarily on immigration from Europe and almost invariably reminds readers that recent waves of immigrants were composed primarily of Catholics who, Klan leaders argued, could not be assimilated into American society. As a national movement, however, the Klan also sought to appeal to Protestants in western states who were concerned with immigration from other parts of the world. One article "reports,"

> Fifty thousand Mexicans have sneaked into the United States during the past few months and taken the jobs of Americans at wages on which a white man could not subsist. All of the Mexicans are low type peons. They are all Catholics and many of them are communists.[38]

Occasional references to Asian immigrants can also be found in the Klan literature. These references, like those directed toward European and Mexican immigrants, point to dire economic consequences of immigration while characterizing the immigrants as inherently inferior to white Protestant Americans.

The Klansmen's writing clearly communicates their view that the nation did not require additional unskilled laborers. One article, for example, complains about how "those admitted are predominantly of the unskilled labor class and those with no occupations at all, the unskilled classification being the largest." The author goes so far as to report relevant data on the skills possessed by recent immigrants. In an address to Klansmen at a national convention (Klonvocation) in Kansas City, a Klansman argued that "Alpines" were unfit for immigration to the United States, describing them in the following manner: "This group forms the bulk of Europe's peasant class. They come here from the Slavic countries and from Southern Germany. They are a stolid, docile, tenacious people—enduring heavy labor, but contributing nothing to leadership, initiative and independence."[39] From the Klansmen's perspective, tenacity and a capacity to endure hard labor were undesirable traits for immigrants, reflecting the Klansmen's concerns about the increased use of unskilled labor in American society and the deterioration of republican ideals.

Evans proposed that immigration policy should be based on social scientific research and consideration of the welfare of the nation as a whole, rather than on the desires of industrialists. In an interview printed in the *Imperial Night-Hawk,* he suggests,

> With exceptions applying only to separated families, we temporarily should stop immigration absolutely. Then we should collect the information indispensable to a wise immigration policy. Such information would contain full knowledge of the causes and the effects of the foreign influx, the facts relative to our needs for rural and urban labor, and scientific counsel concerning how these needs can be met without injury to the all-important principle of ultimate amalgamation into our political and social structure.[40]

Notably, such a "scientific" approach would not only restrict the supply of unskilled labor that could be employed in manufacturing occupations, it would also be sensitive to the labor needs of Klan constituents in rural locations—what Evans elsewhere referred to as "the only legitimate and justifiable excuse for cheap labor."[41]

The Klan leaders' negative characterizations of unskilled labor indicate that they did not view unskilled laborers as a core constituency, regardless of the race or ethnicity of the laborer. However, their argument could be extended, and was extended, in such a way that some unskilled laborers might find it appealing. As noted above, promoting cultural solidarity can be an effective means of combating power devaluation. In addition to criticizing the use of unskilled labor, Klan leaders also argued that unrestricted immigration drove down wages for all American workers. Hiram Evans claimed that competition with immigrants "saps the vitality of leadership, because it makes the struggle for existence such a burden that people stagger under it." Other Klan writers noted that immigrants "come from countries where they have been accustomed to a lower standard of wages and living; they, therefore, compete with American labor, which is already over-crowded."[42] These same sentiments were echoed in the Indiana Klan's newspaper, the *Fiery Cross:*

> Stated in plain terms, the demand of large manufacturers for immigrant labor at the present time is baldly a demand for cheap labor. It is a demand for men who will accept work at wages below that which the American standard of living demands; for men who will work longer hours than American standards of health and comfort insist should constitute a day's work; for men who will undermine the American standard of living, who will tend to break down the labor unions, who will work for a wages so small that the employing class can temporarily reap larger profits from their labor.[43]

Klan leaders attempted to make the case that immigration was detrimental to all "100 percent Americans," regardless of their occupational status. For example, one author wrote,

> Every foreign government realizes that the liberty of the United States and the ease with which the citizens of other countries become enriched, at the expense of one hundred per cent American citizens, makes it a most desirable place to come to. They are anxious, therefore, to send their citizens here to accumulate fortunes and return to their native heath with the wealth garnered from the American people who are careless with their money and never think that it will eventually find its way to the coffers of some foreign banking institution, thereby taking away that which rightfully belongs to the American citizen.[44]

In this way, the Klansman suggests that Americans were unwittingly contributing to the flow of capital from the United States to foreign nations. This argument tapped into the same resentments that many Americans held about how consumer dollars spent in southern, midwestern, and western states enriched large corporations in eastern U.S. cities. Indeed, Hiram Evans claimed that some of the eastern states were already "lost to true Americanism" and that the midwestern, southern, and western states were the new battlegrounds in a fight over fundamental American values and interests.[45]

African American Migration

The way in which Klan writers addressed race relations also indicates that the movement was not primarily concerned about its constituents' direct competition for jobs but was instead focused on the way that unskilled labor strengthened large manufactures at the expense of small-scale manufactures and skilled laborers. The Klan's rhetoric rarely mentions competition with African Americans as a problem in need of redress, in spite of the fact that during this time period industrialists' use of blacks as strikebreakers was a source of racial conflict in many urban locations.[46] In fact, several articles boast of the Klan's efforts to protect blacks from unruly mobs. This is not to say that Klan members did not, at times, inflict violence upon African Americans. Indeed, before assuming the position of Imperial Wizard, Hiram Evans allegedly led a group of Klansmen who brutally assaulted a black bellhop in Texas. Many other instances of Klan-initiated violence have been noted by historians and other scholars. However, when Evans took control of the national organization, he strategically calculated that curtailing Klan violence would be necessary if the movement were to broaden its appeal, especially as it moved into the political arena.[47]

The Klan's leaders characterized blacks as inferior to whites in the same way that they characterized the new wave of European immigrants as inherently inferior to native-born Americans. However, the Klan's literature primarily adopted a paternalistic stance toward blacks and spared them much of the venom that was directed toward Catholics and immigrants. The following passage from the *Imperial Night-Hawk* typifies the way in which the Klan press addressed the race issue:

> We of the Klan are supposed to hate the negro. Nothing could be further from the truth. The negro was brought to America. He came as a slave. We are in honor and duty bound to promote his health and happiness. But he cannot be assimilated. Intermarriage with him on a wholesale scale is unthinkable. There are more than ten millions of him—about a tenth

of our population. He cannot attain the Anglo-Saxon level. Rushing into cities, he is retrograding rather than advancing, and his rate of mortality is shockingly high. It is not in his interests any more than in the interests of our white population that he should seek to assume the burdens of modern government. These are almost too heavy for the strongest shoulders, and their weight is increasing. However much we may regret to state the truth when the truth is otherwise than pleasant, it is better that it be stated and faced. I am sure the interests of all are served thereby.[48]

This passage clearly illustrates the strategic calculations involved in the Klan's official stance in regard to race relations. Certainly, the Klan's assertions of white supremacy were attractive to many Americans, given the deeply entrenched prejudices of the time period. Unlike the immigration issue, however, it was the internal migration of African Americans that contributed to the economic grievances of Klan constituents. The Klan offered paternalism as the optimal strategy for discouraging black migration.

Klan writers, it seems, had resigned themselves to the fact that black Americans composed a significant proportion of the American population and would continue to do so into the foreseeable future. They attributed that reality to mistakes of the past—a system of slavery that they condemned. As Hiram Evans put it, "The negro is here. He was brought here. In love and justice must we ever promote his welfare, his health and happiness."[49] It was the migration of blacks and their potential for moving out of menial positions that was of primary concern. In an article titled "Negroes Flocking to Industrial Centers," a Klan author alarmingly cites an address made by a public figure in Chicago who described how, in the previous ten years,

> Negroes, both men and women, have gained and held places of employment in five or six of the basic industries of the North, such as packing, iron and steel and clothing industries. Formerly they were restricted mainly to domestic and personal service. Today negroes are coming North in numbers comparable to the days of the war labor shortage.[50]

The Klan's paternalism was undoubtedly designed to keep blacks "in their place." It is important to bear in mind that in the early 1900s not all white Americans shared similar strategic interests in regard to African Americans. Some whites were engaged in a competitive relationship with blacks and had an incentive to support racial violence as a means of eliminating and/or driving away competitors. More prosperous whites did not compete with blacks but instead exploited their labor. As Tolnay and Beck point out in their study of lynching patterns in the American South, the Great Migration prompted a shift in the way in which many southern land owners interacted with African Americans. Before the exodus began, when exit to the North was not a viable option for most blacks, white southern landowners could rely upon intimidation and coercion to facilitate the exploitation of black labor. However, once the migration flow was underway, many prosperous southern whites shifted strategies, using paternalistic appeals to dissuade blacks from migrating. In many cases, white landowners intervened to prevent lynching attempts initiated by less prosperous white southerners—something that they had failed to do before the onset of the Great Migration.[51]

The Klan's paternalism is strikingly similar to that described by Tolnay and Beck. As one Klan writer expressed it, "The Knights of the Ku Klux Klan has no fight to make upon the negro. He is recognized as an inferior race and Klansmen are sworn to protect him, his rights and property and assist him in the elevation of his moral and spiritual being and in the preservation of the purity of his race."[52]

In the Klan press, movement leaders consistently discouraged members and supporters from inflicting violence on African Americans. One Klan writer, for example, described how some Klan members aided southern farmers by protecting African Americans:

> The farmers in the southern part of our territory have seen fit to bring in negroes to handle their crops due to the fact that they can't get white labor. Inasmuch as there have not been any negroes in that part of the country before, it has caused a lot of trouble, by a bunch of good for nothing loafers trying to run out the negroes. At —— the other night a negro house was fired on and a negro man killed. The Klan has furnished the authorities sufficient information to lead to the arrest of the supposed murderers. In addition to that fact they have paid the undertaker's bill and mailed the receipt to the negro widow with a letter explaining that the Klan had nothing to do with the murder and also offered her assistance in the future.[53]

Still another article described how Klansmen prevented the lynching of a black man in South Carolina while risking their own lives in the process. This type of protection that the Klan offered to black Americans, of course, came with strings attached. As Mary Jackman has emphasized, paternalism is often an effective strategy in processes of domination and exploitation.[54] Lurking beneath the surface of the paternalistic rhetoric is an understanding that violence may be utilized against members of an exploited group who do not conform to the dominant group's expectations and desires.

The Klan's writings make it very clear that the protection it offered to black Americans extended only to those who were willing to accept a subservient role in society. Klan writers appeared to be particularly concerned about the possibility that blacks would be drawn into radical politics. One article claimed that an organization called the African Blood Brotherhood was being directed from Moscow and was seeking to promote communism in the United States. The article concludes, "It proves that there are black Bolsheviks as well as white ones and that the call of the Klan for the maintenance of White Supremacy is not an idle one."[55] In another lengthy tirade on the threat of communism, a Klan author claims that Communists were secretly organizing blacks as part of a plot to extend their influence to the United States. According to the author,

> To Communists there are but two classes: the working class, and all others. There [sic] ideal is to have the working class absorb the others and to make of the United States a working class republic, a part of similar republics all over the world and all dominated by the central government in Moscow.[56]

Klansmen clearly feared the prospects of labor radicals inciting a revolt among black Americans. Sounding the alarm on this issue also seems to reflect a deliberate strategy used to motivate Klan members and adherents. According to the *Imperial Night-Hawk,* "white-girl followers of the Communists are meeting classes of negro prospects as social equals. These girls are teaching the negroes to demand social equality."[57] Black men who dared to associate with white women, or who dared to challenge racial inequality in any of its dimensions, were immune from the Klan's paternalistic protection. In fact, they were at risk to the type of Klan-initiated violence that movement members administered to those whom the Klan accused of immoral or traitorous behavior.

Through paternalism, the Klan aimed to stem the flow of black migration, which would, in turn, reduce the supply of unskilled laborers in cities while preserving the demand for positions as laborers in rural settings. The paternalistic rhetoric offered by the Klan's national leadership was flexible enough, however, to provide cover for acts of violence against blacks that were carried out in many local settings.[58] As one article expressed it, "The law abiding negro need have no fear of the Klan; but woe be unto the criminal, white or black."[59] African Americans who refused to accept a subordinate position could be victims of the brutality embedded in the Klan's white supremacist views. In an angry response to W. E. B. Du Bois's call for racial equality, a Klan writer declares, "This negro has a wonderful fine opinion of himself. We expect he thinks he would make a black pope, and a good one. The menace of the black brute will never be 'downed' until this [sic] kind of negroes are put where they can never raise their voice."[60]

In the early 1920s, the range of acceptable behavior for African Americans was extraordinarily narrow. Virtually any type of behavior that did not serve the interests of Klan constituents could be defined by Klansmen as a threat to the established order. This established order, according to the Klan, was sanctioned by an almighty God.

Traditional Families and Labor Force Participation

Women, as well as African Americans and immigrants, provided a source of unskilled labor that was needed to fuel the consolidation of industrial capitalism as well as the expansion of retail chain stores throughout the nation. Not unlike the Klan's approach to African Americans, men of the Klan utilized paternalism in an attempt to control the behavior of women and to keep women out of the paid labor force. Klan leaders, for example, criticized businessmen who threatened the family and contributed to immoral behavior by hiring women to work in offices and factories.[61] Kathleen Blee notes that women of the Ku Klux Klan shared the prejudices that the men held, but saw the women's chapters as vehicles for expanding women's rights.[62] However, Blee describes the Klansmen's approach to women as a mixture of paternalism and misogyny.[63] As self-appointed guardians of traditional morality, Klansmen would at times instigate public floggings, victimizing those accused of immoral behavior. Klan posses punished men for not taking care of their wives and children, targeting vagrants, drunkards, adulterers, abusive husbands, and those who abandoned their families. Women were also victimized for offenses such as infidelity, flirting, or neglecting their children. Working outside the home was interpreted, by some Klansmen, as a form of child neglect.[64]

The Klan's paternalistic approach to gender relations was different from its approach to African Americans. While the Klan promoted white supremacy, its leaders argued that women were equal to (or perhaps superior to) men. They did this by advocating separate spheres for women and men while claiming that the roles traditionally performed by women should be valued more in American society. Whenever possible, the men of the Klan liked to have their paternalistic rhetoric conveyed by an object of their paternalism. For example, the Indiana Klan's *Fiery Cross* would, on occasion, publish letters that were said to have been written by black Americans who endorsed the goals of the Klan. Similarly, an article published in the Klan's national magazine, the *Kourier,* was written by the "Imperial Commander of the Women of the Ku Klux Klan." According to the author,

Herein lies the greatest strength of woman's power. Men depend upon her and are, for the most part absolutely, or nearly so, helpless without her. Men do not question her motives. Men do not tolerate abuse of her. Men receive their greatest inspirations from her. They perform their most noble deeds, or they make their most crushing failures, according to her power over them.[65]

This power that women held over men, however, was rooted in women's roles as men's helpmates. The Klan's literature makes it clear that women's primary responsibilities were to care for the home and to raise children—the next generation of Klansmen. In the same article, the writer refers to the American flag and opines,

The white of our flag's folds cries out for unstained purity and virtue in manhood and womanhood, and bears silent testimony that the men of the nation would rise as one to protect and keep spotless the honor and chastity of our home-builders—our women.[66]

The men of the Klan sought to enlist the support of women within the political arena and became advocates of women's suffrage after the fact—a point addressed in more depth in the next chapter. Relevant to a discussion of economic power devaluation is the way that the Klan omitted labor force participation when it constructed its notions of gender equality. A report issued by a committee of Klansmen began to outline "the position assumed by the Knights of the Ku Klux Klan toward the Women of the Ku Klux Klan" by stating, "The women of the nation are an important factor in the development of the moral, educational, ethical and political life of the people. The American men need the co-operation and assistance of the women if the best results are to be obtained."[67] In another article, a Klan writer encourages women to participate in politics because governmental policies directly impact family and home life. He adds,

We know that home life is held in low esteem, and childhood and womanhood are neither protected nor honored, where the forces of radicalism have swept a country and gained the upper hand. We find woman as a home builder, an important and never-failing ally in times of greatest need.[68]

Women of the Klan, at least from the perspective of the men of the Klan, were emancipated, yet also primarily responsible for maintaining the home and rearing children. This dualism is reflected in the following excerpt from the "Klanswomen's Creed," published in the *Imperial Night-Hawk:*

We believe in the American home as the foundation upon which rests secure the American Republic, the future of its institutions, and the liberties of its citizens. *We believe* in the mission of emancipated womanhood,
freed from the shackles of old-world traditions, and standing unafraid
in the full effulgence of equality and enlightenment. *We believe* in the
equality of men and women in political, religious, fraternal, civic, and
social affairs wherein there should be no distinction of sex.[69]

Obviously, the men of the Klan could not attack women, as a category,
in the same way that they rhetorically attacked Catholics and immigrants.
Klansmen, after all, were tied to women through kinship. Men directly
benefited from these ties to women and sought to confine women to subservient roles. By praising women who attended to the home and raised
children, and by defining nonconformity as immoral and un-American,
Klansmen aimed to stem the flow of women into the labor force much in
the same way that they sought to stem the flow of black migration to urban
locales. The Klan's message should have resonated strongly with many men
who were not only concerned about the economic consequences of increasing utilization of unskilled labor, but were also concerned about the power
that they held over their wives (and over women more generally).

The Klansmen's concerns about the family also extended to children
and, more specifically, child labor. Several articles in the Klan press address the topic. One ties the issue to the value of public education, arguing that "one serious cause of illiteracy in America is the fact that parents
frequently let their children stay out of school to work. It is said that more
than a million children between the ages of ten and fifteen years of age are
out of school to work in different industries."[70] In another article a Klansman writes,

It is to the corporations interest that the child labor laws and Sterling-
Reed Educational bill and a rigid immigration measure be kept off the
statute books. By the failure of measures of this nature they are enabled
to secure a cheaper class of labor and hold the price paid to the American
citizen down to a minimum at all times. The un-educated child of today
will be the common laborer of the future and every day the ambition of
men is being blighted when they realize that they are fighting losing battles because they were not as fortunate during their school days as were
their playmates. One of the greatest duties of Klankraft to the American
child is the successful carrying on of an educational program that will
put every child in the United States, of school age, into a Free Public
school.[71]

Similar to the way in which Klansmen discussed immigration, the writer calls industrial capitalists to task for profiting from the use of unskilled labor. However, while the Klan denigrated immigrants in order to supplement its argument on behalf of immigration restriction, it spoke of the importance of protecting innocent children:

> The children whom we expect to be the leading citizens in a few short years are now employed in sweat-shops; their small frames are being stunned and their minds will, sooner or later, become warped, by constant association with a class whose interests are foreign to the United States. A condition of this kind will soon beget a generation of children whose thoughts will be of unclean things and whose acts will be those of the criminal.[72]

Certainly, many of the men and women who were drawn to the Ku Klux Klan were genuinely concerned about the detrimental effects of labor on young children and not simply concerned about restricting the supply of unskilled labor. On this point, and on several others, the Klan aligned with the progressive movement. Economic transformations described earlier in this chapter should have made any argument that advocated restriction in the labor supply appealing to many native-born white Protestant Americans. The potency of these frames rested on the movement's abilities to link these economic arguments to shared cultural values that were deeply held by those whom they sought to recruit.

Prognosis: Stimulate Demand

By constructing interpretive frames advocating restrictions in the supply of unskilled labor, while simultaneously drawing upon cultural values that were shared by many native-born, white Protestant Americans, the Klan made itself attractive to skilled laborers and small-scale manufacturers whose own economic livelihoods were being harmed by the increasing concentration of industry. The resonance of the Klan's economic framing extended beyond these groups. Changes in manufacturing production not only affected skilled workers and small manufacturers, but could also affect entire local economies. As industrial production increasingly became concentrated in large cities, wages and consumer dollars followed. The agricultural recession pushed many individuals off the farm and into urban centers where they were pulled by a growing demand for unskilled labor. Local merchants and professionals residing outside of these urban centers experienced shrinking demand for the goods and services that they offered.

The Klan leaders advocated programs that would benefit individuals residing in towns and cities outside of the industrial centers, but for the most part they did not appeal directly to farmers. In fact, there are some indications in the Klan press that movement leaders did not see farmers as a natural constituency; rather, they sought out ways of including farmers' grievances in their frames to expand their base of support. For example, one writer commenting on the importance of public education noted,

> Those of us who live in the towns and cities must learn to look beyond the family circle and take an active interest in our rural brother and make the country school measure up to the importance of the economic position which the American farmer occupies. The farmer is the wealth producer of the nation, the backbone of all industry. The better educated the farmer, the greater becomes his capacity to produce. The greater the facilities for education in the rural schools, the more attractive the farm life becomes. Let us extend the right hand of fellowship to our rural brother, with our influence, our taxes—and demonstrate the true fraternity of brotherhood.[73]

Although the Klan sought the support of farmers, movement leaders were harshly critical of radical responses to farmers' grievances—responses that would benefit farmers at the expense of their other middle-class constituents. Movement leaders pitched their message to property owners and to those who aspired to own property. Any response to the agricultural crisis that challenged private property rights would have threatened many of the Klan's constituents. Rather than aligning with radical agrarian movements, the Klan leaders instead aligned themselves with progressives and populists. This can be seen in the way in which the Klan press discussed party politics. Several articles in the *Imperial Night-Hawk* are critical of the old guard in the U.S. Congress and speak positively of the progressive insurgents. One article, for example, noted that the progressive insurgents in Congress are greatly outnumbered and emphasized the importance of increasing their numbers in coming elections. Another article complained about how the old guard politicians in Congress were deeply entrenched and described the Progressives (the opponents of the old guard) as "Representatives who would unselfishly put public welfare above personal and political gain."[74]

Klan leaders frequently discouraged supporters from claiming allegiance to a single party. Progressives could be found in the ranks of both the Democrats and the Republicans—as could the Klan's own constituents. The *Imperial Night-Hawk,* for example, offered praise for William Jennings Bryan, the fiery Democratic leader who articulated the grievances of rural Americans and strongly advocated inflationary monetary policies and low tariffs. Yet the Klan also offered positive comments on behalf of Republican progressives such as Theodore Roosevelt and Robert LaFollette.[75] The Klan press would later turn against LaFollette after the Wisconsin senator publicly condemned the Invisible Empire during his third-party presidential bid in 1924.[76] Before LaFollette spurned the organization, it is clear that the Klan's sympathies were with the Democratic and Republican progressive insurgents.

As the election of 1924 approached, an article in the Klan's *Fiery Cross* offered a state-by-state evaluation of each of the U.S. senators (see Figure 12). Notably, progressive Republican Robert LaFollette was characterized as "an outstanding liberal leader." Idaho's progressive Republican senator, William Edgar Borah, is described by the Klan as "an outstanding progressive." In general, the word "progressive" is modified by positive adjectives such as "good" and "dependable." Pro-business Republicans and conservative Democrats, on the other hand, are described as reactionaries or as being "Old Guard" or "machine Republicans." Several of the Progressives whom the Klan writer admired shared the movement's racial and religious bigotries and their support for prohibition. However, the progressives and populists earning the Klan's praise were also advocates of economic policies favored in regions of the country in which agricultural production was vital to local economies. These policies include low tariffs, inflationary monetary policies, tax reduction, regulation of railroads, and better credit terms for debtors. Reflecting the economic interests of its broad middle-class constituency (those whose fortunes were not tied to industrial production in northern cities), Klan leaders aligned themselves with populist and progressive legislators and encouraged their constituents to support independent and progressive candidates, regardless of the candidate's party identification.

Although the Klan press made relatively few specific references to farmers' grievances, the references that do appear reflect progressive and populist goals. The *Imperial Night-Hawk* criticized Kansas gubernatorial candidate William Allen White for taking a stance against the Klan but failing to offer any programs to address farmers' grievances.[77] Articles published in the Indiana Klan's *Fiery Cross* did occasionally comment on difficulties faced by midwestern farmers. They cautioned against radical responses to agrarian grievances and instead endorsed populist and progressive stances such as expanded credit, government aid for more efficient farming techniques, lower taxes, and lower railroad rates.[78] There are some indications in the Klan literature that the leaders and recruiters spoke more directly to farmers' grievances in public appearances delivered in rural settings. For example, an article in the *Imperial Night-Hawk* commented on a joint appearance in Indiana by Hiram Evans and D. C. Stephenson and noted that Stephenson "decried the Federal reserve system 'as the organized betrayal of America,' and condemned them for their inadequacy and failure to render farm relief measures."[79]

Similar language can be found in D. C. Stephenson's July 4 speech in Kokomo, which was reprinted in the *Fiery Cross*. There, Stephenson declared,

> Today we are turning backward in the hope that we might again meet in a common bond of mutual understanding on a basis of hope, and may that hope not be forlorn, that the men who manipulate the affairs of the American government today shall not lose sight of the founding fathers and that they shall now arise to our present need and come forth with a response which will answer the crying need of the farmers of America, who have been neglected and pushed out in the cold; who have been ignored and in a large measure hampered from receiving their just portion of governmental support where the institution of governing found it expedient to protect and defend our industry.[00]

In the same speech, Stephenson adds,

> The manipulators of our national government have seen fit to erect high walls of tariff to protect our industrial interest, which were not justified, and while they have permitted the Federal Reserve Bank to become a tool in the hands of selfish and sordid men, the great agricultural districts of American have been sorely neglected to a point where they have suffered almost beyond hope of repair.[81]

Passionately delivered populist rhetoric such as this was, certainly, music to the ears of many Americans who resided in communities that were bearing the brunt of a sharp decline in demand for agricultural commodities in the aftermath of World War I. Klan leaders were careful to avoid pitting the specific interests of farmers against those held by other Klan constituents.

Vocational Klannishness: The Klan's Boycotting Strategy

In light of the economic changes taking place during the Klan's ascendance, it is understandable why many skilled laborers, small manufacturers, and farmers were attracted to the movement. Yet the Klan's leaders sought to construct frames that would unite all white Protestants in a powerful social movement. Many of the Klan's members and supporters were professionals

State	Evaluation
Alabama	Two Democrats, Underwood, reactionary, and Heflin, progressive.
Arizona	Ashurst, progressive Democrat; Cameron, Old Guard Republican.
Arkansas	Robinson and Caraway, Progressive Democrats.
California	Both Republicans, Johnson listed as progressive with a question mark, and Shortridge a machine man.
Colorado	Has Adams—a recently appointed Democrat, and Phipps, Old Guarder.
Connecticut	Brandegee and McLean—both reactionary Republicans.
Delaware	Bayard, untested Democrat, and Ball, a machine Republican.
Florida	Fletcher and Trammell, both Democrats, the latter more progressive.
Georgia	Has Harris and George, good Democrats.
Idaho	Borah is an outstanding progressive, and Gooding a "me too" Republican.
Illinois	Two machine Republicans, McCormick and McKinley.
Indiana	Ralston is a progressive Democrat; Watson has been a Republican machine leader.
Iowa	Has Cummins, Republican reactionary, and Brookhart, who is his own boss.
Kansas	Curtis as a machine leader, with Capper somewhat on the fence.
Kentucky	Stanley, progressive Democrat on most issues; Ernst, colorless Old Guarder.
Louisiana	Ransdell and Broussard, both very conservative Democrats.
Massachusetts	Lodge is the dean of Republican reactionaries, with Walsh a progressive Democrat.
Maryland	Has Bruce, an untried Democrat, and Weller of the Republican Old Guard.
Maine	Both Fernald and Hale are Republican regulars.
Michigan	Ferris is a progressive Democrat and Couzens, an independent Republican.
Minnesota	Both Shipstead and Johnson are ultra progressive.
Mississippi	Has Harrison and Stephens, good Democrats.
Missouri	Reed is an able Democrat, while Spencer will do anything the Old Guard machine thinks best.
Montana	Walsh and Wheeler, both able Democrats with the latter a real independent.

Nebraska	Has two Republican progressives—Norris and Howell.
Nevada	Pittman is a progressive Democrat and Oddie an Old Guard Republican.
New Hampshire	Both Moses and Keyes are regular Republicans.
New Jersey	Edwards is an untested Democrat and Edge a reactionary Republican.
New Mexico	Has a progressive Democrat in Jones, with Bursum a machine Republican.
New York	Has Copeland, a liberal Democrat, and Wadsworth, Old Guard.
North Carolina	Simmons is an able, progressive, Democrat, with Overman, also of that party, but conservative.
Ohio	Has two regular Republicans—Willis and Fess.
Oklahoma	Checks itself, Owen being a liberal Democrat and Harreld a machine Republican.
Oregon	Both Republicans, with McNary a wobbler and Stanfield dependable from the Old Guard point of view.
Pennsylvania	Has two Old Guarders—Pepper and Reed.
Rhode Island	Gerry is a progressive Democrat and Colt a Republican regular.
South Carolina	Two Democrats—Smith and Dial, with the former more liberal.
South Dakota	Both Republicans, with Norbeck having progressive leanings and Sterling in the camp of the regulars.
Tennessee	Has two Democrats—Shields and McKellar, the latter progressive.
Texas	Both Democrats, Sheppard being a dependable progressive, with Mayfield, a new senator, said to be in that camp.
Utah	King is a fighting, independent Democrat, with Smoot an expert Republican machinist.
Vermont	Has one Republican —Greene—and a vacancy due to the death of Dillingham.
Virginia	Swanson and Glass are good Democrats.
Washington	Hass Dill, a progressive Democrat, and Jones, a sometimes independent Old Guard Republican.
West Virginia	Neeley is an average Democrat, and Elkins a completely colorless Old Guarder.
Wisconsin	LaFollette is an outstanding liberal leader, with Lenroot a regular.
Wyoming	Has one of the highest class Democrats in Kendrick and an Old Guard wheel horse in Warren.
Source: Fiery Cross, Michigan State edition, December 14, 1923.	

Figure 12. A Klan writer's evaluation of the U.S. Senate, December 1923.

and merchants rather than skilled laborers, small manufacturers, or farmers. Yet, many professionals and merchants were affected by the same economic transitions. Their livelihoods were, after all, linked to the strength of local economies. Many suffered from a sharp decline in demand for their goods and services. The Klan's promotion of "Klankraft" or "Vocational Klannishness" should have been especially appealing to any native-born, white Protestant who was suffering from such a decline in demand. Essentially, the Klan attempted to organize a nationwide boycott, insisting that Klan members only do business with other Klansmen, or with other "100 percent Americans."

The foundation of the Klan's boycotting strategy can be found in the Klansman's Creed, which states, "I am a native-born American citizen and I believe my rights in this country are superior to those of foreigners."[82] Although Klan leaders resented the alleged "clannishness" of Catholics and Jews, which was interpreted as a violation of republican ideals, they surmised that they should adopt a similar practice as a necessary defense mechanism. An article titled "The Definition of Klankraft and How to Disseminate It" nicely summarizes the motivation behind the practice:

> Vocational Klannishness is paramount to the ultimate success of our order. All other sects practice it in one way or another, and in many instances to the entire exclusion of the protestant world, and it is apparent that the protestant world has failed to realize the significance of this practice. It is our duty as Klansmen, for self-preservation, if for no other reason, to practice vocational klannishness and I am firmly of the opinion that the time is coming, and not far distant, when we shall be compelled to follow this phase of Klankraft religiously. Otherwise, we shall feel the yoke of utter dissension in our own ranks brought about through our inability to compete in a commercial way with great corporations owned and controlled by men who do not hold their allegiance to one flag and government. Therefore, the seeds of vocational klannishness should be sworn at every opportunity in all meetings of Klansmen, and in carefully worded press items. Klansmen should be taught that it is their sacred duty as Klansmen to always favor a Klansman in the commercial world, whether it be in buying, selling, advertising, employment, political, social or in any way wherein a Klansman is affected.[83]

The Klan's practice of Klankraft draws upon (and constructs) cultural solidarity to stimulate the demand for goods and services provided by white, native-born Protestant Americans. In some instances this practice involved direct boycotts of specific merchants. In other instances it involved professionals and merchants publicly displaying their ties to the Invisible Empire in hopes of attracting customers.[84]

The practice could also be extended to and applied against national corporations. MacLean, for example, describes how a Klan lecturer in Athens, Georgia, railed against the encroachment of large retail chain stores:

> Local Klan lecturers on "Americanism," for their part, blamed Jews and Catholics for the chain-store peril. One speaker dared his listeners to "find out who owns stock" in companies like the "A & P Grocery stores." Jews and Catholics, it seems, hid behind the initials. He further complained that "department stores, all of which are principally owned by Jews or foreigners," were pushing out "American" businesses. He raved against the inroads made into Georgia by Sears & Roebuck, which he insisted was owned by "Jews. Jews. Jews." Its entrenchment would "spell ruination" for the state's independent merchants. He told listeners to find out whether their druggists, undertakers, grocers, butchers, and clothing and shoe merchants were "JEWS OR CATHOLICS," and if so, to boycott them and organize others to do the same.[85]

The boycotting strategy, a recurrent theme in the movement's discourse, was ideally suited for the task of uniting a socioeconomically diverse constituency and providing an economic motivation to support the Klan. Regardless of whether one was a professional, merchant, farmer, artisan, or small manufacturer, many stood to benefit from a massive boycott of all commercial enterprises that could be linked in some way to Catholics, Jews, or immigrants. The Klan justified its tactics by making positive claims about the cultural heritage of its own constituency and derogatory claims about their cultural enemies. Klansmen even offered a religious rationale for boycotting. In one article, the writer asserts, "Above all else, Jesus Christ was a Klansman. Christ, according to the Klan's author, "sought, first of all, to deliver the people of his own race, blood and religion from bondage of ignorance, tradition and superstition." After quoting from the book of Romans, the author then instructed his readers, "Real Klankraft requires that Klansmen be knit together as the members of our body, each cooperating with the other; so closely and vitally connected that when one member suffers the whole body suffers."[86]

Vocational Klannishness applied not only to trade, but also to employment. Klan publications frequently published notices where individuals were seeking a "100 percent American" worker or a "100 percent American" employer. A notice in the *Imperial Night-Hawk*, for example, sought to help a small Georgia town attract a physician:

Klansmen of a thriving Georgia town are anxious to get in touch with a first-class, one hundred percent American physician who wishes to locate in a town in which Klankraft predominates. The physician, as a citizen of the Invisible Empire, will receive the endorsement of the entire Klanton. For further information, address The Imperial Night-Hawk, Post Office Box 1204, Atlanta, Ga.[87]

The Klan's practice of vocational Klannishness could backfire. One article in the *Imperial Night-Hawk* noted, "In communities where Protestants are in the minority, Klansmen dare not let their identity be known, lest they be boycotted or Ostracized."[88] Indeed, in Chicago, the National Unity League used its publication *Tolerance* to expose the names of thousands of local Klansmen. In response, local merchants and businessmen rushed to the newspaper's office to apologize for their involvement in the Klan. The National Unity League's tactics caused thousands of Chicago-area Klansmen to abandon the order. Similarly, in Buffalo, New York, the local Klan organization virtually disintegrated when the names of its members were exposed.[89] Chalmers notes that Klan-friendly businesses, such as the Budd Dairy Company in Columbus, Ohio, were crippled when their association with the Invisible Empire was brought to light.[90]

The effectiveness of "vocational klannishness" hinged, to a great extent, on the ethnic composition of local communities. Klan-sponsored boycotts would be of little value in communities that were completely homogeneous. Boycotting Catholic merchants would not generate new business for Klan constituents if there were no Catholic merchants in the community. The strategy could backfire in communities where its enemies were numerous enough to stage an effective counter-boycott. However, in many Klan strongholds conditions were such that the promise of klankraft would have been appealing. Vocational klannishness was also used as a weapon against large corporations with headquarters in distant cities that, according to the Klansmen, were run by Jews, Catholics, and foreigners.

Conclusion

Founded in 1915, the Ku Klux Klan struggled for five years. When professional organizers were placed in charge of recruiting, the movement began its phenomenal ascendance. Millions of new members were enlisted, Klan chapters were organized in every state in the Union, and the movement grew particularly strong in America's heartland. The growth in the Klan coincided with major shifts in the organization of economic life. During and after World War I, labor conflict intensified and industrialists intensified efforts to rationalize manufacturing production, relying on unskilled labor and machinery to increase profits. After the war ended, a deep agricultural recession gripped rural America, generating widespread hardships and uncertainties. Klan leaders discussed economic conditions in the frames that they constructed, combining progressive and populist discourse with militant expressions of white supremacy, nativism, and religious bigotry.

The Klan's discussion of economic conditions was cognizant of the way in which the movement's constituents were experiencing power devaluation by virtue of declining demand for what they offered in exchange and from increasing supplies of competitors. While drawing on cultural solidarity, movement leaders advocated programs and policies that would restrict the supply of what its constituents offered in economic exchange and also stimulate the demand for what its constituents offered in exchange. The strategy, as I will argue in the next chapter, was enhanced by the way in which movement leaders addressed their constituents' political power devaluation.

5

National Politics and Mobilizing "100 Percent American" Voters

*The vote is the instrument by which each man exercises his equality.
When the vote is given those who are not entitled to it, its value to the real
American citizen is depreciated and his equality is encroached upon.*
—*Imperial Night-Hawk,* September 19, 1923

The vast majority of the Klan's members and supporters were neither rich
nor poor. Many recognized, however, that economic transitions taking
place in the early 1900s were redistributing wealth in American society and
they would have to organize to preserve advantages they previously enjoyed.
Rationalization of manufacturing production and a severe agricultural recession directly affected small-scale manufacturers, skilled laborers, and
farmers. These changes also disrupted exchange relationships for merchants
and service workers whose fortunes were linked to the strength of the local
economy and to the economic prosperity of their clients and customers. As
the Klan's recruiters fanned out across the nation in the early 1920s, they
recognized an opportunity. Incorporating economic grievances into their
collective action frames could help the movement grow. And the movement
did grow. In only a few short years, the Klan was transformed from a relatively small organization, teetering on the brink of bankruptcy and confined
to two southern states, to a mass movement with chapters established in all
forty-eight states and with millions of members nationwide who enriched
the national headquarters with their membership dues and their purchases
of robes and other Klan paraphernalia.

The Klan's rhetorical response to its constituents' economic grievances drew inspiration from the Progressive movement, the populist movement, and a republican tradition. Yet the Klan added its own twists and turns and, as a result, bore a stronger resemblance to fascism than to progressivism or populism. Movement leaders promised to deliver a classless society, united by a common racial, ethnic, and religious heritage and committed to promoting the welfare of the people—its people—rather than the welfare of all citizens or of members of a particular social class. Klan leaders capitalized on the intuitive appeal of microeconomic logic as they drew on deeply rooted cultural values to construct frames advocating policies and programs that would restrict the supply of individuals competing with the Klan's key constituencies while also stimulating demand for what Klan constituents offered in economic exchange.

It would be a mistake to attribute the Klan's recruiting success solely to the way in which it appealed to the economic self-interest of its supporters. As the power-devaluation model stipulates, incentives to support right-wing mobilization should be especially strong when members of clearly identifiable social groups are experiencing power devaluation on multiple dimensions. Economic grievances, after all, are often addressed and satisfied through participation in institutionalized politics. However, if those who are experiencing economic power devaluation are simultaneously experiencing political power devaluation, it becomes increasingly difficult for them to solve economic problems through normal channels. Political power devaluation provides an incentive to supplement participation in political institutions with extra-institutional right-wing activism.

As was true of the movement's discussions of economic conditions, Klan leaders often railed against Catholics and immigrants when they described political problems facing their supporters. The fact that the Klan often thrived in communities where Catholics and immigrants were few in number has led some scholars to argue that the movement's recruiting success can be explained in terms of status politics or as a form of low-status backlash.[1] This view rests on an assumption that all "real" political struggles are local. If the movement's declared political enemies pose no real threat within the community, the declared enemies must be symbolic of something else. This type of thinking, however, when applied to the Klan of the 1920s, misses the national scope of the religious and ethnic conflicts of the time period and fails to consider the extent to which religious and ethnic boundaries overlapped with competing economic interests in a national economy.

These same scholars also argue that status anxiety resulted from a prevailing sense that rural and small-town values were being replaced by urban cosmopolitan values, contributing to the Klan's political mobilization.[2] An apparent contradiction to this argument—that the Klan thrived in many urban locations as well as in small towns—is attributed to white migration patterns. Based on some rather sketchy evidence, they argue that urban Klansmen were predominantly recent migrants to the city. These migrants looked favorably on the Klan, the argument goes, because they viewed it as a vehicle for imposing law and order and small-town values on the chaos of urban life. Chalmers, for example, writes, "The internal migrant brought his heartland values and defensiveness with him to the metropolis. . . . Poorly educated and unsure of himself, he was a likely recruit for the Klan."[3]

More recent research calls this thesis into question. Rhomberg's analysis of the rise of the Klan in Oakland, California, for example, presents persuasive evidence that the Klan drew its support in that city primarily from an upwardly mobile middle class rather than from poorly educated rural migrants.[4] In general, the Klan's heavy recruitment from Protestant congregations and fraternal orders strongly suggests that most of the movement's members had established some roots in the communities in which they resided, whether those communities were rural or urban.

While much has been made about the Klan's capacity to attract members in both urban and rural locations, the urban-versus-rural dichotomy is not very useful when trying to understand the growth of the Klan. A more relevant distinction has to do with whether the local economy was linked primarily to agricultural production or to industrial production. In the early 1920s, even large cities that were located outside of core industrialized regions of the country had yet to break their ties with the agricultural economy. As Sanders describes it,

> The role of cities in the core was fundamentally different from the role of cities in the periphery. The great industrial cities of the manufacturing belt existed as loci of factories and of those who worked in and otherwise supported them. There were, and are, agricultural areas within the manufacturing-belt states, but they are dependent on the industrial cities for their raison d'être and not the reverse. The dairy, truck, and poultry farms outside the industrial cities existed to supply city residents with foodstuffs, particularly perishables. In the agriculture/extraction-based periphery, on the other hand, the engine of economic growth lay in the surrounding country side. Cities here existed to supply surrounding farms, ranches, mines, and forests with banking, storage, and transportation services and essential commodities.[5]

Rural dwellers residing in the industrial core regions, therefore, shared many of the same economic interests as their proximate urban counterparts. Similarly, the interests of urban and rural residents overlapped substantially in the "periphery" because agricultural production drove both the urban and rural economies.

When viewed from this perspective, the Klan's political attacks on Catholics and immigrants take on an entirely different meaning. In terms of national politics there were, essentially, two different economies housed under the same political roof. Kathleen Schwartzman persuasively demonstrates that these same conditions (intense sectional economic conflicts) contributed to the collapse of the first Portuguese Republic. Barrington Moore sees the same conditions as the determining factor leading to the American Civil War. According to Moore, there was no inherent conflict between the slavery-based agricultural economy of the southern states and the industrial economy of the North, were it not for the fact that the two economies coexisted within a single nation-state. An irreconcilable conflict, he argues, resulted from a struggle between representatives of two different regional economies as they attempted to secure national policies that would favor their sectional interests over those of the other sector.[6]

The Civil War put an end to the slavery-based economy, but competing sectional interests would continue to shape political conflicts at the national level. In the years following the Civil War, several social movements emerged to address agrarian grievances, most notably the cooperative enterprises of the Grange and the Farmers' Alliance. Organizing in the 1880s and 1890s, the Farmers' Alliance promoted a platform wherein the federal government would underwrite a local farmer cooperative system, and would regulate banks, railroads, and manufacturers.[7] Farmers' grievances also found expression in the third-party challenge of the People's (or Populist) Party in the 1890s. While the party failed in its bid for the presidency in 1896, it had some success in other campaigns. Seven U.S. senators and thirty U.S. congressmen elected in 1896 were either Populists, fusionists (populist candidates running under the Democratic banner), or Silver Party members. The gains were short-lived, however. The Party splintered into competing factions, and much of its agenda was co-opted by the Democratic Party.[8]

To absorb the Populist Party support, Democrats adopted the rhetoric of agrarian protest, articulated by the party's new figurehead, William Jennings Bryan. Bryan and other Democratic leaders argued against industrial tariffs and argued for inflationary monetary policies. The new agrarian agenda of the Democratic Party drove many industrial workers to the Republican Party—workers who feared higher food prices and who tended to benefit from protective tariffs on industry.[9]

The Republican and Democratic parties became institutionalized vehicles for sectional conflict, pitting states in the industrialized core against states in the agrarian periphery. By the 1920s, the link between sectional interests and party alignments was becoming more complex. After suffering a severe nationwide beating in 1920, the Democratic Party staged an impressive comeback in the off-year elections of 1922, gaining seventy-eight new congressional seats. The new Democratic support, however, came primarily from northeastern cities. These cities, previously dominated by the Republican Party, were quickly shifting to the Democratic camp. Immigrants and Catholics, in particular, were pouring into the Democratic Party. Twelve of New York's thirteen newly elected congressmen in 1922 were elected from districts with high percentages of immigrants.[10]

Increased Catholic and immigrant participation contributed to a virtual stalemate in the Democratic Party between core and periphery states. In fact, the balance of power within the party had shifted, for the first time, toward the core. Hostility between the two factions made it virtually impossible to come up with any meaningful agenda that could garner the support of the majority of Democrats. Senator Nathaniel B. Dial of South Carolina expressed the viewpoint of many in the periphery when he stated:

> We have infected ourselves and our party with political miasma and pestilence, brought here from fetid and sickening atmospheres of the old countries. We have permitted the great Democratic Party to be degraded and used by a small alien faction. . . . The Democratic Party must declare whether it will serve high, straight, outspoken American democracy or some kind of shambling, bastard, shame-faced mixture of so-called democracy and alien-conceived bolshevism or socialism or hell broth and all.[11]

The strong resemblance between the senator's words and those expressed by leaders of the Ku Klux Klan is not coincidental. Both were responding to similar political grievances. Prior to the Democratic National Convention in 1924, a Klan writer sized up the Democratic Party in the following manner:

> On the one side will be the drys and against them the wets. On the side of the drys will be the progressives and on the side of the wets will be arrayed the conservatives. The drys and progressives, so[-]called, will come largely from the west and south, while the wets and reactionaries, so called, will come from the north and east. The Klan will be found fighting with the drys and liberals.[12]

The article describes how the fault line in the Democratic Party had played out since 1896, with the Klan's favored progressive or populist candidates, such as William Jennings Bryan and Woodrow Wilson, contending with "reactionaries" and "conservatives" whose strength was rooted in Tammany Hall and, more generally, in the northeastern states.

Klansmen were not the only ones who recognized the way in which immigration contributed to the political clout of the industrialized core at the expense of the agrarian periphery. This was a central issue of contention in the early 1900s. Sanders describes the situation when speaking of debates about immigration restriction:

> As for periphery agrarians, they had two strong reasons to support immi-
> gration restriction with few, if any, to oppose it. In the first place, many
> southern and Midwestern rural and small urban communities had tried,
> without success, to entice more European settlers. Most immigrants
> settled in cities in the industrial core where, given the region's propen-
> sity to vote Republican, their numbers expanded the political power of
> the farmers' chief rivals. Second, ethnic prejudice led agrarians, along
> with most other contemporary citizens (including AFL and Socialist
> Party leaders), to argue that the newer immigrants could not easily be
> assimilated into American society and culture. Even the most idealistic
> and humanitarian of the agrarian progressives—like George Norris of
> Nebraska—saw the "immigration problem" in these terms.[13]

The fact that Catholics and immigrants were moving into the Democratic fold only compounded the problem for many in the periphery. Although there was a bloc of progressive Republicans in Congress, the majority of Republican legislators remained committed to advancing and protecting the industrial economy ("old guard" or traditional Republicans). Meanwhile, the Democratic Party was becoming increasingly factionalized and unable to mount an effective national level challenge to the Republicans.

Expansion of Suffrage

Expansion of suffrage also helped strengthen the political hand of the in-
dustrial core. The 1920 election was the first national election in which women in all forty-eight states were eligible to vote. The Klan began its phenomenal growth throughout the nation in the same year. Notably, new women voters were not randomly distributed across geographic and political space. Many western states had extended voting rights to women prior to the Nineteenth Amendment. In the more restrictive southern polities, passage of the Nineteenth Amendment did not immediately lead to a substan-
tial increase in actual votes cast. In South Carolina, where women's suffrage had been strongly resisted, there was only about a 4 percent increase in the number of total votes cast in the 1920 presidential election relative to the

Figure 13. Percent increase in total votes cast for U.S. president by state, 1916–1924.

election of 1916. The percentage increase in voters was substantially higher in many northern industrialized states such as Rhode Island (91.2 percent) and Massachusetts (86.7 percent). The migration of African Americans from southern states to northern industrial cities also contributed to this substantial geographic redistribution of eligible voters. Blacks migrated from southern states where they were disfranchised to northern industrial cities where there were fewer restrictions on voting (see Figure 13).

A Challenge from the Left

As Elisabeth Clemens's work emphasizes, the historical time period in which the Klan emerged was characterized by significant changes in the way that citizens approached the polity. Republican ideology espoused by the leaders of the Klan was being undermined as groups increasingly organized around their specific interests (e.g., as industrial laborers, farmers, or women) and pressured legislators to satisfy their collective demands. In addition, farmers and industrial laborers were increasingly pressing their demands at the national, rather than at the local, level.[14] Individuals who were not part of an organized group contending for influence had much to lose in emerging zero-sum struggles in national politics. Those who were neither farmers nor industrial laborers, for example, faced the prospect of footing the bill for any new benefits secured by the "producing class." Not surprisingly, republican ideology was particularly appealing to the middle class because of the way it condemned the pursuit of class-based interests, thereby protecting the interests of an unorganized middle class.[15]

While middle-class interests were threatened by the way in which laborers and farmers pressed their specific demands on representatives of the major political parties, more radical forms of political organizing also posed a significant threat. Prior to World War I, support for left-wing political parties tended to come from the West rather than from the northeastern industrialized core. Industrial workers, for the most part, were engaged in trade unionism and often attached themselves to urban patronage machines. Accordingly, the Socialist Party agenda, to a great extent, reflected the grievances of the agrarian periphery. Eugene Debs, a gifted orator, came to symbolize America's unique brand of radical politics in the early 1900s. Debs, a former leader of the American Railroad Union, offered rhetoric that combined Marxist thought with heavy doses of American populism and progressivism.[16] Although his presidential candidacies never posed a realistic threat to the two dominant parties, he consistently captured between 3 and 6 percent of the popular vote, having his best outing in 1912.

Figure 14. A rally held by a women's auxiliary in New Castle, Indiana, 1923. Women played a vital role in the Klan's mobilization. W. A. Swift Collection. Courtesy of Ball State University. Copyright 2006. All rights reserved.

Debs was the most widely recognized national figure of the Socialist Party in the early 1900s, but his popularity overshadowed, to some extent, the strength that the party had at the local level. Debs's advocacy of independent political action placed him in the left wing of the party. Other more conservative Socialist leaders, such as Victor Berger and Morris Hillquit, preferred to work within the dominant political parties and to forge alliances with the American Federation of Labor (AFL). Support for socialism in the United States ran deeper than electoral support in national elections would indicate. With the failure of the populist challenge fresh in their minds—a failure that illustrated the difficulties of mounting a third-party challenge in the American electoral system—most Socialists operated within the two dominant parties. This was a practice used effectively by the Non-Partisan League and by various farmer-labor coalitions that were also promoting socialist goals.[17]

The structure of the political left in the United States was abruptly reshaped in the late 1910s by World War I and the Russian revolution. As America entered the war, the Socialist Party was one of the few large domestic organizations that openly criticized the nation's involvement. Socialist opposition to the war led to substantial state-sponsored repression. After a speech in Canton, Ohio, in 1919, Eugene Debs was arrested and sentenced to ten years in prison. Numerous other Socialists were also imprisoned for openly voicing their opposition to the war. But while the party's antiwar stance attracted the wrath of the federal government, it also attracted many new members. Party membership grew during the war years in spite of state repression.[18] As the war ended, the Socialist Party was stronger than it had ever been. In 1920 Debs managed to secure over 4 percent of the popular vote for the presidency, running a makeshift campaign from his prison cell.

Although the war strengthened the party, the Russian revolution splintered it. The key issue of contention was whether American workers should follow the Soviet model and organize for militant action, or work for progressive reform within American labor unions and within conventional political institutions. A compromise could not be reached, and the relative harmony that once characterized the left came to an end. In 1921 many in the left wing of the Socialist Party defected to the Communist Party, causing membership in the now more conservative Socialist Party to plummet.[19]

Those who favored gradual reform within the electoral process still outnumbered those who were promoting a more militant strategy. By 1922, farmer-labor parties, rather than the Socialist Party, were taking the lead in promoting the socialist platform. Farmer-laborism was particularly strong in Minnesota, which elected two of its candidates to the U.S. Senate. The farmer-labor movement was having a significant impact in state-level politics outside of Minnesota as well, particularly in the western states.[20] Most of the leaders were either Socialists, former Socialists, or at least sympathetic to the cause.

Prior to 1924, the organizational focus of farmer-labor parties had been at the local and state level. In 1920, a Farmer-Labor candidate from Utah did make a tentative move into the national political arena. Parly Parker Christianson only polled 1 percent of the vote nationwide in his run for the presidency, but his support in several states was impressive considering the limited resources at his disposal. Christianson received 19.4 percent of the vote in the state of Washington and nearly 7 percent in Wyoming. Still, neither Debs nor Christianson posed a legitimate threat to the dominant parties' nominees. The results of the 1920 election convinced all factions of the left that a more mainstream candidate with name recognition and popularity was needed to have an impact in national politics and to establish a competitive third party devoted to the interests of laborers and farmers. As the 1924 election year approached, all eyes on the left turned to Robert LaFollette Sr., the progressive Republican senator from Wisconsin.

LaFollette was more conservative than the Socialists would have preferred. Strong support from middle-class Wisconsin Progressives prevented him from declaring that he was exclusively a representative of farmers and industrial laborers. Nevertheless, he shared many of the Socialists' goals and Socialists and Farmer-Laborites hoped to capitalize on his considerable nationwide popularity to launch a third-party challenge on their behalf. In 1923, even the American Communists, who had temporarily moderated their stance on electoral politics, fell into the movement to draft LaFollette as a third-party presidential candidate.[21] It appeared that a LaFollette candidacy could bring together the deeply factionalized political left and draw enough support from the middle to establish a viable third party devoted to the producing classes and to progressive reform.

LaFollette was ready to run. He was becoming increasingly frustrated in his attempts to operate within a Republican Party that appeared to be moving further and further to the right.[22] His progressive minority report to the party platform was shouted down vociferously at the 1924 Republican National Convention and was rejected without a vote. LaFollette saw a third-party bid as his only option. The only question was who would sponsor his candidacy. The Minnesota Farmer-Labor Party was busy preparing for a run at the presidency, and its leaders assumed that LaFollette would be their candidate.[23] William Mahoney, the party's leader, decided to allow the full participation of Communists within the national campaign—a move that was against the better judgment of many of the party's members. The Communists, led by William Z. Foster, were intent on having influence within the party in excess of their numbers.[24] Even more damaging, however, was the reaction that communist participation prompted from LaFollette. LaFollette denounced the Communists, once again splintering the left, and chose to run as an independent Progressive rather than as a Farmer-Labor candidate.

LaFollette's decision to run as an independent Progressive caught the Farmer-Labor Party leaders and the Socialists off guard. Yet with nowhere else to go, they fell in line behind him, committing their organizations, resources, and members to his campaign. Eugene Debs, rather than making his usual bid for the presidency, threw his support to LaFollette. Debs gave his formal endorsement on July 7. In a letter to Socialist leaders in New York, he wrote that while he was not in full accord with the Convention of the Conference on Political Action (LaFollette's initial sponsors), the Socialist Party need not blush for supporting LaFollette, who "all his life had stood up like a man for the right according to his light; he has been shamefully maligned, ostracized and persecuted by the predatory powers of the plutocracy yet his bitterest foe had never dared to question his personal integrity or his political rectitude."[25]

LaFollette and his running mate, Burton Wheeler, a progressive Democratic senator from Montana, also received the endorsement of the American Federation of Labor. This is the first time that the AFL had endorsed a presidential candidate. In justifying this unusual move, the executive committee for the AFL issued the following statement: "Mr. LaFollette and Mr. Wheeler have throughout their whole political careers stood steadfast in the defense of the rights and interests of the wage-earners and farmers."[26] The AFL's endorsement of LaFollette, which meant cooperation with Socialists, represented a significant leap for the relatively conservative labor organization. The AFL leadership was being radicalized to some extent by attacks from organized capitalists, continued setbacks in the court system, and by the lack of sympathy that the unions were receiving from either of the two dominant parties.[27]

La Follette's third-party challenge created ambivalence for the types of individuals who were drawn to the Klan. He was one of the nation's prominent progressive legislators, and he was a forceful opponent of monopolies, trusts, and exploitative capitalism. He was outspoken in his opposition to industrial tariffs. LaFollette's alliance with Socialists and his growing radicalism, however, were problematic for many who feared that they would come out on the losing end if the polity became an arena of conflict between organized classes. And, although the Klan's leaders criticized capitalists for exploiting unskilled labor, they were staunch defenders of private property rights and spoke disparagingly of unskilled laborers. The challenge from the radical left threatened the interests of many of the Klan's members and adherents. Klan supporters' ambivalence was resolved when LaFollette condemned the Invisible Empire soon after launching his presidential campaign. The Klan press then characterized LaFollette as someone who had abandoned progressive principles and had instead chosen to become a representative of Catholics, immigrants, and radicals. Because LaFollette and left-wing parties did, in fact, draw strong support from immigrant populations, Klansmen could wage political warfare with cultural weapons.

Machine Politics

To understand sources of political power devaluation confronting many of the Klan's constituents, it is useful to give attention to national-level politics. Immigrants and Catholics settling in northeastern industrial cities adversely affected the political power of those residing outside of the industrial core regions of the country. Immigrants settling in western states, on the other hand, could potentially strengthen left-wing political organizations. Similarly, with new women voters being concentrated in northeastern industrial states, there were incentives for national politicians to give extra attention to these new voters when formulating policies and when making campaign promises. States that were not gaining new voters might be ignored in the process. As important as national politics were, it is also necessary to consider how local political conditions contributed to the rise of the Ku Klux Klan.

In the early 1900s, the urban political machine was a primary target of progressive reformers. Opposition to patronage politics was especially popular among the middle class. Fighting the corruption of urban patronage machines was a task perfectly suited for the Klan's constituencies because the machines often represented an alliance between powerful corporations and working-class immigrants. Those in the middle class were often denied benefits and services provided by local government because they were not connected to patronage networks established in working-class neighborhoods. Those who opposed machine politics also had cause to oppose immigration because a steady flow of new immigrants could potentially strengthen the position of the party bosses. Clemens points out:

> Notwithstanding conflicts among themselves, the middle classes, therefore, viewed their mounting public burdens as the alarming portents of a new democracy, a democracy mobilized around two predatory

constituencies. One constituency was composed of "vulgar" hordes of workingmen and immigrants substantially devoid of a real stake in society; the other comprised the corporate rich and their "unproductive" retinues. Both constituencies were believed to be drawing power from the debasement of traditional morality and from the confiscation of established properties. In respectable quarters, moreover, the aggressive agent in the advancement of this destruction was identified with party organization, usually symbolized by bosses, rings, and machine politics.[28]

Machine politicians essentially served as middle-men between the business elite and industrial laborers. The former could provide jobs and other valued resources that could be passed along to laborers in exchange for their political support. Patronage networks tended to be organized along ethnic lines due to the high concentration of immigrants and Catholics in working-class occupations. The system, of course, was ripe for corruption and could generate widespread resentment among those who were left out of the patronage loop. Because of the way in which immigrants and Catholics were incorporated into machine politics, it was easy for contemporary observers to attribute the machines' corrupt practices to "foreign influences." Link and McCormick note that many progressive reformers concluded that taking on patronage politics on behalf of "clean and efficient" government would require restraining the unruly behavior of immigrants and even placing restrictions on political participation for immigrants, Catholics, African Americans, and the poor.[29]

Corporate funding was especially important in establishing and maintaining patronage machines in western cities, where politicians could not always count on establishing ties in relatively stable immigrant neighborhoods.[30] Dynamic population growth in western cities could make elections unpredictable. Under such conditions, resources from large corporations were especially useful in helping the local machine to maintain power. The Ku Klux Klan, for example, battled machine politics in Oakland, California, in the early 1920s. As Rhomberg describes it,

> The franchise corporations formed the core of the urban regime in Oakland. Through them, local politicians satisfied public demands for both low taxes and basic city services. Corporate elites, in turn, protected their profits and privileges by forming alliances with the ward bosses who controlled the votes of the dependent working class.[31]

As the city expanded, a growing middle class grew increasingly frustrated as their suburban neighborhoods received low priority from local government when it came to providing basic services.[32]

Middle-class voters in cities such as Oakland confronted political power devaluation from multiple sources. The size of the national electorate (the overall supply of voters) had increased substantially due to women's suffrage, yet California women had been eligible to vote in national elections prior to passage of the Nineteenth Amendment and the new women voters who were concentrated in the industrial Northeast. Immigration had declined in the latter half of the 1910s but was on the rise again after the war, preceding the Klan's growth spurt. Returns to high levels of immigration would strengthen the hand of northeastern core states but would also be consequential in urban politics. A rise in the number of immigrants settling in cities such as Oakland, Denver, or Portland, for example, would add to the strength of the political machine that the Klan opposed. Population growth in general, even that which could be attributed to an influx of native-born, white Protestants, also contributed to power devaluation by increasing the overall supply of voters. New voters in the electorate can represent both a threat and an opportunity to those who were previously in the electorate. To benefit from population growth, groups must organize and they must take steps to ensure that the new voters are not captured by political competitors.

The Klan's Prognosis: Supply Restriction

According to the power-devaluation model, political power devaluation can result from an increase in the supply of, and decreases in demand for, that which is offered in political exchange. In a political market, mediums of exchange include votes, money, representation, and patronage. The theory does not presuppose that any particular collectivity (e.g., the capitalist class, the proletariat, or Protestants) will always act together based on some common interest that is inherent to group membership. Instead, it focuses on how extant exchange relationships are affected by shifts in supply and demand.

It is important to be clear that power devaluation can result from supply increases even when new entrants to the political arena appear to be similar to those who are already established within a political market. A simple example will illustrate the point. A small group of friends (Mary, Jane, and Charlie) are attempting to decide whether to go out for pizza or for Chinese food. If the friends wish to solve the problem democratically, each one of them controls one-third of the votes. Mary must only reach agreement with one of her two friends in order to secure her preferred outcome. If three more friends (Bob, Amy, and Norman) decide to join them, then Mary, Jane, and Charlie each experience political power devaluation.

Mary now controls only one-sixth of the votes in the group and her capacity to influence the outcome has been diminished. It may be the case that Bob, Amy, and Norman all share her love for pepperoni pizza. But Mary cannot assume that initially. The addition of three new friends provides her with an incentive to take political action, off-setting her diminished political power by persuading the newcomers to join her in the pizza vote. If Mary knows in advance that Bob, Amy, and Norman are craving Chinese food, she would have an incentive to prevent them from joining the group for dinner.

It is this simple intuitive logic that made the Klan's message resonate with so many Americans in the 1920s. At a time when many of the Klan's constituents were undergoing economic power devaluation, the pool of eligible voters was expanding in ways that generated incentives to advocate restrictions in the supply of voters. Klan leaders capitalized on these circumstances, constructing collective-action frames that noted how their constituents' political purchasing power was being diminished. Indeed, they often used language that directly applied the logic of market dynamics. In reference to voting rights, for example, one article in the *Imperial Night-Hawk* complained, "We have cheapened American citizenship until it has become worthless." Another Klan writer, directly applying microeconomic logic, wrote, "The vote is the instrument by which each man exercises his equality. When the vote is given those who are not entitled to it, its value to the real American citizen is depreciated and his equality is encroached upon."[33]

Klan leaders frequently commented on how immigration affected the political power of their own constituents. One article cautioned,

> Americans should regard with alarm the fact that nearly one half of the population of the United States is composed of Poles, Russians, Greeks, Italians, Negroes, and European Asiatics. If these nationalities were to combine their votes, they could gain control of the American government.[34]

Similarly, another Klan writer warned,

> The total foreign vote has grown until its combined strength is sufficient to control a national election, and this does not take into consideration the influence of the un-naturalized foreigners, who may, in some localities wield a power practically equivalent to the strength they would have if they were allowed to vote. This is done by bringing pressure to bear on local politicians.[35]

This writer also noted that "the foreign born multiply their political power by settling themselves in cities, and that is why their leaders and their newspapers are loath to see the racial groups break up."[36]

The Klan's strong advocacy on behalf of immigration restriction was motivated by political as well as economic concerns. By restricting immigration or by changing voter registration laws, the Klan hoped to stem the flow of new voters into the electorate. As Colorado's Grand Dragon expressed it, "I hope to see the day when every foreigner must live in this country twenty-one years before he or she becomes a voter. We have to do it, why not they?"[37] The fact that immigrants tended to vote differently from the Klan's constituents only compounded the problem from the Klansman's perspective. Klan leaders frequently commented on how recent immigrants were from Catholic countries, and the Klansmen, quite simply, did not like the way that Catholics tended to vote.

Drawing on a deep vein of anti-Catholic bigotry that existed in the United States long before the Klan resurfaced in the 1920s, movement leaders argued that Catholics should not be allowed to participate in democratic institutions because they allegedly placed loyalty to the pope above loyalty to the United States. This argument, that Catholics received their political marching orders from Rome, contrasted Catholicism with republican virtue. Catholics, the argument assumes, were subject to coercion from religious authorities and were, therefore, unable to act in the best interest of the nation as a whole.[38] As one Klan writer put it,

> The time has full come when this country, and every other country ought to serve notice on the Catholic church that its days in politics has passed, that so long as it meddles in affairs of state its activity will be an insurmountable barrier to official preferment for any man who owes allegiance to its authority. This, we repeat, is no discrimination against Catholicism as a church. It is simply saying that we do not approve of the brand of politics that Catholicism represents, and that we do not mean to have it.[39]

Similarly, another Klan writer claimed,

> It is a significant fact, borne out by the pages of history, that the effort of the Roman Catholic hierarchy in the past to dominate state affairs has led to more wars and more unhappiness throughout Christendom than any and all other causes for seven hundred years. In this country it is ideas and votes, rather than sword, battle-axe or gun, with which we fight.[40]

When discussing the movement's political goals, Klan leaders often presented their arguments as being motivated by patriotism and a deep concern for the welfare of the nation rather than by hatred or bigotry. Speaking at the Klan's national convention in 1924, Hiram Evans emphasized, "We have no fight to make upon the Catholic church, no fight upon the Catholic creed, no fight upon the Catholic religion. We are here to protect as the fundamental of our American government, and the basis of our American Constitution, the right of religious freedom in America." One article described, in detail, how Klansmen rescued a six-month-old baby from a kidnapper and returned the child to its Catholic mother. Again, the point of the story was to demonstrate that the Klan held no ill will toward individual Catholics; the Klan only opposed their involvement in politics.[41]

The Klan leaders' attempts to display pure motives in their political fight with Catholics were often contradicted by words and deeds. Direct appeals to anti-Catholic bigotry could be valuable tools when it came to attracting members and spurring members to action. Klan recruiters and lecturers often made false claims about atrocities committed by Catholics in order to stir up their audiences. One recruiting tactic involved having women pose as former nuns, delivering public lectures describing depraved sexual acts committed by Catholic priests behind convent walls.[42] The Klan press at times supplemented its "high-minded" arguments against Catholics' participation in politics with more blatant appeals to anti-Catholic bigotry. This was especially true of some of the movement's local or regional papers. Hiram Evans characterized such practices as strategically flawed, however. Speaking at the Klan's national convention, he noted, "A few of the editors waste no time preparing constructive articles since it is much easier to stick their pens in the vitriol bottle and anathemize everyone who does not think precisely as they do."[43] Here, Evans's strategic calculations are transparent as he went on to emphasize the importance of presenting the Klan in a positive light in order to gain favorable publicity from the non-Klan press.

Rather than resorting to "vitriolic" attacks on Catholics, the Klan press more commonly presented its own members and constituents as victims of poorly behaved Catholics. One particularly interesting article describes how Catholic students at the University of Notre Dame rioted against the Klan in South Bend, Indiana. According to the Klan writer, the college students "showed no regard for sex or age, beating up men, women and children. . . . One old man, an old lady and a little child were so badly beaten up and trampled that the attention of a physician was necessary."[44]

By advocating clean government at both the national and local level, Klan leaders were free to take numerous potshots at Catholics for their alleged involvement in corrupt practices. Combining the themes of immigration and Catholic corruption, one article claimed, "In certain Texas towns like El Paso, and Corpus Christi, and in many towns in Arizona and New Mexico where the Roman Catholic influence is a power in politics, these Mexicans are voted at the polls like sheep in order to thwart government by loyal Americans."[45] Klan leaders articulated the grievances of many middle-class Americans who were growing increasingly frustrated by patronage-based urban politics. A "prominent minister" addressed Klansmen at a Klonvocation in Kansas City, asserting, "If we look out into the political realm we discover in many places, and many localities, that they have no government by the people. There is a government by political machines that are corrupted by shyster politicians, government by clique." An "Exalted Cyclops" from Monroe, Louisiana, noted that the Klan "strenuously objects to any church being used as a political machine and its members voted to warp, annul or set aside a highly cherished American institution."[46] And lest any of the Klansmen forget, the Exalted Cyclops reminded readers that

> A large percentage of the foreign immigrants pouring into this country, during the past few years, have been Roman Catholics and a big percent of these immigrants are from the lowest strata of Italy, Poland and other Roman Catholic countries. As fast as these immigrants land upon our shores they are "corraled" by the Catholic church, herded into conjested [sic] sections of big cities, naturalized as soon as possible and voted in order to elect men to office who will do the bidding of Rome.[47]

Compared to Catholics and immigrants, African Americans were not viewed by Klan leaders as a serious political threat. On this point, Evans's paternalism is evident:

> The Negro is not a menace to Americanism in the sense that the Jew or Roman Catholic is a menace. He is not actually hostile to it. He is simply racially incapable of understanding, sharing in or contributing to Americanism. Booker T. Washington, the greatest of Negro leaders, exhorted his brethren to cast aside their political and social ambitions. The Klan stands where he stood upon this phase of the question.[48]

Disenfranchisement in southern states minimized any political threat posed by African Americans south of the Mason-Dixon Line. In northern states, Klan leaders banked on black voters' loyalty to the Republican Party as a factor that would at least make their vote predictable. In Indiana, where the Klan forged strong ties with the Republican Party, movement leaders even hoped to enlist black voters as allies or, at the very least, to dissuade them from defecting to the Democratic Party.[49]

Attacking the Political Left

Klan leaders also recognized that immigration contributed to the strength of a growing coalition on the political left. While concerns about public perception led them to tone down their rhetorical attacks on Catholics (especially in their national publication), the gloves came off in the fight against radicals. In the wake of the Russian revolution and on the heels of the red scare in the United States, movement leaders could harshly attack groups on the left in the name of patriotism and civic virtue. One Klan writer noted, "Trotsky was spawned in a New York slum, and who can hazard how many more future communist, bolshevik, and anarchist leaders are now sheltered in this and other great American cities, by grace of our lax immigration laws."[50]

For Klansmen, the threat from the left was not only in the slums of great American cities. The *Imperial Night-Hawk* cautioned,

> Out in California the IWW's are threatening armed revolution and sabotage against the lumber companies, while in St. Joseph, Mich., in trials of communists, it is proved that the Russian Soviet government still continues its attempt to forment [sic] revolution in America. So it looks as if there is a very real need for a hundred-percent-American organization after all.[51]

Indeed, the Klan writers seemed particularly concerned about the threat posed by the Industrial Workers of the World (IWW or "Wobblies"). The IWW was particularly threatening to the Klan because, unlike the American Federation of Labor, it was committed to organizing unskilled laborers, immigrants, African Americans, and women along with other workers into "One Big Union."[52]

Radical groups such as the IWW provided Klan leaders with an opportunity to use scare tactics to motivate their own supporters by exaggerating the threat posed by the radicals. For example, one article in the *Imperial Night-Hawk* printed what it claimed to be "The I.W.W. Oath":

> I do solemnly swear that I hold in contempt all institutions of capitalism, including ecclesiastical and secular; and its laws, its flag, its courts, its codes, its churches and its religion; that I will obey all summons and commands of the elected officials of this order under penalty of death, and spare neither my time, effort or money to obey, even to the last drop of my blood.

This "I.W.W. Oath" was juxtaposed against "The Klan Oath," which read,

> I most solemnly declare and affirm that to the government of the United States of America and any State thereof, of which I may become a resident, I sacredly swear an unqualified allegiance above any other and every kind of government in the whole world. I most solemnly pledge my life, my property, my vote and my sacred honor to uphold its flag, its constitu-

tion and constitutional laws, and will protect, defend, and enforce the same unto death.[53]

Numerous articles in the Klan press sound the alarm about the threat posed by political radicals. When writing on the topic, Klansmen almost invariably conveyed a sense of urgency. One article described the Bolshevist threat in the following manner:

> Their object is to tear down the Stars and Stripes and supplant it with a red rag. To destroy all capital and slaughter the "b[o]urgeois[i]e" who are every man, woman, and child who loves God and the United States. To agitate strikes, bloodshed and anarchy, that the work of our forefathers in establishing the glorious free republic of America may be brought to naught at the hands of such foreign revolutionary swine as dominate un-fortunate Russia today.[54]

The Klan writer's extraordinarily inclusive definition of the "bourgeoisie" is particularly notable given the Klan's criticisms of large-scale capitalists and the way it targeted its appeal toward the middle class or the petite bourgeoisie. Movement leaders clearly wanted to emphasize the way in which class conflict threatened the interests of the middle class. Later in his article the same writer added, "To Communists there are but two classes: the working class, and all others. Their ideal is to have the working class absorb the others and to make the United States a working-class republic, a part of similar republics all over the world and all dominated by the central government in Moscow."[55]

Although the Klan often relied on scare tactics when describing the threat posed by the political left, the Klan press also made it clear that the movement opposed any political group that was organized on behalf of a social class. Movement leaders emphasized the way in which their own middle-class constituents would pay the price for policies and programs designed to address the particular interests of farmers or unskilled laborers. The Klan declared its opposition to "Universalism, Sovietism, Communism, Socialism, Anarchism, Judaism, and especially Roman Catholicism," arguing that "each is fundamentally different from, and is opposed to, Americanism. Each is personal, selfish or sectional—sometimes all three." Calling for a return to republican values, a Klan writer declares, "We must educate our people to a knowledge of the fact that statutes are not a panacea for social and economic ills. By precept and example we must create anew among the people the idea that government is for all, and not for a clamorous, organized few."[56]

Klan leaders argued that class-based political mobilization was un-American and could be traced to foreign influence and to vast Jewish conspiracies. Immigration, they argued, was the primary cause of the problem. Restricting the supply of voters was offered as a solution. One article, titled "Restricted Franchise," proposed that "Klansmen believe that the time is at least near when American citizenship must be protected by restricting franchise to men and women who are able through birth and education to understand Americanism." Another writer recommended deportation or imprisonment for those advocating "Bolshevism, Sovietism, Anarchism, Communism, and every other 'ism.'" A more feasible remedy, however, was immigration restriction: "If we are to preserve unsullied the ideals, the principles, and the government transmitted to us by our forefathers, America must close the door to the diseased minds and bodies and souls of the peoples of foreign lands."[57]

Prognosis: Stimulate Demand

For many Klan constituents, political power devaluation resulted not only from an increase in the supply of voters but also from a decline in demand for their votes. As other societal groups began to organize to pressure political representatives to act on behalf of their specific interests, those running for political office faced greater pressure to satisfy the demands of these constituencies and, in the process, become less attentive to the needs of an unorganized middle class whose votes were split among the two major political parties. Klan leaders condemned interest-group politics and appealed to republican ideals. To address the problem, Klan leaders proposed that it would be necessary to abandon republicanism and to form their own interest group. Much in the same way that they advocated "vocational Klannishness" to address economic grievances, movement leaders argued that they must counter interest group politics by forming their own bloc of voters—a huge bloc that would bring together all of the nation's native-born, white Protestants. Only then would "100 percent Americans" be able to compete with other groups that were "clamoring" to influence the political process. In other words, Klan leaders aimed to stimulate demand for their constituents' votes by organizing them in to a solid bloc that would be large enough to elect or defeat candidates running for office—depending on the candidates' stances on issues near and dear to the hearts of the Klan members.

Klan leaders frequently commented on the way in which other groups organized in politics. Catholic voting habits were of particular interest: "It is a significant fact that in matters of politics the Roman Catholic Church stands peculiarly united." The Klan writer added, "A block vote in America is a dangerous thing, and that is the trend of the times today."[58] However, the Klan's reactive response to interest-group politics extended beyond their opposition to Catholics. The Klan's stance on this issue is nicely summarized in a speech attributed to Elmer D. Brothers, president of the Board of Trustees at Valparaiso University. The *Imperial Night-Hawk* noted that Brothers was not a Klansman but that his remarks were both timely and in line with the Klan's principles.[59] Brothers argued that it was essential to

> Restore the fundamental idea that this is a government of majorities, within constitutional limitations and provisions; learn to respect the opinions of the majority when enacted into laws, and to seek changes ther[e]in, if any, only through constitutional and orderly processes; cease the practice of arraying interest against interest, section against section, passion against passion, and of exaggerating the miseries of the poor and the comforts of the rich; confine governmental activities to governmental functions, and dedicate ourselves anew to the principle of the Fatherhood of God and the Brotherhood of Man—a principle upon which this government was founded.[60]

Similarly, another Klan writer asserts, "Class legislation is unconstitutional; then let us enforce the Constitution that the interests of the weak and the poor may be as well provided for as are the interests of the strong and the rich."[61]

Klan leaders recognized that before they could exert full influence on political representatives they must first unite public opinion behind their movement and its goals. Speaking of the immigration issue, for example, South Carolina's Grand Dragon noted,

> America is largely governed by public opinion, and the sources of that opinion concerning the problems of immigration are of vital importance. To deal with so complex a national situation and so profound an international situation requires the public to be intelligently informed before we can have a united public opinion. This can be acquired only by a great movement, such as the Knights of the Ku Klux Klan, which is willing to gather this information and to see that the public is properly and correctly informed of the true facts.[62]

Similarly, Colorado's Grand Dragon argued,

> A Klansman's obligation to his country is to lead public opinion in the right direction, for public opinion is the force that moves the wheels of

government for good or for evil. What excuse is there for the American citizen who allows public opinion to be swayed by every wind of foreign sentiment from abroad?[63]

Klan leaders understood that as long as their members and supporters divided their votes among Democratic and Republican candidates, they would have very little leverage against those who held political office. One article noted, "In our councils are found as many, if not more, Republicans than Democrats." Klan leaders criticized "partyism" as a fundamental evil in politics and promoted their own brand of nonpartisan politics.[64] In a column titled "Christian Citizenship: The Gospel according to the Klan," a Klansmen declares,

> Blind obedience to partisan politicians of two hostile camps—the bartering of the people's interests to partisan advantage—the placing of the crown of party servitude above the diadem of American sovereignty and placing party banners above Old Glory's star-gemmed promise of everlasting unity have brought this great democracy near the rocks.[65]

Klan leaders expressed dissatisfaction with both major parties and were frustrated by the way in which the progressive candidates that they admired represented numerical minorities in each party. According to one writer,

> Partyism in politics has long hindered our national progress. The Klan's educational program is already modifying this deplorable condition, and the signs are that before many years pass the real citizen of our great country, no matter where he resides, will regard himself as an American first and a Democrat, Republican or something else second.[66]

As late as September 1924, the *Imperial Night-Hawk* expressed dissatisfaction with the presidential candidates. A Klan writer complained, "Neither party will put their best men forward. The men nominated must subserve the political machine and the machine goes in always for the spoils of office." The article concludes, "The Ku Klux Klan is for no particular party. The Ku Klux Klan is for America—an America awakened to patriotic citizenship."[67] By persuading Klansmen to abandon party loyalty and be loyal, instead, to the Ku Klux Klan, movement leaders hoped to demonstrate that they represented a formidable voting bloc that could determine the outcome in any election. This would restore the demand for the votes and political support of their middle-class constituents.

In addition to breaking down party loyalties, it was also important to increase voter turnout among the faithful. Citizens who do not vote can be safely ignored. At the Klan's national convention, a speaker noted with dismay,

> Many of our people do not exercise their right of suffrage, with the result that a few tricky scheming politicians often control whole sections of our nation. What is the great duty of Klansmen on the political situation? It is to arouse our fellow citizens to their civic duty and responsibility, in order that government of the people, for the people, by the people, shall not perish from the earth.[68]

Another Klan writer encouraged his readers to "ponder these statistics: In 1920 there were 54,421,823 men and women in this country entitled to vote in the presidential election. Only 26,705,246 voted. When you reflect that we punish crime by disfranchising people, somebody is guilty of the crime of disfranchising themselves. Who is asleep?"[69]

In this respect, promoting voter turnout among women who were sympathetic to the Klan's agenda was especially important. Many members of the Women's Ku Klux Klan had experience with the suffrage movement, and men of the Klan understood that the votes of native-born, white Protestant women would be needed to counter new women voters who opposed the goals of the Invisible Empire.[70] The same writer who reported voter turnout statistics added,

> The exercise of women's rights in the affairs of the state is inevitable. The women's day is here. The right to vote carries with it the obligation to vote. The power of the ballot now granted to women is a challenge to our real one hundred percent American women to join the men of the nation in laying the axe of the ballot at the root of every American tree which does not bring forth American fruit.[71]

The Klansmen's paternalistic approach to gender roles carved out a role for women in the political sphere. One article claimed that "woman has now come into her own through the 19th Amendment."[72] The author explained that women are perfectly suited for voting and engaging politics because they have given birth to the world's greatest leaders, and they are more practical than men and, therefore, "she is needed to combat the forces of radicalism that are ever increasing in America." The article concludes,

> We find woman as a home builder, an important and never-failing ally in times of greatest need; we note with ever-increasing gratitude that she has not been found wanting in places of important trust, and has proved that her patriotism and loyalty are above reproach.[73]

Conclusion

Claiming to represent the viewpoint of the nation's majority—native-born, white Protestants—Klan leaders sought to gain new members and motivate their current members by drawing attention to ways in which their constituents were losing their capacity to influence political outcomes at both the national and local levels. Although they considered a wide range of political problems, their discussions were structured by an overarching logic: an increase in the supply of voters was contributing to a substantial geographic redistribution of voters that was detrimental to many of the Klan's constituents. Immigration was, without question, the issue that received the most attention from the Klan press. On that front, the Klansmen claimed a victory when national legislation was enacted in 1924 that sharply curtailed immigration. One Klansman boasted,

> It is seen that there was no time to be wasted if America was to be saved from the evil effects of the lax immigration laws. If the flow of foreigners into this country had not been checked, it would have been but a short time until they would have made of America a country far different from the ideals on which it was founded. The Klan has taken the lead in teaching and expounding the ideals of true Americanism, and to it is due most of the credit for warning and protecting the country from the alien hordes that have threatened to overrun it.[74]

Attention to the historical context in which the Klan operated reveals why the Klan's advocacy of immigration restriction was appealing to so many Americans, even in communities where immigrants and Catholics were few in number and posed little or no challenge in local politics. Klan spokesmen articulated what many Americans of the time understood—their lives were affected by what took place in the nation's capital just as much as they were affected by what took place in the town hall. Yet the general logic of their argument could just as easily be applied, and modified, in the urban context to fight local battles. Restricting the supply of voters and promoting a solid voting bloc among native-born, white Protestants would have been an attractive political strategy for many Americans, and it is a strategy that could be applied in many different political struggles, given the way in which ethnic, religious, and racial boundaries overlapped substantially with class boundaries and occupational boundaries in the early 1900s.

In addition to advocating supply restriction, Klan leaders attempted to organize a solid bloc of voters composed of all native-born, white Protestant Americans. To members of the cultural majority group who stood on the sidelines of intensifying class conflict and who could expect to pay the costs of any new benefits that would be awarded to farmers, industrial laborers, or industrial capitalists, becoming part of such a voting bloc would have been appealing. By organizing the majority racial, ethnic, and religious group—and by making special efforts to encourage political participation among native-born, white Protestant women—the Klan stimulated the demand for what its constituents offered in exchange and became a force to be reckoned with in both national and local politics.

6

Fights over Schools and Booze

One of the principal duties of the Klan today is to build up a great free educational system. Fifty percent of our taxes should go towards education instead of only five per cent. Go home and talk education among the Klansmen and soon your representatives in congress will see the light and will be voting to make America the best educated country on earth so that through education our children and our children's children can care for themselves and be of value to their state.

—Hiram Evans, speaking at a national convention of
Grand Dragons and Grand Titans held in Asheville,
North Carolina, *Imperial Night-Hawk,* July 25, 1923

Few social movements in the history of the United States have been as successful as the Ku Klux Klan in recruiting members and supporters. With the leverage that comes from enlisting millions of dues-paying members, the movement forced political representatives, including those who had their sights set on the presidency, to take a stand in regard to the Ku Klux Klan and its agenda. In spite of the movement's successes, scholars have been reluctant to give the Klan credit for its accomplishments. Rather than investigating how the movement was able to develop a program that appealed to so many people, many scholars have instead approached the problem by trying to figure out what was wrong with the people who joined. The Klan's popularity is presented as a lesson on how easily the masses can be deceived by leaders who exploit common fears, anxieties, and resentments.

Some writers have, tautologically, supported their arguments by pointing to the movement's ultimate demise. Chalmers, for example, argues that the Klan went into decline because it appealed to "negative, defensive feelings which, though strongly rooted in the American life, did not prove sufficient to long sustain a major movement."[1] Jackson echoes these sentiments, claiming,

> Without a meaningful *raison d'être* the Invisible Empire was exposed as a ludicrous sham, for neither its infantile mumbo jumbo nor its exaggerated claims could bear objective scrutiny, even among those it counted as Knights. The genuine American sense of decency finally asserted itself and consigned the once mighty Klan to obscurity.[2]

Richard Hofstadter, one of the first scholars to comment on the Klan's popularity, helped set the tone for later studies that would characterize the movement as a classic example of low-status backlash. Hofstadter described the Klansmen as "gullible nativists" who sensed that their rural values were being ignored and even ridiculed by those residing in the "wicked cities." The same type of interpretation was later offered by Lipset and Raab who proposed that "the backlash of the 1920's demonstrated again the simple phenomenon of status substitution."[3] Like Hofstadter, these authors argued that changes in society at large were viewed as threatening to traditional values and that individuals joined the organization because they perceived a decline in their status. Numerous other studies attribute the Klan's growth to the fears and anxieties of its members or to the way in which Klansmen felt that their core values were being threatened.[4]

Motivations for joining the organization were far more complex than the status anxiety argument suggests. More recent scholarship has focused on how the Klan became a vehicle for pursuing political interests of its constituents in local settings and has revealed complex ways in which race, class, religion, and gender interacted to produce both support for, and opposition to, the movement.[5] Those who have explained the Klan in terms of status anxiety focused on the movement's racism, religious bigotry, and xenophobia and failed to consider how these characteristics of the movement were deeply intertwined with its other political goals. The Klan's other goals were either ignored or dismissed as being irrelevant to the central task of explaining why a white supremacist movement could become so popular in the United States. In the process, these scholars neglected to consider many of the issues raised in the preceding two chapters—they failed to consider how economic and political power devaluation generated incentives to join the organization and how the leaders of the Klan constructed collective-action frames that resonated strongly with those who were experiencing power devaluation.

Does this mean that concerns about status had nothing to do with the movement's growth? I believe the answer is no. The Ku Klux Klan was, among other things, a moral reform movement. The Klan sought not only to defend the core cultural values of its own adherents but also to impose those values on others and at times resorted to violence as a means of punishing transgressors.[6] More commonly, the Klan sought to work with local law enforcement agents who were sympathetic to their goals, helping them to root out and punish bootleggers, drunkards, adulterers, gamblers, and anyone else who violated the moral code promoted by the movement. It is hard to explain these actions solely in terms of economic and political incentives, as they seem to indicate that social esteem derived from adhering to a particular code of moral behavior was an important motivating factor.

Nicola Beisel has criticized students of moral reform movements for constructing a false dichotomy between class-based interests and status-based interests. Marxist scholars, she argues, have mistakenly dismissed the significance of status because they tend to view a movement's rhetoric about cultural values as a mask used strategically to obfuscate a group's pursuit of class interests. Other scholars have gone too far in the other direction by focusing solely on status and neglecting to consider the interdependence of status and class interests. High levels of cultural capital, for example, not only garner social esteem but also connect individuals to social networks that can be useful in maintaining a position (or advancing) in a class hierarchy.[7] Yet the values themselves are not simply tools for obtaining material wealth. They represent core beliefs about how one should live one's life, and they often carry with them powerful emotions because they define, to a great extent, collective identities and one's sense of self. Interpretive frames that forge connections between class-based interests and core cultural values, particularly if they pertain to children and the family, Beisel argues, are especially potent when it comes to motivating collective action.

In agreement with Beisel, I believe it is important to consider how status and class concerns interacted to generate support for the Ku Klux Klan. Indeed, Klan leaders appealed to both when they discussed issues such as patriotism, Prohibition, and public education. Their arguments in support of public schools, for example, typically emphasized their view that the schools should instill core Christian (i.e., Protestant) values in all students, but also noted that such values would contribute to the students' well-being and economic prosperity. In this chapter, I consider the role that status played in the Klan's mobilization by focusing primarily on one key issue, public schooling, which was centrally featured in the Klan's agenda. The Klan's recruiting success was not simply a case of status backlash. Instead, applying the logic of the power-devaluation model reveals how status concerns contributed to the movement's growth.

The Klan's Defense of Public Schools

When considering the role of status in social movement mobilization, education is a logical starting point. Klan leaders took pains to present their movement as one composed of individuals who were well educated and highly regarded in their communities, and they often ridiculed their enemies for their lack of educational credentials. Articles written in the *Imperial Night-Hawk* were clearly intended to convey a sense of intellectual sophistication (but not elitism); they often referred to philosophers, biblical passages, scholarly work, and speeches made by prominent political figures. Perhaps more important, movement leaders frequently identified public education as the most pressing issue requiring the Klan's attention. Speaking to "seventy-five thousand Ohio Klansmen," Hiram Evans declared that saving, enlarging, and expanding the free public school system was the greatest necessity currently facing the movement. Evans clearly saw the issue as one that could be useful in attracting more members and supporters. Speaking to Grand Dragons and Grand Titans at a national convention held in Asheville, North Carolina, he advised his fellow Klan leaders to "go home and talk education among the Klansmen," and he addressed the topic in depth in numerous speeches and public addresses.[8]

Early in the Klan's ascendance, movement leaders discovered that concerns about public schooling provided them with an ideal issue to generate support for their organization. The Klan entered the state of Oregon in 1921 and quickly became involved in political controversy. The movement backed a ballot initiative sponsored by Scottish Rites Masons that essentially outlawed private schooling. The Scottish Rites Masons served, it is widely believed, as a front for the Klan in the state. The initiative, which was later found to be unconstitutional, passed with 115,506 votes in favor and 103,685 votes opposed.[9] The public school issue was also central to the gubernatorial campaign of 1922. Siding with the Klan on the issue, and declaring himself to be a 100 percent American candidate, Democrat Walter Pierce won a bitterly contested contest in a state that had previously been dominated by Republicans.

What was it about public education that captured the hearts and minds of Klansmen and Klanswomen in the early 1920s? Why did leaders of the Klan feature public education prominently in their collective-action frames? The Klan's rhetoric creates the image of an educational system in crisis. Movement leaders frequently commented on high rates of illiteracy, poor attendance in the schools, poorly funded schools, and underpaid teachers as problems in need of immediate attention. Certainly there was room for improvement in public education in the 1920s, and issues related to schooling can generate powerful emotions because parents are concerned about their children's prospects for social mobility.[10] Yet to understand the role that public education played in the rise of the Klan, it is important to ask whether conditions were improving or worsening in the 1920s. Were Klan members responding to new objective grievances (increasingly poor performance of the public schools) or were they reacting instead to status-based power devaluation resulting from gains made in education in the years prior to the Klan's emergence?

Available data suggest that to a great extent the Klan's discussions of an educational system in crisis were more an exercise in the social construction of a social problem than an accurate assessment of worsening conditions in the United States. This is not to say, of course, that Klan members were not genuinely concerned about the quality of public education. Certainly, many were. And clearly the educational system had significant deficiencies in the 1920s. In fact, in the 1919–20 school year the average annual salary of teachers, principals, and supervisors was only slightly higher than the average annual income of manufacturing wage earners.[11] However, these and other deficiencies in public education represent a cross-sectional snapshot of what was generally a positive longitudinal trajectory. According to U.S. census data, total salary paid to teachers, principals, and supervisors increased by 133 percent from 1910 to 1920. Salaries continued to rise during the years of the Klan's growth, showing a 70 percent increase from 1920 to 1925.[12] Census data show a similar trend in total expenditures on public schools. Expenditures per student (for the population aged five to seventeen) nearly doubled from 1909 to 1919 and nearly doubled again during the decade in which the Klan began its phenomenal growth (see Figure 15).[13]

While public spending on education was on the rise, so were rates of enrollment. In 1900 72.4 percent of the population from age five to seventeen was enrolled in public schools. By 1920 that figure had risen to 77.8 percent. Although this change is not dramatic, a state-by-state examination of census data provides a more interesting story. Table 3 ranks states according to the change in the percentage of school-age population enrolled in public schools from 1900 to 1920. Many northeastern states, such as New Hampshire, Vermont, Massachusetts, Maine, Rhode Island, and New York, experienced a decline in public school enrollment. Much of the change can be attributed to the expansion of parochial schools in these states where Catholics comprised a sizable proportion of the total popu-

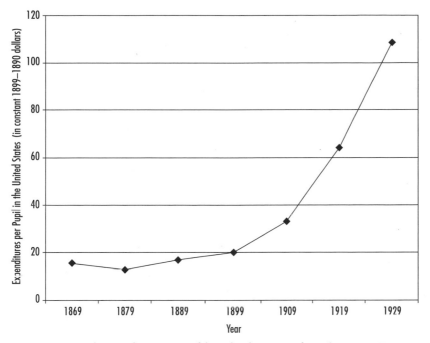

Figure 15. Total expenditures on public schools per pupil, 1869–1929. Figures are based on average daily enrollment. U.S. Department of Education, 120 Years of American Education: A Statistical Portrait.

lation. However, several predominantly Protestant states such as Indiana, Kansas, and Oregon also lost ground to other western and especially southern states. In 1900 the enrollment rate for Indiana was higher than rates of all eleven states of the former Confederacy, but by 1920 Indiana had been surpassed by Arkansas, Florida, North Carolina, South Carolina, and Tennessee.

Increases in rates of public school enrollment in southern states can be attributed to several factors. Relatively few Catholics resided in the South, so the public schools faced little competition from parochial schools in these states. Also, urbanization and northern migration certainly played a role. As long as a majority of black Americans were confined to positions as sharecroppers, subsistence farmers, or laborers in rural locales, there were few opportunities to secure a quality education for their children.[14] Urbanization generated additional incentives for white migrants to enroll children in schools. The low rates of school enrollment in southern states at the turn of the century reflect the low priority placed on public education

Table 3. Percentage of school-age population (five to seventeen years old) enrolled in public schools, by state

State	Enrolled 1900	Enrolled 1920	Change in Enrollment	State	Enrolled 1900	Enrolled 1920	Change in Enrollment
Arizona	51.9	88.0	36.1	North Dakota	81.3	84.6	3.3
Wyoming	65.7	91.6	25.9	New York	69.6	72.8	3.2
South Carolina	60.7	83.9	23.2	Pennsylvania	68.9	71.5	2.6
Louisiana	43.6	63.5	19.9	Michigan	77.1	79.3	2.2
Montana	72.8	92.2	19.4	Oregon	82.1	84.1	2.0
North Carolina	63.6	82.4	18.8	West Virginia	78.6	79.8	1.2
Nevada	63.6	82.4	17.4	Ohio	75.4	76.6	1.2
Florida	66.6	82.6	16.0	Nebraska	89.5	90.5	1.0
Idaho	79.2	94.8	15.6	Kentucky	75.3	76.2	0.9
Arkansas	71.0	85.7	14.7	Maryland	67.0	66.9	-0.1
New Mexico	61.4	75.4	14.0	Missouri	78.6	78.3	-0.3
Oklahoma	79.8	92.6	12.8	Illinois	72.7	72.1	-0.6
Tennessee	75.1	87.6	12.5	Kansas	89.2	87.9	-1.3
Alabama	61.7	74.1	12.4	Rhode Island	66.8	65.4	-1.4
Virginia	63.2	73.3	10.1	Indiana	81.1	79.4	-1.7
New Jersey	68.5	77.4	8.9	Delaware	75.3	73.3	-2.0
Georgia	65.3	74.0	8.7	Iowa	89.1	86.1	-3.0
Texas	64.7	73.4	8.7	Mississippi	73.3	69.8	-3.5
Colorado	88.2	95.0	6.8	Wisconsin	72.5	68.2	-4.3
Utah	81.0	87.2	6.2	Massachusetts	76.2	71.3	-4.9
Washington	87.9	94.1	6.2	Maine	81.4	76.3	-5.1
Connecticut	74.5	80.3	5.8	Vermont	82.2	73.4	-8.8
Minnesota	77.6	81.8	4.2	New Hampshire	74.0	64.3	-9.7
South Dakota	79.5	82.9	3.4				

Source: U.S. Department of Commerce, Statistical Abstracts of the United States, 1925.

in an agrarian economy in which a privileged few possessed most of the land, the wealth, and the political power and had little incentive to promote educational opportunities for those who labored in the fields. Most northern and midwestern states had passed compulsory education laws prior to the turn of the century, while southern and southwestern states were holdouts.[15] That began to change in the early 1900s. By 1920 all southern states had enacted compulsory education laws with most of these laws enacted in the 1910s.

Although these laws were not enforced as aggressively in southern states as they were in northern states, and while expenditures on black schools continued to lag behind spending on white schools, new educational opportunities were opening up for southern blacks.[16] Census data show evidence of a sharp reduction in illiteracy among black Americans in southern states from 1900 to 1920. Although the census figures on illiteracy are not completely reliable, they do show a consistent trend toward increasing literacy. For example, the census reports that 54.7 percent of adult black males in South Carolina were illiterate in 1900. By 1920 black adult male illiteracy had decreased to 37.7 percent. In Arkansas the illiteracy rate for adult black males dropped from 44.8 percent to 25.4 percent during the same period. Indeed, all southern states show a sharp drop in black illiteracy in the years prior to the Klan's resurgence.

In the nation as a whole, enrollment in public schools was on the rise but so was enrollment in Catholic schools. Indeed, the Klan emerged during a time of rapid expansion of parochial education, which began in the mid-1870s. There were approximately 1,400 Catholic schools in the nation in 1875; within ten years, there were more than 2,500 schools.[17] By 1920, the year in which the Klan began to spread across the nation, the number of Catholic schools had reached 8,706. An increase in the number of Catholic high schools was particularly sharp in the years leading up to the Klan's rise: in 1915 there were 1,276 Catholic high schools in the United States, and by 1922 that number had nearly doubled to 2,129. Perhaps more telling, the number of teachers in Catholic high schools increased by 298 percent, and the number of students enrolled in Catholic high schools jumped by 106 percent during the same time period.[18]

Although Klan leaders criticized Catholic schools for their failure to promote assimilation of European immigrants and for not instilling core American values in students, these criticisms were leveled at a time when Catholic schools, ironically, were becoming more and more like the public schools. The Catholic school system in the United States originated and developed in a larger context characterized by deep-seated and intense religious animosity. To a great extent, Catholic schools emerged in response to teaching and practices in public school that Catholics viewed as hostile to their faith. Many Protestants drew on republican theory to argue that (Protestant) religion must serve as a foundation for public education. According to this line of thought, the fate of the republic rests on participation of moral citizens in the public sphere. The public schools, therefore, must draw on core religious values to produce successive generations of moral citizens. As Tyack and colleagues express it, nonsectarian public schooling in this context "meant that the Protestant churches agreed to suspend their denominational quarrels within the public schoolhouse." However, reading from the Bible in public schools was quite common throughout most of the nineteenth century.[19]

Catholic and Protestant disagreement over the role of public schools provided impetus for the development and expansion of a parochial school system:

> So deep were the differences of religious outlook between Protestants and Catholics in the mid-nineteenth century that they often seemed incapable of understanding one another. Enraged by compulsory reading of the King James Bible and by textbooks that derogated Catholicism and often the lands from which Catholic immigrants had come, Catholics in many communities came to believe that they must build their own school system.[20]

In spite of such conditions, many Catholics continued to send their children to public schools. Limited resources possessed by Catholic immigrants and other working-class Catholic families put the Catholic schools at a competitive disadvantage, and Protestants, in most instances, successfully resisted public funding of Catholic schools.

In the nineteenth century, Catholics were divided on the role of parochial education and how Catholic schools should relate to the public school system. In some communities Catholic schools did receive public funding. This typically resulted from local conditions that required cooperation between the public school system and the Catholic Church. In Poughkeepsie, New York, for example, Catholic schools were in danger of closing due to lack of funding. Closure of the schools would have resulted in a 50 percent increase in public school enrollment, severely straining the resources of the public schools. To avoid such a crisis, public money supported the failing Catholic schools, while the Catholic schools agreed to refrain from offering religious instruction during normal school hours.[21]

In most instances, Catholic schools had to make do without public funding but still had to come to terms, in some way, with the public school system and with the larger society in which they were embedded. Many Catholics believed that the schools should provide religious teaching but should otherwise be closely modeled after the public schools.[22] Proponents of this model argued that Catholic schools should not only cover similar nonreligious content in the classroom but also should strive to surpass the public schools in terms of the quality of the overall educational experience. Other Catholics believed that parochial schools should avoid convergence with public schools. From this perspective, the schools were charged with preserving not only the Catholic faith within a hostile environment but also the language and culture of the immigrant parishioners' home countries.[23]

By the turn of the century an expanding and increasingly structured parochial school system ran parallel to the public school system. It served many of the same purposes and was subjected to many of the same state-imposed regulations. As the size of the Catholic middle class expanded, so did the demand for high academic standards in parochial schools. To prevent defection to public schools, Catholic educators had to convince parents that they could do a better job than the public schools in preparing students for higher education.[24]

Catholic schools also converged with public schools in their efforts to promote citizenship and patriotism within the classroom. In part, this reflected the preferences of second- and third-generation Catholic immigrants who were reaching middle-class status and valued assimilation into the larger society. But outside pressure to promote patriotism and assimilation became intense during World War I and in the war's immediate aftermath as a strong nativist current swept across the nation. Veverka notes that during this period Catholic educators generally agreed that Americanization was an important function of Catholic schooling.[25] The following statement from a diocesan school superintendent in Pittsburgh in 1919 is strikingly similar to statements made by Klan leaders about the role of schools in American society:

> To strengthen our national life, to perpetuate our liberties under the Constitution, to guard against insidious attacks upon republican institutions, we advocate a vigorous and holy spirit of Americanism in our schools, a deep and intelligent love of our institutions, reverence for our flag and respect for our laws. The lessons of patriotism based on religion should be made a part of our daily school life so that our educational system should maintain a strong national character and be a powerful aid to the true development of our national life and national ideals.[26]

Status-Based Power Devaluation

As the Klan's leaders and recruiters opportunistically searched for issues that they could exploit to attract members and supporters, they soon discovered that public education fit the bill. The Klan's leaders generated the impression that schools were failing miserably during a period in which educational opportunities were actually improving for many Americans. Because the Klansmen made exaggerated, inaccurate, and misleading claims about the state of education in the United States, it is tempting to concur with early scholars who argued that the movement exploited the irrational fears and anxieties of individuals that it hoped to recruit. If the educational system was not actually collapsing, then why did so many American Protestants embrace the Klan's message? Close scrutiny of the Klan's rhetoric can reveal a solution to the puzzle. The Klan's message resonated strongly because changes in the educational system (both public and private) taking place in the early 1900s generated status-based power devaluation for many middle-class, white Protestants.

Labaree points out that rapid industrialization in the United States led many middle-class Americans to embrace public education as the key to maintaining a favorable position for oneself and one's family within a fluid class structure. The middle class

> was caught between two advancing dangers. On the one side, the encroachment of successful entrepreneurial competitors threatened bankruptcy. On the other side, the rapid growth of wage labor threatened proletarianization. As the reliability of economic property as a guarantee of social reproduction decreased, the middle class's dependence on cultural property increased.[27]

Middle-class Americans recognized that education set them apart from industrial laborers and that education was vital in terms of ensuring that their children would not fall into the ranks of the proletariat. As Lynd and Lynd point out in their classic study of "Middletown," by the early 1920s the topic of education evoked "the fervor of a religion" among many Muncie residents, as they saw education as salvation from a hard working-class existence.[28]

A high school diploma, and for some a college diploma, had utilitarian value but also generated a considerable amount of social esteem for those who possessed one. The status derived from a high school diploma was a function, to a great extent, of the relative scarcity of degrees awarded.[29] High school graduation rates were very low in the late 1800s and early 1900s, but began to rise sharply around 1910 (see Figure 16). The Klan emerged in a time when a high school diploma was becoming increasingly common and this, in the language of the power-devaluation model, meant that the status-based purchasing power of those who gained social esteem by virtue of their educational credentials was undergoing devaluation. What is more, levels of educational attainment for the Klan's enemies were converging with those of the native-born, white Protestants whom the Klan hoped to recruit. The gap between white and nonwhite Americans in school enrollment began to close rapidly in the years leading to the Klan's mobilization (see Figure 17). As discussed earlier, the parochial school system was also expanding, with the growth in secondary schooling being especially striking. Growing Catholic prosperity and Catholics' commitment to build a school system that could compete with, and surpass, the public school system understandably led many middle-class Protestants to worry about whether the education provided by the public schools would be sufficient to allow their children to maintain their position within the class structure.

College enrollment was also on the rise in the early 1900s, although the most dramatic increases in college enrollment would not occur until

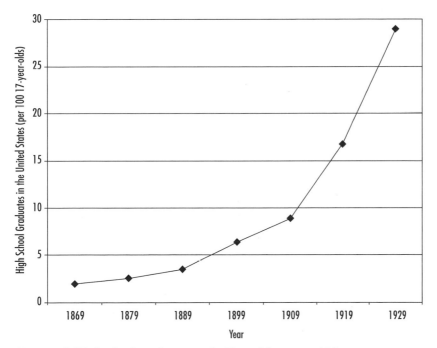

Figure 16. High school graduates in the United States per 100 seventeen-year-olds. U.S. Department of Education, 120 Years of American Education: A Statistical Portrait.

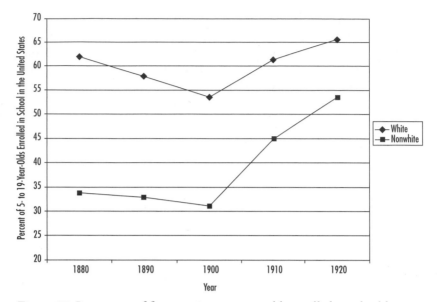

Figure 17. Percentage of five- to nineteen-year-olds enrolled in school by race, 1880–1920. U.S. Department of Education, 120 Years of American Education: A Statistical Portrait.

several decades after the Klan's mobilization. Notably, in the years leading up to the Klan's mobilization, women were beginning to comprise a larger proportion of the undergraduate population. In 1900 close to 20 percent of bachelor's degrees in the United States were conferred to women. By 1920 women earned approximately 35 percent of conferred bachelor's degrees.[30] Many white, middle-class Protestants, men in particular, were experiencing status-based power devaluation in the early 1920s resulting from increases in the supply of others who were gaining educational credentials. These conditions provided a framing opportunity for the leaders of the Ku Klux Klan.

Prognosis: Supply Restriction

The Klan's arguments on behalf of public education were deeply rooted in republican ideology. One Klan writer lays the groundwork for an argument to improve the public schools system by writing,

> The greatest American problem is to learn how to have voters and taxpayers recognize the fact that the children of today will be the responsible government of tomorrow and that governments reflect the character of individual constituents. Unless the child's character is founded on good

principles, mental and moral trustworthiness, he can not attain the full measure of responsible citizenship. The public school is the training school for the potential responsible citizen.[31]

The writer praised the founders of public schooling for developing a system that provides an "equal chance for all," and reminded readers that it was every citizen's duty, even those without children, to support public schooling with tax dollars. Klan writers, including the one cited above, also expressed concern that the value of education in the United States was being "cheapened."

The Klan's framing of education conveys deep concern that the public schools were losing ground. One article describes a speech delivered by Hiram Evans in Pennsylvania, where the Imperial Wizard "pleaded for action to guard this country against a recurrence of the conditions found in the world war, where 24 percent of the men in the army were found to be illiterate. This disgrace of the nation, not fully appreciated before, would be wiped out if compulsory education were required of all children."[32] Evans was referring to tests administered to servicemen that revealed high rates of illiteracy. The issue was covered extensively by the national media, and groups such as the National Education Association (NEA) capitalized on the media attention to demand that greater investments be made in education.[33] Klan leaders sought to capitalize on the publicity to advance their own agenda. Hiram Evans advocated compulsory education as a cure but was quick to point out that the solution lay in public rather than parochial schooling. According to Evans, "Children taught in parochial schools, Roman Catholics or otherwise, can not grow up with open minds. They have been taught what to think . . . rather than how to think."[34]

Although Evans and other Klan leaders criticized Catholic schools, it is clear that they sensed that the public schools were losing ground to parochial schools. One article addressed this issue in considerable depth, noting,

> The Catholics, who number in the United States considerably over eighteen million, against eighty million Protestants, are awake to the advantages of an education and have established their schools at central points where every child of the Catholic faith is enabled to attend and secure the benefits that are being denied the majority. Of course the schools are owned and controlled by the Catholic and Catholicism is drilled into the children from the day they first enter school until their education is completed. If this is good for the minority of the population of the United States, then why should not the Protestant citizen see the point and work with the idea of developing their children into leaders? The illiteracy of Protestant America is not so astounding after a careful study

of the school system without a compulsory education or child labor law. On the other hand, the Catholic does not have to be forced to send his child to school. He is training him to dominate the child who is raised a Protestant and in this manner they will be enabled to completely control economic conditions after a few years of intensive education. Our schools will then fall into the hands of the Catholic and the wonderful system that our forefathers have labored to build up and turn into a most efficient system will become a thing of the past. Our children's children will be taught the religion of the Catholic in our own schools and in a few generations the United States will be a Catholic country.[35]

Klan leaders expressed grudging admiration for the way in which Catholics were taking advantage of educational opportunities and expressed fear that Catholics would translate superior educational training into economic and political power. They raised concerns about individual Catholics influencing the public schools by gaining seats on the school board or through teaching in the public schools. The Klan leaders' diatribes often spoke of Vatican-inspired conspiracies to take over public education. One such article ends by instructing the Klan's followers to "see to it that no boards of education are elected who, directly or indirectly, come under the influence of the Vatican, so that teachers may be selected and employed who will teach the principles of real Americanism." Another article warned of Catholic propaganda creeping into public school textbooks: "Take a look at the youngsters' school books when they bring them home. Maybe you will find the hierarchy at work."[36]

Klan leaders' framing of education tapped into a general feeling among members of the racial and religious majority that they were losing ground to subordinate groups. While Catholic competition generated the most concern, race also came into play. One article chastises white Protestants for spending more on cigarettes, movies, and cosmetics than they do on education, while "eighty percent of the negroes are now able to read and write, yet, there are thousands of whites that cannot. No one will deny that the negro has the right to an education, but are one hundred per cent Americans willing to allow whites to group up in ignorance while negroes are educated?"[37] Clearly, Klan leaders knew how to push their constituents' buttons when it came to constructing collective-action frames. Given the prejudices of the day, and the prejudices held by members of the Klan, the prospect of being surpassed by black Americans in educational achievement was, undoubtedly, a powerful motivator.

Although Klan leaders noted the educational progress made by Catholics and African Americans and criticized fellow Protestants for being complacent about public education, they argued that problems in the public schools resulted in part from the burden of having to incorporate blacks and Catholic immigrants into the system. Doing so, they argued, resulted in a lowering of standards that, in the language of the power-devaluation model, diminishes the value of public education as a source of social esteem. As one Klan writer put it,

> Many of our public schools, I am told, do not teach English. Few of the emigrants past thirty years of age ever gain a speaking acquaintance with our language as it is spoken or written. Go to a foreign district in any city and see them reading their particular newspaper or books printed in their particular language. With that state of affairs, how in the name of God can they learn what Americanism means?[38]

To emphasize the magnitude of the problem, another Klan writer claimed that the task of educating immigrants was even more complicated and serious than a world war. The immigrants, he argued, were

> A stupendous army of downtrodden, landless peasants, illiterate for a thousand years, submerged and warped in mind and body and spiritual estate by their cramped existence and the absolutism under which they have lived—the very flood from the cesspools of that old continent boiling and reeking with the filth of ten centuries of plundered, profaned and disinherited mankind.[39]

The Klan's arguments in favor of immigration restriction had implications for public education as well as for economic and political struggles. If the status derived from a public education was being diminished by increasing numbers of individuals receiving similar educational credentials, then immigration restriction would reduce the supply of individuals in the public schools. It would also reduce the number of students who might fuel the growth of a parochial school system that, Klansmen feared, was outperforming the public schools in many respects. Public schools, from the Klansmen's perspective, were burdened with educating poor immigrants, many of whom were Catholic, while the Catholic schools could devote their resources to training relatively prosperous Catholic students.

Interestingly, the Klan did not argue that Catholic or black students should be prohibited from attending the public schools. They were more concerned about the possibility that Catholics would control or influence public education. Klan leaders advocated a form of compulsory education that would not only compel all school-age children to attend school but also force them to attend *public* schools. They advocated sharp increases in spending on public schooling that, through public taxation, would require all Americans (including Catholics) to fund a school system that would be completely under the control of Protestants. Evans argued that 50 percent of taxes, rather than 5 percent, should go toward education.[40]

To address status-based power devaluation resulting from changes in education, the Klan did much more than advocate immigration restriction. Indeed, the movement's leaders embraced a failed effort to establish a federal department of education in the 1920s. Efforts to create a department of education preceded the Klan's growth in the early 1920s and, as Dumenil notes, it was an issue that stimulated intense debate throughout the nation. According to the *New York Times,* the debate could be characterized as a "controversial discussion that spreads in an accelerating wave over the whole country, until every village is lined up pro or con."[41]

The attempt to create a federal department of education was an outgrowth of the progressive movement and was closely linked to ongoing efforts of education reformers who were promoting expansion, centralization, and standardization in public schooling—what Tyack refers to as an effort to develop the "one best system." The Smith-Towner Bill, introduced in 1919, not only sought to create a federal department of education but also aimed to raise educational standards through research and through the provision of federal funding. Similar bills, the Towner-Sterling Bill and the Sterling-Reed Bill, were introduced in 1921 and 1924. The legislation also included provisions to promote "Americanization" in the public schools. Klan leaders viewed the legislation as an opportunity to secure a Protestant monopoly on the administration and delivery of education, and, as Dumenil notes, they were also attracted to the proposed legislation because of the way in which it would elevate the public schools at the expense of parochial schools. Using federal influence and federal funding to raise standards in the public schools could go a long way toward restoring the status-based purchasing power of a public education.[42]

Several lengthy articles in the *Imperial Night-Hawk* describe the Klan's rationale for supporting legislation that would establish a department of education. These articles clearly demonstrate the Klan's view that federal aid was required to guarantee that a public school education would be superior to a parochial school education. One writer enthusiastically supported the Sterling-Reed Education Bill, reasoning that its passage "will mean that the public schools will rank along with the best of sectarian schools and be efficiently controlled with the highest of American ideals and usages being taught, making, in the end, a completely Americanized government."

Another author noted that the bill was opposed by the "corporations" because of a desire to maintain a supply of cheap labor. The Klansman added, "The un-educated child of today will be the common laborer of the future and every day the ambition of men is being blighted when they realize that they are fighting losing battles because they were not as fortunate during their school days as were their playmates."[43] Arguments such as this one surely resonated strongly with middle-class Protestant Americans who feared that their children would fall into the ranks of the proletariat while Catholics experienced upward mobility due to superior educational opportunities.

Klansmen noted that the Sterling-Reed Bill would accomplish two general goals. First, it would establish a department of education with a Cabinet secretary at the head, and second, it would provide badly needed federal funding to the schools. One writer argued that the first goal was the most important: "The big thing, the fundamental, all important thing, to be accomplished for the cause of democratic education in America is to give it the recognition, the dignity, the established standing, of a high place in the Cabinet." Klansmen believed that increasing federal involvement in public education would prevent Catholics from influencing public schools, even in communities where Catholics represented the numerical majority. By enacting the Sterling-Reed Bill, the Klan argued, "we will find that Protestant Americans will cease to be discriminated against because of their affiliations with those things that are purely of America and for America."[44] Especially appealing to the Klansmen, in this regard, was $7,500,000 earmarked for promoting Americanization in the public schools.

While the Klan embraced legislation that would establish a federal department of education, the movement also backed efforts in states such as Michigan, Oregon, and Alabama to require all children to attend public, rather than private, schools. By advocating immigration restriction and by seeking ways to establish a Protestant monopoly on education, the movement offered a remedy for status-based power devaluation that resulted from increasing supplies of individuals possessing educational credentials at a time when the educational gap separating white Protestants from Catholics and African Americans was rapidly closing.

Prognosis: Stimulate Demand

Although the Klan raised concerns about public schooling, arguing that the quality of education had been "cheapened," the movement's frames also forcefully argued that a public education, if properly supported and funded, was inherently superior to private education—parochial education in particular. In essence, the frames aimed to demonstrate that those who were educated in the public schools had a superior educational experience and were therefore more worthy of social esteem than were individuals who were either uneducated or were educated in private schools. By promoting Protestant values and patriotism, the Klansmen argued, public schools not only produced better citizens but also produced citizens better equipped to succeed in life. One article, titled "Christian Citizenship: The Gospel according to the Klan," makes the following argument:

> The Klan insists that education must lead to a larger realization of citizenship; a deeper spiritual, a broader intellectual preparation for its privileges and duties. This is placing education on a higher plane than the Old World system. There they train a man into a machine, the soul into a pair of hands. We believe that citizenship in a democracy like ours is essentially Christian therefore, we insist on the Bible being placed in the public schools. We want every child in America to become intimately acquainted with the Christ, the most uplifting personality in all history.[45]

The quotation above exemplifies the way in which Klan leaders spoke to the special role that public education played for middle-class Americans. The public school represented a bulwark against intergenerational downward mobility. Bible reading and Protestant teaching in the public schools, they argued, were not only good for the soul but also good for the pocketbook. Acquaintance with Christ, in other words, was "uplifting" in a material sense as well as in a spiritual sense. Klansmen argued that even if Catholic schools could teach basic academic skills as effectively as the public schools, the Catholic schools were inferior in other important respects. One article, for example, characterized Catholic schools, and more generally the Catholic faith, as being antidemocratic. According to the writer,

> To attempt to institute a "parallel" system of sectarian or culturally and spiritually separate schools is to undertake something which, gloss it over as you wish, is "not specifically national" and furthermore is essentially un-American and un-democratic. A parochial school or any separate school which is educationally equal, or even superior to a public school, is its hopeless inferior as a democratic school.[46]

Quality education, according to the Klansmen, involved much more than the transmission of academic skills. As one writer expressed it, "Today, we need something more than grammars and fractions and geographies to prepare our youths and maidens for good citizenship. The great curse of the whole world today is the educated villian [sic]. These men know enough, they know everything, they know too much, but they have no moral principle."[47] Given the historical context, arguments such as this could help restore (or shore up) the social esteem that individuals derived by virtue of their public education. Indeed, for small businessmen, craftsmen, shop owners, and other middle-class Protestants targeted by the Klan's recruitment, a reputation for being honest and dependable was as least as important in securing a livelihood as was possession of reading, writing, and math skills.

Klan leaders criticized Catholicism and, more specifically, parochial education for allegedly promoting superstition and ignorance. According to the Klansmen, Catholics were taught to obey the pope's commands and were discouraged from thinking for themselves. According to Hiram Evans, in Catholic schools "memory has been developed at the expense of reason. Graduates of such schools can not be so well fitted for public life as those who grow up with minds keenly trained to reasoning who can face problems and decide them free of bias or prejudice."[48]

Klan leaders viewed secularism, as well as Catholicism, as a threat to the public schools. They countered this threat by arguing that Christian spirituality was a key ingredient in a superior educational experience. Protestantism, they argued, promoted free thinking and creativity but also grounded students in certain fundamental truths pertaining to the natural world. In one article critical of the theory of evolution, for example, a Klansman writes,

> All true knowledge of consciousness, the gaining of which is the correct evolution, is the enlightenment of the mind by the application of Truth as taught by the Bible, and not by Darwin. When education has lost its element of spiritual truth it is not worth having.[49]

The same author passionately concludes,

> With unselfish hands we must guard well the portals of knowledge. We must purify every avenue with the philosophy of the Man of Nazareth. For in such philosophy rests all human hope, all the elements which go to make a great people, who can stand the storm of assault, of envy and religious intolerance in its organized effort to enslave.[50]

Klan leaders spoke positively about the value of education in science, mathematics, literature, and history. However, they resented attempts to remove the Bible from the schoolhouse. The Bible, according to one Klan writer who was also a Protestant minister, "is a book which is the basis of every other book that is worth while. Books of science, which were the basis of scientific investigation ten years ago, are now discarded, but this book has been true in all ages. It is the one book that sets a standard for moral culture in every age."[51]

Faced with the prospect that public schools were losing ground to parochial schools, and that Catholics and black Americans were gaining ground on native-born, white Protestants, Klan leaders embraced public education as an issue that could rally the troops and motivate members of the racial and ethnic majority to join their cause. Klan leaders sought not only to gain a Protestant monopoly on the administration and delivery of education in the United States, but also to elevate public education as a source of social esteem. The public school system, if generously funded, could not only provide children with specific academic skills required to succeed in life but also arm them with a strong moral character. Catholics, the Klansmen

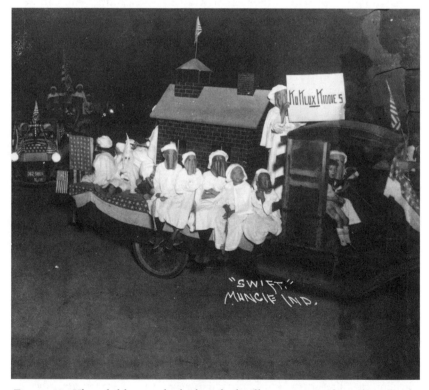

Figure 18. Klan children and a little red schoolhouse on parade in New Castle, Indiana, 1923. W. A. Swift Collection. Courtesy of Ball State University. Copyright 2006. All rights reserved.

argued, were hostile to these laudable goals. At a time when many Catholics were experiencing upward mobility and at a time when a Catholic—New York's governor, Al Smith—had his sights set on the presidency, Klan leaders sought to stimulate the demand for values that they claimed were the exclusive property of Protestants while characterizing Catholicism as an imminent threat to those values. Speaking before an "immense gathering in Ohio," Hiram Evans posed the following question: "What are the agencies and who are the people that would try to circumscribe the educational possibilities and prevent the enlightenment of mind and conscience which comes from a free and broad education?" Answering his own question, the Imperial Wizard asserted,

> During all ages a brutal and religious priesthood has sought through superstition, ignorance, and passion to prevent the emancipation of the human souls who come within the spread of their influence. Slowly from age to age the proponents of real liberty have come to see and to know from the history of their past and the acts of their present that the only sure way to insure to a people independence of thought and action is separation of church and state and the broad education of the masses of the people.[52]

Conclusion: Other Sources of Status-Based Power Devaluation

The Klan's mobilization in the early 1920s represents, in part, a response to a perceived decline in status for many native-born, white Protestants. However, theoretical arguments that explain the Klan in terms of status anxiety or status substitution badly mischaracterize the movement. These arguments mistakenly assume that Klan members were downwardly mobile and that they were irrationally clinging to a worldview that was becoming obsolete in a rapidly changing world. Contrary to such explanations, the Klan was attractive to many members of the cultural majority because the organization provided them with a political vehicle for engaging in ongoing cultural conflicts and the stakes of these conflicts were high. For middle-class Americans who were targeted by Klan recruiters, social esteem was valuable in its own right, but it was also vital in maintaining a position in a class hierarchy. Cultural capital, like other forms of capital, is subject to deflationary pressures.

The Klan's fight on behalf of public education was, in some respects, ahead of its time. The movement strongly backed a failed attempt to establish a federal department of education, and the Klan's leaders advocated dramatic increases in spending on public schools with the federal government, rather than local governments, providing the bulk of the funding. On these issues, they were aligned with Progressives and with educational reformers of the era who recognized the increasing relevance of education in a modern economy. As argued earlier, the Klan's rhetorical stance struck a chord with many individuals because it connected with a prevailing sense that the esteem derived from a public education was in decline. This devaluation occurred, in part, because of improvements in the educational system. A high school diploma, once a scarce commodity, was becoming increasingly common. Adding insult to injury, from the Klansman's perspective, increasingly large percentages of these diplomas were earned by Catholics and African Americans. In addition, a rapidly expanding parochial school system offered a different type of educational experience that, Klansmen feared, would come to be viewed as superior to that which could be experienced in the public schools.

As was true of most issues addressed by the movement, Klansmen argued that immigration restriction was one remedy for the problem. Many problems in the public schools, they argued, resulted from the burden of incorporating immigrants into the system—immigrants who, the Klan claimed, were not eager to learn the language of the land and who were unfamiliar with, and even hostile toward, the republican tradition in the United States. Klansmen also sought to secure a Protestant monopoly on the administration and delivery of education. They clearly recognized the advantages that would come their way if the public schools were to be generously funded through tax revenue. Catholics (as well as Protestants) would be compelled to enrich the public school system to a point where Catholics schools could no longer be competitive. These "supply side" tactics were complemented by an attempt to stimulate demand for public education in a status-exchange market, as Klansmen argued that public schools were inherently superior to private schools because of the way in which they instilled morality and patriotism in students.

I have focused on public education in this chapter because of the central role that the issue played in the Klan's agenda. Klan leaders wrote extensively on the topic, making it possible to observe the way in which movement leaders constructed frames that offered a remedy for status-based power devaluation. However, Klan members concerned themselves with several other issues that are related to status. Klansmen, for example, were staunch defenders of Prohibition. Interestingly, the Klan makes relatively few references to the subject in the *Imperial Night-Hawk* in issues published in 1923 and 1924. This may reflect a strategic calculation by Klan leaders who thought that the issue was best suited for specific local contexts where

anti-liquor sentiment was especially strong. Klan leaders opportunistically
sought ways to add new items to their agenda—what Snow, Rochford,
Worden, and Benford refer to as "frame extension"—to broaden their base
of support.[53] In doing so, they had to take care not to alienate preexisting
members and supporters.[54] Klan leaders, for example, purposefully glossed
over denominational distinctions among Protestants to avoid narrowing
the movement's appeal.

When the Klan did address the Prohibition issue in its national publication (and also within the pages of Indiana's *Fiery Cross*), the writers typically addressed the topic in terms of the movement's role in helping law enforcement agents crack down on bootleggers and, more generally, to enforce
the Volstead Act. Law enforcement was an issue that most of the Klan's
constituents could support, even if they were not enthusiastic supporters of
Prohibition. The "Great Titan" of the Realm of Texas expressed the Klan's
position in the following way:

> Klansmen are sworn not only to obey the laws themselves but also to
> aid the constituted law authorities in enforcing them. Many a bootlegger
> and illicit narcotic dealer, many a trafficker in the shame of womanhood,
> many a vagrant loafer and thief has met his downfall directly owing to
> information lodged with the proper authorities by Klansmen. Klansmen
> by thus aiding the officers of the law are making their home cities hap-
> pier, safer, brighter and cleaner places in which American women and
> children may live.[55]

Although Klan leaders publicly cautioned their members that they
should assist constituted authorities and not take the law into their own
hands, Klansmen often resorted to the latter.[56] In the states of Indiana and
Ohio, the Klan acted as an armed, militant, and highly organized vigilante
force. The movement's militant wing operated under legislation enacted in
the 1870s that allowed vigilante groups to form in order to protect against
horse theft. The new "Horse Thief Detective Association," over 20,000
members strong, answered only to the Klan, not to the state governments.
The armed Klansmen took it upon themselves to perform vice raids, and
they stopped and searched automobiles on the highway attempting to con-
fiscate liquor.[57]

How did the Klan's support for Prohibition fit into the movement's
overall recruiting success? The power-devaluation model suggests an answer. Many of the Klan's constituents exchanged abstinence for social esteem. With passage of the Volstead Act, abstinence became a common trait
in the general population—the supply of abstainers increased dramatically

and literally overnight. Abstaining from consumption of alcohol (not unlike refraining from homicide) lost some of its luster as a source of respect and admiration. Protestants who deeply believed that sobriety signaled respectability and virtue were suddenly indistinguishable from a Catholic who abstained not because he viewed abstinence as virtuous but because alcohol was illegal and no longer readily available. I am not arguing that Klan adherents were not genuinely angered by bootlegging and by lax enforcement of Prohibition laws. I am arguing that the Klan's vigilantism and its emphasis on law and order was particularly appealing to many of the movement's supporters because it helped to generate the impression that "true abstinence" remained a scarce commodity. The more that the Klan's members and leaders drew attention to Prohibition violations, the more they symbolically restricted the supply of abstainers.

It also seems likely that the Klan's position on Prohibition attracted members and adherents because of a shift in the demand side. Most notably, a significant proportion of the industrial elite began to redefine abstinence and its relation to economic prosperity and progress during the time in which the Klan gained strength. Historically, much of the initial support for Prohibition and for shutting down saloons came from the industrial elite who sought a stable and dependable workforce and bemoaned losses in productivity (and industrial accidents) that could be attributed to drink. Alcohol could cut into the profit margin, and employers, therefore, were motivated to construct a narrative that emphasized the virtues of sobriety. Abstinence was good not only for the individual but also for business and the nation.[58] As Beisel's work emphasizes, abstinence, and more generally avoidance of all forms of vice, became particularly important to many middle-class Americans in the late 1800s and early 1900s.[59]

In a fluid class structure, middle-class parents feared that their children would be tempted by illicit activity. They could be drawn into activity that would bring shame on the family, thereby diminishing the family members' cultural capital and severing network ties to those who might otherwise help them to advance (or maintain a position) in the class hierarchy. For many middle-class Protestants of the time, abstinence served as a marker distinguishing them from members of the working class. Protecting children from exposure to alcohol seemed to be particularly important to Klansmen. One article in the *Imperial Night-Hawk* describes how a Texas statute would result in up to ninety-five years in the penitentiary for "giving intoxicants to a girl." According to the Klansmen, "Such a law will go far towards placing the fear of God in the hearts of libertines and should prove a powerful deterrent to juvenile delinquency."[60]

After passage of the Volstead Act, capitalists' desires for a sober and re-liable workforce had to be weighed against their desires to avoid antagoniz-ing workers to the point of open rebellion. Indeed, concerns about stirring up working-class anger motivated some capitalists to form the Association Against the Prohibition Amendment (AAPA) in 1918, and the organization began to gain strength in the early 1920s.[61] Blatant disregard for Prohibition legislation in many communities also concerned capitalists who feared that social disorder threatened the legitimacy of their dominance in American society. Middle-class Americans were also troubled by an apparent dis-regard for the law, but the Klan's supporters advocated strict enforcement of the law rather than compromise and concessions. The Grand Dragon of the Klan's South Carolina Realm disdainfully noted,

> There is an effort being made by certain organizations and individuals to amend the Volstead law in order to include light wines and beers. The Klansmen of South Carolina are called upon to make a united effort in opposition to any amendment of the Volstead law and to stamp their ap-proval upon the prohibition law as it now stands.[62]

As mentioned above, the Klan's national publications did not delve deeply into the topic of Prohibition. Perhaps this is because the merits of abstinence would have appeared obvious to the Klan's supporters, but there are some indications that the movement's leaders sought to capitalize on a general sentiment among middle-class Protestants that the economic and social elite had betrayed the noble cause. Klan leaders seemed to be particu-larly incensed when teetotalers were ridiculed in the movies or by other pub-lic figures (not unlike the way in which contemporary social conservatives resent Hollywood for being out of touch with their traditional beliefs and values). They also complained about how Catholics were overrepresented in motion pictures and presented in a positive light, while Protestant funda-mentalists were caricatured and ridiculed.

Clearly angered by the way in which it seemed that the "demand" for abstinence was declining, Klan leaders pushed back by reasserting the view that abstinence was an admirable trait and one that should be emulated by all Americans. One Klan writer approvingly described a circular being distributed in Kansas that presents a view of how the issue will be discussed forty-four years in the future.

> Officers and private citizens are agreed that prohibit[i]on is the state's best business asset. Many crimes that are common in communities that toler-ate liquor are absent from Kansas. Conviction of violators is easier now

than at any time in the past, due to the years of proof that intoxicating liquor is a commercial and social detriment to any community. Many undesirable influences that attend liquor were banished from the state when liquor was banished. Liquor sales are not even permitted in Kansas on doctor's proscriptions. Liquor is an outlaw in Kansas. Kansas is forty-four years removed from the thought of ever returning to the saloon.[63]

From the Klansman's perspective, movement members already understood what others would eventually discover about the social and economic consequences of liquor. Klansmen were, in other words, ahead of their time.

7

How to Recruit a Klansman

More than seven hundred members of the Ku Klux Klan attended services at the First Methodist Church in Wellsville, Ohio, recently and presented a silk American flag and a purse of money to the pastor. The minister in receiving and thanking the Klansmen for the gifts spoke of the work of the Knights of the Ku Klux Klan as being "the world's greatest movement."
—*Imperial Night-Hawk,* January 16, 1924

According to the theory advanced in this book, structural changes that produce devaluation in economic, political, and status-based exchange markets provide incentives to participate in right-wing movements. Individuals who are experiencing power devaluation are likely to be receptive to a proposed course of action that aims to restore their power. This is especially true when power devaluation is not distributed randomly in the population but instead appears to be disproportionately affecting a clearly identifiable social group. In preceding chapters I have identified several ways in which structural changes related to immigration, transformations in manufacturing production, an agricultural depression, women's suffrage, public and private schooling, and Prohibition legislation, along with other factors, contributed to power devaluation for many native-born, white Protestant Americans in the years leading up to the Klan's mobilization.

Yet power devaluation by itself does not automatically translate into right-wing mobilization. Individuals respond to power devaluation in a variety of ways. Some may not even be aware of their own depreciating power. Others may understand (on some level) that they are experiencing power devaluation but are unable to identify the source of the devaluation and, therefore, are uncertain as to how they should respond. Many will simply accept their fate and accommodate to their new circumstances. Interpretive processes are required to transform collectively held grievances into collective action. As Snow and Benford point out, collective-action frames are most effective when they provide both a diagnosis and a prognosis for problems confronting potential members and adherents while simultaneously motivating them to take action. To be effective, these frames must resonate with those who are targeted for recruitment, and they should appear credible in light of their perceptions and lived experiences.[1]

Collective-action frames constructed by leaders of the Ku Klux Klan addressed a wide variety of topics. At first glance, the Klan's framing may appear to be incoherent and disarticulated because it addresses so many different issues seemingly in a piecemeal fashion. However, I believe that the Klan's framing succeeded because of a consistently applied overarching logic embedded in the frames. Klan leaders opportunistically sought to identify problems confronting potential members and adherents and capitalized on the intuitive appeal of simple microeconomic logic to gain their support. If power devaluation results from an increase in the supply of that which individuals have to offer in exchange and from a decrease in demand for that which they offer in exchange, cultural attacks and cultural appeals could be used to restrict the supply and to stimulate the demand.

Power devaluation and effective framing can generate a large pool of individuals who are favorably predisposed toward right-wing mobilization. In Klandermans's terms, they have become a part of the "mobilization potential."[2] If mobilization is to occur, organizational resources must be available and the political context must be conducive to collective action. Because right-wing movements represent relatively advantaged groups rather than those facing extreme poverty and political oppression, resources and political opportunities are typically available. Right-wing mobilization does not require the infusion of new, previously unavailable resources or a favorable shift in political opportunities. However, growth in the size and strength of a right-wing movement does depend heavily on how effectively movement leaders exploit preexisting resources and political opportunities.

Organizational Models: Fraternal Lodges and Protestant Churches

When analyzing a social movement, one should not assume that the membership is homogeneous in terms of motives for participation or in terms of the intensity of their commitment to the cause.[3] The Ku Klux Klan was not an exception to this general rule. Klan leaders cast a very broad net and were constantly seeking to identify new issues that would attract members and adherents. Some individuals were attracted to the movement because of the way in which it addressed their economic grievances, while others were drawn to the organization because they opposed political machines and because they felt Catholics were gaining too much political clout. Still others sided with the Klan's approach to issues such as public schooling and Prohibition. Some Klansmen and Klanswomen were so committed to the movement that they were willing to contribute substantial time, energy, and personal resources to help the Klan to achieve its goals. As is true of most social movements, however, many participants sided with the Klan but their commitment to the cause was not so great that they would participate without receiving something in return.

The economist Mancur Olson pointed out years ago that those who wish to organize collective action must overcome a "freerider dilemma."[4] Social-movement organizations aim to secure collective benefits for constituents. If the movement succeeds, individuals can enjoy the benefits without participating. The American civil rights movement sought to secure fundamental rights and privileges for all African Americans, not just for those who marched in the streets and sat-in at southern lunch counters. The Ku Klux Klan aimed to secure benefits for all native-born, white Protestants, not just for those who joined the organization. Because individuals can enjoy the benefits of a collective effort without participating, and because participation entails personal costs, many people will rationally choose not to participate. It is more rational to free-ride on others' efforts.

To overcome the free-rider dilemma, according to Olson, participation must be enticed by offering selective incentives. The term "selective incentives" refers to benefits that individuals receive only through participation in the collective effort. These benefits may be "hard" (e.g., material) or "soft" (nonmaterial or social).[5] Building on Olson's logic, resource mobilization theorists have emphasized the importance of an organizational infrastructure in social-movement activism. Organizations provide not only a base for staging protest rallies, marches, meetings, and other movement activities but also communication networks and the resources needed to supply the selective incentives that draw people into collective action. As Oberschall points out, preexisting organizations are also an important source of members and leaders. It is much more efficient to recruit blocs of individuals who are already organized for some other purpose than it is to recruit isolated individuals one by one.[6]

The Klan's leaders aimed to enlist 10 million dues-paying members, recognizing that it would be difficult for political representatives to ignore any social movement that could boast of such a large membership.[7] Although the Klan ultimately fell short of its goal, its recruiting success was nevertheless impressive in terms of both the number of people who joined and the speed of the movement's growth. In only a few years, several million Americans joined an organization dedicated to white supremacy and, more generally, to advancing the interests of native-born, white Protestants. The capacity to offer selective incentives was crucial to the movement's recruiting successes.

In comparison to many social movements, the costs of participation in the Ku Klux Klan were high. In some locations, for example, Klansmen were on the receiving end of mob violence. Indeed, a few Klansmen were killed in skirmishes with the movement's enemies. In Carnegie, Pennsylvania, an industrial town on the outskirts of Pittsburgh, ten thousand Klansmen attempted to march through the town. They were met by a barrage of rocks and bricks. A Klansman was shot and killed, and his fellow marchers were forced to retreat. Klansmen were also bombarded with bricks in Boston. In Perth Amboy, New Jersey, Klansmen who were assembled in the city's Odd Fellows Hall came under siege as a mob five thousand strong gathered outside of the building. The local police were unable to protect Klan members from attack. Car windshields were smashed, and Klansmen attempting to escape were chased down and beaten in the streets.[8] These attacks mostly took place in northeastern cities where the Klan's Catholic enemies were concentrated, but the movement also faced similar opposition in some midwestern and western locations where the Klan's opponents were more numerous than its supporters.

In many communities, however, the Klan enjoyed broad support, and its members were free to reveal their ties to the movement without fear of violent retaliation. Even so, membership entailed significant costs. Klansmen paid a ten-dollar initiation fee and also had to foot the bill for their robes and other components of Klan regalia worn in parades and ceremonies. There were significant opportunity costs involved as Klansmen and Klanswomen took time away from other activities to attend frequent meetings and other Klan-sponsored events. To gain mass support, Klan leaders had to offer something more than simply a promise to address their constituents' collective grievances.

The content of the *Imperial Night-Hawk* reveals an impressive range of creatively conceived activities sponsored by the movement designed to attract new members to the organization and to maintain the interest and loyalty of those who had already joined. The leadership also made many mistakes, and corruption and factionalism would continually threaten the movement's growth—even its very existence. Nevertheless, the phenomenal growth of the Klan is much easier to understand after examining the way in which the movement exploited preexisting organizational resources and offered a variety of selective incentives to participants.

Elisabeth Clemens's work demonstrates that preexisting organizations provide not only resources and participants for activism but also organizational models that can be co-opted by social movements.[9] Transplanting a particular organizational form into a social movement provides a familiar script that is useful in coordinating the activities of many people. But the organizational form may also serve as a symbolic expression of core values that the movement wishes to convey.[10] A social movement, for example, may opt for a decentralized and democratic form of organization because that organizational form maps (ideologically) onto its goal of challenging hierarchical systems of dominance and oppression.[11] In contrast, the Klan was organized in a military fashion, and its leaders frequently invoked "war" analogies to describe it. Hiram Evans once claimed that "the Klan literally is once more the embattled American farmer and artisan coordinated into a disciplined and growing army."[12] "Onward Christian Soldiers" was one of the movement's favorite anthems. Klan leaders constructed a world in which "100 percent Americans" were locked in battle with formidable foes. As one Klan writer expressed it,

> If the time shall come when the purposes for which the Klan was organized have all been accomplished, then its members need no longer be a militant, fighting organization, and they may possibly revert into an organization something like the veterans of foreign wars, or the veterans of any other crusade; but until such time, and until the purpose for which the Klan was organized have been accomplished, the military feature of the Klan must be maintained.[13]

Although the Klan adopted a military style, later on its organizational form, fraternal lodges, rather than the military, were the most influential models. Indeed, Klan members conceived of their organization as a fraternal order not unlike the Masons and the Odd Fellows. The Klan's founder, William Joseph Simmons, had considerable experience with fraternal organizing, as did many of the Klan's recruiters. Not unlike fraternities of the era, the Klan's internal hierarchy tended to reinforce class-based distinctions among members, in spite of rhetoric that denied the significance of class in evaluating the worth of a Klansmen.[14] Based on her study of the Athens, Georgia, Klan, MacLean observes,

> The fact that the Law Enforcement Committee included none of the Klan's poorer, less prominent members is significant. The order seems to

have purposely staffed the committee with men whose claim to authority would be difficult for their non-Klan peers to question. In so doing, Klan leaders most likely aspired to attract others of the same class. Whether intentional or not, the composition suggests a clear hierarchy within the Klan. It replicated internally the chain of command it prescribed for the rest of society. Indeed, internal Klan documents indicated that only better-off members were trusted to plan activities and speak publicly. These practices illustrated how intimately the quest for respectability was tied to class differentiation.[15]

The Klan's self-comparisons to mainstream fraternal organizations were not always appreciated by its models. In some cases, fraternity officers spoke out against the Klan. One Klan writer noted that an Elks lodge in Atlantic City, New Jersey, had voted to expel any members who were also Klan members. The Klan writer warned that because many Klansmen belong to the Elks, it would be foolish for other Elks lodges to follow suit. As Chalmers points out, the rank-and-file fraternity members often embraced the Klan in spite of their officers' stance toward the Invisible Empire. One Klan writer describes how some leaders of the American Legion failed in their efforts to "ramrod through a resolution" that condemned the Klan at their national convention.[16] Even among the leadership, however, most members of fraternal orders and other voluntary associations had no fight to pick with the Klan, and many were themselves Klansmen.

Fraternal organizations offered fertile recruiting ground for the Ku Klux Klan, and Klan leaders vigorously sought to reap the harvest. To help promote their own movement, and to stake a claim for the Klan's respectability, Klan leaders took pains to call attention to the Klan's fraternal ties. For example, one article in the *Imperial Night-Hawk* describes a funeral ceremony of a Dr. Bobo in Pisgah, Alabama. Bobo, a "prominent Mason," had apparently requested to have a Klan funeral rather than a Masonic funeral. Several articles make a point of describing how members of organizations such as the Kiwanis Club, Masons, and Elks paid visits to the Klan's Imperial Palace in Atlanta when their conventions were being held in the city. Each of these articles notes that many of the visitors were Klansmen taking advantage of an opportunity to visit the national headquarters. The Klan went so far as to decorate the Imperial Palace with purple and white bunting, the national colors of the Elks, "in recognition of another great fraternal order."[17]

The Klan, on occasion, staged joint meetings and ceremonies with other fraternal organizations. Klansmen in Loogootie, Indiana, attended services at a Methodist church and then marched along with Masons, Odd Fellows, and Knights of Pythias members to a cemetery to honor the dead on Memorial Day.[18] One Klan writer describes activities staged during a special "Klan Day" at a Shriner's Circus in Akron, Ohio, and points out,

> The friendly relations of the Masons and the Klan was greatly emulated in this incident when Klansmen from far and near attended the circus and during the evening staged an open-air ceremony at Summit Beach Lake. Thousands of Klansmen and Masons expressed their appreciation of the work that is being accomplished by these two fraternal orders.[19]

The *Imperial Night-Hawk* even announced plans to construct a meeting hall that would be shared by the Klan and by the Odd Fellows of Stigler, Oklahoma.[20]

While the Klan sought to strengthen its ties to various fraternal lodges, movement leaders worked just as diligently to forge strong bonds with Protestant churches and church leaders. Using religious oratory to recruit new members seemed to come naturally to Simmons, the movement's founder and a former preacher, and to many Klansmen who would follow in his footsteps. Klan-sponsored lectures drew large crowds and often produced substantial membership gains in their wake. Religion was a popular theme addressed in the lectures. One article in the *Imperial Night-Hawk* describes the Klan's new "National Program of Education," designed to enlighten Klansmen and also the general public. Titles of some of the planned lectures include "Christ, the Klansman's Criterion of Character" and "The Relation of the Klan to the Protestant Church." Another article emphasizes the importance of scheduling lectures for the winter months so that the movement would not lose momentum when harsh weather prevented staging outdoor ceremonies. Suggested topics included "History of Protestant Christianity" followed by "History of Roman Catholicism."[21] Klan rallies and ceremonies often resembled church services, characterized by solemn rituals and featuring sermon-like lectures that drew on broad Christian themes to inspire and motivate the Klan faithful and to make converts among those who had yet to join.

Reciprocal Ties between Protestant Churches and the Klan

Klan leaders recognized that Protestant churches were an important potential source of resources and members. Both resource-mobilization theory and the political-process model have drawn attention to the way in which social movements rely on preexisting organizations (including churches) to provide resources required for mobilization, and that dynamic was certainly important in the Klan's recruiting success. Less attention has been given to the motives underlying the transfer of organizational resources. Why would members and leaders of any organization allow their resources to be directed toward social-movement activism? In some instances, the answer to that question is rather straightforward. If the organization's constituency and the movement's constituency are one and the same, then few would object if the organization's resources are temporarily used to fund social-movement activities. Decisions would still need to be made about how the organization can most appropriately utilize its resources, but at least there would be general consensus in regard to the movement's goals and its worthiness for receiving organizational support. In other instances, the movement and its organizational sponsor might not be so tightly coupled, and movement leaders would have to invest energy in nurturing a stronger relationship.

In the case of the Ku Klux Klan and Protestant congregations, constituency overlap was not so great that the movement could simply assume that churches and church members would willingly redirect resources to fund the Ku Klux Klan. The relationship had to be nurtured and church leaders had to be courted. Klan leaders did not simply approach the churches with hat in hand but came bearing gifts and promises. Klan recruiters offered clergymen free membership, complimentary subscriptions to Klan publications, and a promise to actively promote the supremacy of Protestant Christianity.[22] Beyond that, the Klan promised to increase church attendance and even increase cash donations in the collection plate. As one Klan writer expressed it, "It is a very noticeable fact that in communities where the Knights of the Ku Klux Klan are active, Protestant church attendance has shown notable increase and church work generally has taken on renewed vigor."[23]

The Klan's strategic courting of Protestant clergymen is clearly evident in numerous articles in the *Imperial Night-Hawk*. One article was directly addressed to clergymen, stating, "We have the welfare and progress of every Protestant pastor and every Protestant congregation in the United States at heart." Another article describes how an "Exalted Cyclops" begins Klan meetings in Chattanooga, Tennessee, by asking every Klansman who went to church the previous Sunday to stand up. Following that, he would ask all those who pledged to go to church the next Sunday to stand up. According to the Klan writer, "Sunday school and church attendance has been increased in every Protestant church in Chattanooga by this activity of the Klan and the men's Bible classes have grown rapidly."[24]

The Klan also made a practice of publicly rewarding ministers who were deemed to be friendly to the movement. One article praises the bold response of a Methodist minister in West Virginia who ignored a death threat while delivering a sermon on Americanism. Frequently, such praise would be delivered in person as the Klansmen, dressed in full regalia, would unexpectedly appear at a church service. The *Imperial Night-Hawk* describes how Klansmen dropped in on a Calvary Baptist Church revival tent in Jacksonville, Florida, to express appreciation for the work being performed by evangelist Allen C. Shuler.[25] These Klan visitations were designed not only to befriend the minister but also to impress the congregation. The events were carefully staged to maximize the dramatic effect. Describing visitations in Altoona, Pennsylvania, a Klan writer instructs:

> These visitations are made by committees numbering from fifty to one hundred robed men, who make contributions to the church and get in close contact with the Christian element. They are telling the church-goers just what the Knights of the Ku Klux Klan stand for and of the many duties they have voluntarily allotted to themselves. These visitations are proving very successful in combating the un-American and anti-Klan influences.[26]

The Klan's church visitations were calculated to solidify a strong tie between the social movement and Protestant Christianity. Movement leaders purposefully downplayed denominational differences, hoping to unite all white Protestants behind their cause. The Klan leaders seemed to appreciate the symbolic value of downplaying racial distinctions among Protestants. Although the movement continued to claim white supremacy and advocate white separatism, on several occasions they praised black individuals for being on the "right side" of the religious battle. One article describes how a group of fifty white-robed Klansmen in Princeton, Kentucky, paid a visit to a "Negro Baptist church" to present the pastor with an envelope containing sixty-five dollars for the church building fund. The article makes a point of noting that the minister had been told of the visit in advance so that his congregation would not be alarmed by the sight of hooded Klansmen entering the church.[27]

The Klan press makes many references to less dramatic ways in which the movement sought to win favor with Protestant congregations so that they could rely on churches to provide members, adherents, and resources. Klansmen in Casper, Wyoming, initiated a drive to increase attendance in local Sunday schools. Klansmen in Wichita Falls, Kansas, donated an American flag and flagpole to a Protestant church, which then prompted several additional requests from other local churches. An American flag made from silk, along with a "purse of money," was donated to a pastor in Wellsville, Ohio. Klansmen in Coraopolis, Pennsylvania, made a substantial donation to the building fund of the "Fifth Avenue Negro Church" and presented a number of Bibles to the faculty at Coraopolis Heights School. Many similar donations are mentioned in the Klan's publications, and readers were encouraged to adopt similar practices in their own communities.[28]

In return for the Klan's support of Protestant churches, Klan leaders expected (and received) endorsements from Protestant clergy. According to the *Imperial Night-Hawk,* even the black minister in Princeton, Kentucky, publicly thanked the Klansmen for their cooperation and assistance and commended the movement for its decision to admit women into the organization. But, of course, most endorsements came from white clergymen. A short letter from a Baptist minister in Alabama informs the editor of the *Imperial Night-Hawk* that he had become a Klan member soon after reading a copy of the Klan's publication. Another issue reports that a concerned minister had sent telegrams to fellow pastors asking if the Klan should be "regarded as a menace." In response, the paper published numerous ringing endorsements from Protestant ministers and from political representatives— including Oregon's governor, Walter Pierce. While the Klan was careful not to claim that Billy Sunday was a member of their organization, movement leaders sought to capitalize on the evangelist's immense popularity. One article describes how hundreds of Klansmen in full regalia attended a revival meeting in West Virginia and slipped $226 into the collection plate. According to the Klan writer, Billy Sunday told the world "in his unique and emphatic way that he endorses the Klan Kreed and everything the order stands for."[29]

While having a Klan-friendly pastor in a particular church clearly aided the movement in its recruiting, even better results could be obtained when an actual Klansman manned the pulpit. One article notes with pride that a Methodist bishop addressed the eighty-eighth annual New Jersey Methodist conference and "flatly denied" that he would take action against any minister who was a member of the Ku Klux Klan. On special occasions, Hiram Evans was invited to deliver the Sunday sermon to Klan-friendly congregations. One article reports that the Klan's Imperial Wizard drew a large crowd in the First Christian Church in Hot Springs, Arkansas, when he served as the guest minister. Another article describes how the minister at Foss Memorial Methodist Church in Minneapolis ignited a fiery cross that was erected near the pulpit before delivering a sermon titled "The Development of the Protestant Church."[30] In cases such as these, where the Klan had successfully forged a strong bond with the minister and his flock, extraction of organizational resources was especially nonproblematic. The pastor's constituency and the Klan's constituency were, in essence, one and the same.

Ceremonies, Parades, and Social Gatherings

Strong ties to fraternal lodges and Protestant churches gave the Klan access to millions of potential members and the vast resources that were under their control. As a result, the movement was able to offer selective incentives to draw even more people into the movement and to maintain the interest and loyalty of preexisting members. Part of the movement's allure stemmed from the mystery that surrounded it. The secretiveness of the order freed members of their inhibitions. Klansmen paraded through the streets of their hometown, yet their identity was known only to fellow members. In frequently held meetings, Klan members engaged in secret rituals and shared a secret language that solidified distinctions between insiders and outsiders.

Klan leaders clearly understood the value of staging elaborate ceremonies, marches, and rallies. They used the *Imperial Night-Hawk* to solicit ideas from members who were dispersed across the nation and to share "best practices" with its readership for staging events. On several occasions, the editor asked Klansmen to submit photographs of local Klan activities, and each issue of the *Imperial Night-Hawk* contained photos of various Klansponsored events. The editor expressed particular interest in receiving photographs and information pertaining to ceremonials, parades, charitable activities, and other meetings of general interest, and he promised to devote as much space to these events as possible.[31] Plans to erect new Klaverns (Klan meeting halls) also received significant coverage in the weekly publication.

The movement pulled out all the stops for initiation or "naturalization" ceremonies. The initiation ceremonies were often so spectacular that Klan members would travel great distances to attend. As one Klan writer describes it, "Klansmen the count[r]y over are getting the special train habit. Almost daily reports tell of the chartering of special trains or interurban coaches for the purpose of carrying Klansmen on visits to adjoining territory for parades and naturalizations." The program for one initiation ceremony held in Pueblo, Colorado, offers a glimpse into how a typical ceremony was organized. The event began with singing of the national anthem followed by an invocation. After lowering the American flag and lighting a giant cross, the Klansmen sang "Onward Christian Soldiers." Next, the new members were "naturalized." Following more singing, Colorado's Grand Dragon made a speech. One more song—"Blest Be the Tie That Binds"—and a benediction brought the formal ceremony to a close. Before returning home, Klan members (both old and new) enjoyed a barbecue supper.[32]

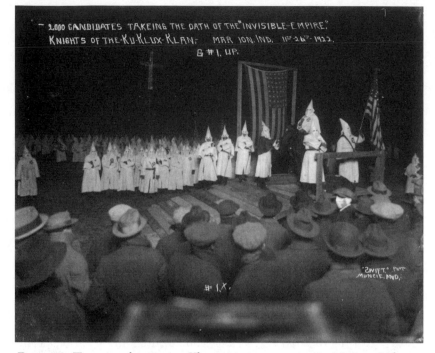

Figure 19. Townspeople witness a Klan initiation ceremony in Marion, Indiana, 1922. W. A. Swift Collection. Courtesy of Ball State University. Copyright 2006. All rights reserved.

Frequently, the initiation ceremonies were combined with family entertainment. A ceremony in Birmingham, Alabama, caused severe traffic jams throughout the day. As a Klan writer tells it:

> Edgewood Park was crowded by noon. Klansmen and their wives and families enjoyed a great barbecue, went swimming, dancing and picnicking. There were airplane stunts during the day with band concerts thrown in for good measure. At night there was a wonderful display of fireworks following the initiation and the address of the Imperial Wizard.[33]

Fireworks and airplane stunts were regular features of major Klan ceremonies and parades. The *Imperial Night-Hawk* reports that a novel feature was introduced at a meeting in Kansas City, Missouri, that was attended by ten thousand Klansmen. "Powerful searchlights suddenly illuminated a white-robed horseman on a white steed standing on a hill near the meeting while an airplane bearing a huge fiery cross swooped low above the celebration."

Figure 20. Klansmen frequently took to the sky to draw attention to their organization. National Photo Company Collection. Library of Congress.

Another article mentions that residents in Seattle received a thrill "when a brilliantly illuminated airplane flew over the city at night. The plane carried a Fiery Cross on one wing and the letters K.K.K. on the other." Many articles boast of magnificent fireworks displays. To celebrate Easter, Klansmen in Hamilton County, Kentucky, ignited three hundred fiery crosses across the countryside just before midnight, and "throughout this spectacular scene aerial bombs were discharged from a high point of vantage which added greatly to the effectiveness of the affair."[34]

While fireworks displays and aerial stunts were tried-and-true crowd-pleasers, Klan writers eagerly described other innovative ways in which local Klan chapters made ceremonies memorable and even awe inspiring. In one locale, members created a "human fiery cross" as "one hundred Klansmen in full regalia aligned themselves in the form of a cross as they stood on a hill side. At a given signal, each Klansman in the formation lighted a red torch forming a moving fiery cross visible for miles. It was a most striking spectacle." A variation on the theme was carried out by Klansmen in

Clarksburg, West Virginia, where three thousand Klansmen "formed themselves into an immense human group of letters reading 'Ku Klux Klan' beneath the light of three large fiery crosses."[35]

Klan leaders also took care to select scenic locations for initiation ceremonies to add additional drama to the events. Klansmen ignited a fiery cross on top of Pikes Peak for a ceremony attended by "several hundred Klansmen," which, a Klansmen noted, broke all records in Klan history "so far as altitude is concerned." On several occasions, Klan members capitalized on the majesty of crashing waves and moonlight reflecting on the ocean, staging late-night ceremonies on scenic beaches. One article notes that Klansmen in Kentucky held "a most impressive ceremonial on the cliffs which tower three hundred feet above the Kentucky river." Klansmen at times added their own manmade diversions when exploiting the wonders of nature. At an initiation ceremony in Santa Monica, California, "A fiery cross suspended from an immense gas balloon floated above the naturalization field, which was marked by a forty-foot electric sign bearing the letters 'K. K. K.' attracting thousands of automobilists to the scene. Five thousand robed klansmen took part in the exercises."[36]

In addition to scenic landscapes, the movement experimented with a wide array of venues. In Durham, North Carolina, Klansmen staged an initiation ceremony at a local amusement park. In several other locations, initiation ceremonies were held during special "Klan Days" at state and county fairs. An initiation in Terre Haute, Indiana, featured a Klan wedding. Klansmen and Klanswomen frequently celebrated life transitions with elaborate rituals. A Klan chapter in Lenoir City, Tennessee, was recognized for having the oldest Klan member (101 years old). The movement also made a practice of awarding a special "hero cross" to members who had belonged to the original Ku Klux Klan in the 1860s and 1870s. The Klan press noted that a Klansman in Gainesville, Georgia, not only was a member of the original Klan but also frequently wore the same robe that he wore when he rode for the Klan during the Reconstruction. Klan members honored the young as well as the old. In Tullahoma, Tennessee, the Women of the Ku Klux Klan presented a miniature robe and helmet to the newborn baby of Klan parents.[37]

While many of the Klan's ceremonies were designed primarily to forge strong bonds between the movement and its members, other activities were developed to capture the attention of those who might be enticed to join. Parades and public rallies were perfectly suited for this task. As was true of initiation ceremonies, Klan leaders were eager to identify innovative means of capturing attention and providing dramatic flare to public events.

They were especially pleased when their activities captured the attention of various media outlets. One Klansmen boasted of a "most successful and impressive" parade in Shreveport, Louisiana. "Moving picture operators took pictures of the Klansmen by the light of powerful magnesium torches. These pictures were displayed at local theaters during the week." The writer could not resist the urge to add that the theaters, which were "owned and controlled by Jewish interests," were packed with customers who were eager to see the Klansmen march.[38]

In some instances, the Klan aimed to impress community members with the sheer size of a parade or rally. An impressive show of strength could be used to convince bystanders that they should become part of an increasingly powerful movement. For example, the *Imperial Night-Hawk* describes a parade in Indianapolis that, the paper claimed, included 55,000 Klansmen and was witnessed by 300,000 people. "One hundred and thirty beautifully decorated automobiles were in the parade, to which were added more than one hundred floats of great beauty. Music was provided by thirty-nine bands and there were eighteen drum corps in line. A squad of motorcycle policemen led the way."[39]

High drama could substitute for raw numbers to produce the desired effect. A Klan writer describes one such event that was held in Kirksville, Missouri:

> Although a drizzling rain was falling at about six-thirty a lone robed horseman rode through the business district with a megaphone announcing that the parade would take place at nine o'clock, rain or shine. As a result the spectacle was witnessed by a huge crowd. The Fiery Cross which shone from the court house was made of powerful red electric light bulbs and the light was so strong it reddened the public square and gave an uncanny effect to the street-lights on the public square through the misty rain that was falling.[40]

Klan members often strategically linked their parades and rallies to public events taking place in the community at large. Klan members in Dayton, Washington, became part of a parade celebrating "Pioneer Day." Klan members in Pawnee, Texas, staged a rally from midnight until 2:00 a.m. on Flag Day so that they could be "the first Klan in the country to pay their respects to the national colors on the anniversary of our flag's origins." Klan members across the country sought to participate in numerous Independence Day celebrations. In Stockton, California, the Klan was not allowed to participate in the city's parade and instead staged a parade of its own. A photo published in the *Imperial Night-Hawk* captures an awkward moment as parading Klansmen crossed paths with Knights of Columbus members who, unlike the Klansmen, were given permission to march in the regular parade. In many instances, in communities where the movement had few enemies, the Klan entered floats in public parades. A favorite theme for Klan floats depicted Klansmen protecting a red schoolhouse.[41]

The Klan press eagerly reported news of other innovative ways in which local Klan chapters captured public attention. Klansmen in Yell County, Arkansas, staged an "auto tour":

> One hundred automobiles, each carrying Klansmen, started from Danville, Arkansas, early in the morning. They toured the Fourche Valley in the Southern part of the County, stopping at every small town and holding a meeting at which various speakers described the patriotic aims and purposes of the Klan. At night the tour ended in Gravelly, Arkansas. The tourists, donning their regalia, attended the religious meeting conducted by Rev. J. W. Ashmore and presented him with $350 to be used towards rebuilding his church which had recently been destroyed by a cyclone. As the result of the trip, many applications are being filed by aliens who wish to join the two Yell County Klans.[42]

Another Klan writer boasted of "many novel features" planned to coincide with a Klan parade in Trenton, New Jersey. Among these novel features was a sightseeing tour of the Trenton area, including a visit to Princeton University.[43]

Kathleen Blee points out that the social activities planned by the movement's leaders played a vital role in the Klan's growth.[44] For many Klansmen and Klanswomen, the movement offered fun, excitement, and fellowship, and these selective incentives more than compensated for the costs of participation. Throughout the nation, Klan members organized baseball teams, marching bands, drum and bugle corps, and choirs. The Klan developed a regulation band uniform that could be purchased by local chapters. It was described by the *Imperial Night-Hawk* as "one of the most colorful and most handsome uniforms yet worn by Klansmen of any rank or station, being made up entirely of real satin with a pleasing distribution of white, gold, crimson, and purple." Space for recreation was also an important consideration in the construction of Klan meeting halls. A Klavern constructed on a farm in New Philadelphia, Ohio, included "a golf course, baseball diamonds, tennis courts, a football field and two swimming pools."[45]

Klan leaders understood that "fun" was an effective selective incentive that could help them build their movement. In Fresno, California, Klan members staged a nine-day "fun frolic." Arkansas Klansmen held a "seven-

Figure 21. Klan musicians posing in Muncie, Indiana. W. A. Swift Collection. Courtesy of Ball State University. Copyright 2006. All rights reserved.

act Klan circus" along with other recreational activities "to assist in keeping the spirit of the klansmen to the highest pitch of enthusiasm." In January 1924, San Antonio Klansmen held their third annual cowboy contest and Klan Karnival. In addition to seeing the "world's greatest bronco busters, bull-doggers, [and] ropers," Klan members in attendance would have a chance to win a "new Jewett touring car."[46]

As discussed in previous chapters, Klan leaders sought to identify grievances of potential members, and they developed collective-action frames designed to motivate action. However, they also understood that collective incentives were needed to build a mass movement. Some Klan members were drawn into the organization primarily because they were persuaded by the movement leaders' rhetoric, and they placed high value on the collective goals pursued by the movement. Others, while sharing many of the movement's general goals, were primarily drawn into the Klan by something as simple as a pleasant Sunday afternoon picnic. The following quote illustrates how the Klan developed a knack for mixing business with pleasure:

> Warm weather brings thoughts of fried chicken, pies, cakes, sandwiches, and numerous other goodies to be found when the family and friends assemble in some wooded space and enjoy a picnic. Brazil, Realm of Indiana, Klansmen recently became so enthused over the picnic idea that

Figure 22. Klan members pay final respects to one of their own in Muncie, Indiana, 1923. W. A. Swift Collection. Courtesy of Ball State University. Copyright 2006. All rights reserved.

> they pulled off a big two-day feast at which time a huge ceremonial was staged and a large Kavalkade marched through the streets. At night a Klan photo-play "A Traitor Within," was shown at the auditorium.[47]

By offering simple pleasures such as a Sunday picnic, and by staging dramatic rallies and ceremonies, Klan leaders provided enticing incentives for participation and then used these occasions to speak to the collective grievances of those whom they hoped to recruit. The availability of organizational resources made it all possible.

Communication Networks

As might be expected, the rapid growth of the movement and the vast geographical dispersion of the Klan's chapters made it difficult to keep all of the local organizations in line and to promote a united front. Indeed, the national leadership was itself struggling to maintain a semblance of unity as the movement expanded. The Klan's founder, Colonel Simmons, was ousted in 1922. A rift between Hiram Evans and D. C. Stephenson developed as Stephenson's northern realm began to surpass the southern realm in terms of members enlisted and revenue raised. Throughout the Empire, local Klan leaders would at times question Evans's legitimacy or, more commonly, express resentment about dues extracted by the national organization. While we should not ignore the factionalism that plagued the movement, the Klan's organizational shortcomings should not overshadow its successes. There were bumps in the road, some of them substantial, but the Klan was able to hold a mass movement together for several years during a period of startling growth. This was made possible in part because of the way in which movement leaders utilized the vast resources at their disposal to establish communication networks that could be used to spread information, to promote unity, and to quell (or at least contain) internal rebellion.

Resource-mobilization theorists have called attention to the value of establishing alternative media in the diffusion of social-movement activism.[48] Through alternative media, movement leaders can stay in touch with members and supporters while simultaneously exerting control over the information they receive. This is especially important when the movement is portrayed negatively in the mainstream media as was often the case with the Ku Klux Klan. The *Imperial Night-Hawk* played a vital role in terms of helping national leaders maintain control of the movement. The first published issue noted that the magazine was established to "carry a weekly message from the Imperial Palace to every Klansman in America."[49]

The *Imperial Night-Hawk* was also used to assure readers that the national leaders were working diligently on behalf of local Klan chapters and that they were exercising fiscal responsibility—doing all that was possible to reduce fees and expenses. The magazine reported the financial assets and liabilities of the national organization and drew attention to impressive revenue surpluses accumulating in the Klan treasury after the fiscally irresponsible Simmons had been replaced. According to the *Imperial Night-Hawk,* Hiram Evans's wise stewardship made it possible to reduce prices on Klan robes and other materials and to allow local chapters to hold on to a larger share of revenue derived from membership fees and other sources. Numerous articles boasted about how the Klan's newly constructed buildings in Buckhead, Georgia, which consisted of a printing plant and a plant to produce Klan robes and other paraphernalia, would save thousands of dollars for the organization. One article noted that "skilled workers, all Klansmen, will be employed to operate both plants" and that the money for construction of the plants was "made available through the great saving of expense in propagation work effected by Dr. H. W. Evans and his cabinet from the abolishment of useless departments and the cutting of needless expenses found both at Atlanta and in the field during the past six months."[50]

The *Imperial Night-Hawk* provided movement leaders with a venue for disseminating collective-action frames designed to have a broad appeal among the movement's constituency. Perhaps just as important, the publication made it possible for Klansmen in Durham, North Carolina, to read about activities staged by Klansmen thousands of miles away in locations such as Elgin, Oregon, or Modesto, California. A virtual flood of information about Klan events and activities taking place throughout the United States helped to ensure that Klan members would see themselves as being a part of a large, powerful, and thriving social movement, thereby strengthening their commitment to the organization.

Of course, the Klan's resources were not unlimited. Copies of the *Night-Hawk* were mailed weekly to each Klan chapter so that they would be available "without cost to Klansmen." Klan readers were encouraged, however, to recycle the magazine for the benefit of the movement—"Don't throw it away. Give it away. Put it where it will do the most good for Klankraft." To emphasize the importance of broadly circulating the Klan's publication, one article described how a copy of the *Imperial Night-Hawk* traveled eight hundred miles, passed from Klansman to Klansman, and eventually wound up in the hands of eight readers in Wyoming.[51]

As a national publication, the *Imperial Night-Hawk* mainly addressed broad themes that would appeal to Klan members and adherents. A local problem that had Klansmen up in arms in Lorain, Ohio, after all, may be of little interest to a Klansman in Shreveport, Louisiana. To address local concerns, the movement relied on numerous regional Klan newspapers. One article in the *Imperial Night-Hawk* listed twenty-four of these local papers and encouraged Klan members to read them and distribute them. Of the editors of these local Klan papers, the *Imperial Night-Hawk* proclaimed, "They are the shock troops of the Klan armies. They are the buttresses against which beat the waves of anti-Klan venom and hatred. They have thrown their own money and personalities into the cause and it is up to the Klansmen of the nation to help them to make good." As the number of local publications increased, the national Klan tried to impose some uniformity by establishing a Bureau of Publication and Education. The bureau, located in Washington, D.C., was charged with "serving as a medium of expression and furnishing publicity and information for the Knights of the Ku Klux Klan" and supervising the content of all official Klan publications.[52]

In addition to its national and regional newspapers, Klansmen and Klanswomen were encouraged to publish bulletins and newsletters to keep members informed of local activities and meetings. The *Imperial Night-Hawk* approvingly noted that the Milwaukee Klan was publishing a "series of pamphlets regarding the purposes and principles of the Knights of the Ku Klux Klan" titled "The Abraham Lincoln Series of Public Information." According to the author, the pamphlets were in demand and were doing "much good for the cause." Another article describes how many local chapters were using mimeograph machines to produce bulletins to keep members informed of local meetings and activities.[53]

While the Klan's development of alternative media was vital to the movement's growth and diffusion, local movement leaders were encouraged to exploit the mainstream media whenever possible to draw attention to movement activities. The *Imperial Night-Hawk* noted that in communities where the Klan enjoyed broad support, the editors of local newspapers were often willing to publish information about the movement and its activities. One article instructs, "If the editor of your newspaper believes in fair play ask him if he will permit your Klan to edit a weekly Klan Kolumn, giving news of activities of the order and carrying constructive arguments for patriotic Protestant Americanism." Another article commends Klansmen in Evansville, Indiana, for "'selling' the organization to the desirable citizens by the use of much good printer's ink, mixed with brains" because they had taken out a full-page advertisement in the Sunday paper to promote their organization. In Pekin, Illinois, the Klan went so far as to purchase the town's newspaper, the *Pekin Daily Times*.[54]

When it came to utilizing media, Klansmen were not limited to the printing press. One Klan writer reports that the Klansmen in Texas were airing a program on radio using "the powerful broadcasting station of the Fort Worth Star Telegram." Klansmen in Raleigh, North Carolina, rented billboard space "in various good locations" to promote the movement. One article described plans to develop a major motion picture titled *Armageddon,* which would "depict the patriotic work of the Knights of the Ku Klux Klan." According to the Klan writer, D. W. Griffith would be asked to direct the film and "picture stars of international fame will take the leading roles."[55]

In general, the Klansmen's writing reveals an infatuation with modern technology. For example, when it came to providing security, writers boasted of how the Klan used the most efficient and up-to-date techniques. One article describes how members had installed two telephone poles in a field outside of Morgantown, West Virginia, so that Klansmen at an initiation ceremony would be able to communicate with Klan headquarters to check credentials of those seeking admission.[56] Klansmen and Klanswomen used media technology as well as good old-fashioned gossip networks to keep tabs on the movement's enemies and to spread information about businesses deemed to be unfriendly to the Klan that would be targeted for boycott.[57] The Klan even established an Intelligence Bureau, under the direct control of Hiram Evans.[58]

The growth and diffusion of the Ku Klux Klan cannot be explained in terms of new resources becoming available to the movement's constituents. Klan members had access to these resources long before the movement emerged. What was needed was an incentive to activate and exploit these resources to promote collective action. Power devaluation provided the incentive and effective framing motivated action. Yet the movement could not have spread so quickly and attracted so many members and supporters if its leaders had not exploited the vast resources at their disposal.

Exploiting Openings in the Political Opportunity Structure

The Klan's mobilization did not require a favorable shift in political opportunities. The movement's constituents, as members of the racial, ethnic, and religious majority in the United States, enjoyed free access to the polity prior to the movement's emergence. They had little reason to fear that they would be violently repressed by the government if they were to engage in collective action. There was, however, local variation in the way in which authorities responded to the Klan, and at the national level there were limits to the political freedom that the movement enjoyed. The Klan's growth and diffusion, therefore, did depend in part on how effectively its leaders were able to strategically exploit opportunities that existed in the political terrain on which they operated. Just as important, movement leaders had to take care to avoid actions that would prompt a crackdown from the federal government.

The Klan posed a dilemma for political representatives. The movement was, after all, named after a violent terrorist organization that had wreaked havoc throughout the South during Reconstruction. And, in spite of denials issued by Klan leaders, members of the second Ku Klux Klan did commit violent acts. Especially in southern states in the early years of the movement's growth, Klan-initiated violence could be brutal and disruptive. In 1922 the governor of Louisiana called in federal law-enforcement agents to restore order after two murders committed by Klansmen had the population in an uproar.[59] Oklahoma's governor Jack Walton declared martial law in his state in response to the Klan's skirmishes with Socialists, Wobblies, and other groups on the political left.[60] Although the Klan promoted white supremacy and spoke disparagingly about Catholics and immigrants, much of the movement's violence was directed toward fellow native-born, white Protestants.[61] Klansmen would, at times, engage in public floggings to enforce "morality" and traditional gender roles.[62]

Public concern about violence could provide political authorities with some cover if they chose to act against the movement. As discussed in chapter 2, the *New York World*'s 1921 exposé detailing violent acts allegedly committed by the Klan led to congressional hearings. During those hearings, Colonel Simmons assured members of Congress that the Klan was a nonviolent organization. Simmons and other Klan leaders came to understand that political authorities would give the movement free rein as long as the Klan kept the violence under control. As one Klan leader expressed it,

> I have watched, with no small degree of interest, at least three Federal investigations of this order, with a view of stopping its "illegal activities" and dispersing its membership. The Post Office Department, the Department of Justice and the Congress of the U.S. have each looked carefully into its workings. Three times the Federal Government has said, as Pilate said of Christ, "We find no fault in them." But still the angry, blood-thirsty, lawless, un-American mob cries outside the Halls of Justice, "Crucify them. Crucify them. If you turn these white-robed, hooded monsters loose, you are no friend of the pope."[63]

Hiram Evans seemed especially cognizant of the way in which the Klan's violent reputation could provoke the government and impede his efforts to win broader support for the Klan as it became involved in politics. Evans repeatedly denounced the use of violence and reminded other Klan leaders to do the same. At the first annual meeting of Grand Dragons (state-level leaders) held in Asheville, North Carolina, in 1923, Evans commented on the Klan's reputation for vigilantism:

> The first time one of your Klansmen violates the law, thus breaking his obligation, thus doing a thing in direct conflict for which we stand, let us administer on him as Klansmen for breaking his obligation. Let us get them outside of the Klan and let the judge and the jury and the penitentiary take care of them. When we do that, this thing will fade like the morning dew.[64]

Although Klan leaders condemned violence, it was really the unorganized and nonselective use of violence that they sought to curtail. According to Pennsylvania's Grand Dragon, "selective and active intolerance is necessary to defend liberty." Klansmen drew inspiration from the Populist legacy and from the writings of Thomas Jefferson, claiming that it was the duty of every citizen to rebel if the government was ignoring the will of the people. Klan leaders argued that the federal government was being challenged by "alien" forces and it was their patriotic duty to restore order, with force if necessary.[65]

Under Evans's leadership, the Klan increasingly sought to institutional-ize (rather than forgo) violence. Klan members were encouraged to offer their assistance to local law-enforcement agencies, and in many cases their assistance was welcome. Movement leaders took special pride in their ability to recruit policemen. Membership lists confiscated in a raid on Klan headquarters in Inglewood, California, revealed that Klansmen were deeply rooted in law-enforcement positions throughout the state, including the chiefs of police in Fresno and Los Angeles, a U.S. attorney general, and the Los Angeles County sheriff.[66] California was not unusual in this sense. Wherever the Klan was strong, it seemed to draw law enforcement officers into its ranks.[67] The movement's leaders drew attention to these ties as way of legitimizing the Klan's activities. One article in the *Imperial Night-Hawk* describes a funeral ceremony for a Klansman who had been a police officer in Indianapolis.

> Uniformed police officers and Klansmen in full regalia marched side by side in the funeral cortege. . . . The funeral procession was headed by the Police and Firemen's Band and a detail of fifty police officers who stood at attention as the three hundred and fifty robed Klansmen passed through their ranks on their way to the cemetery.[68]

The Klan's selective use of violence contributed to the movement's strength in many regions of the country, especially where its violence was institutionalized and legitimated. Where the movement's enemies were weak, the Ku Klux Klan was able to use violence to alter individual behav-ior. More important, the threat and reality of violence increased the costs of individual resistance to the movement. The Klan also made effective use of rumor and gossip networks to either destroy or to gain information about potential foes.[69] Violence, however, was a two-way street. Typically, the Klan would victimize individuals who had violated community norms in locations where the movement enjoyed broad support. In such instances, Klan-sponsored violence was unlikely to create problems for the move-ment, but in communities where the movement had significant opposition, Klansmen could themselves be targeted for violence.

In some locations the movement was confronted with nonviolent ob-stacles. An article in the *Imperial Night-Hawk* reports that the movement's enemies tried to put a damper on a Klan march in Sherwood, Tennessee, by turning off the streetlights. The writer boasts of the Klansmen's resourcefulness as they "provided themselves with hundreds of red torches and their ceremonial went off without a hitch." Klan members faced opposition from local politicians who sought to prevent them from staging public events. According to one Klan writer, the mayor of Youngstown, Ohio, had given "shoot to kill" orders if Klansmen attempted to parade in his city. The parade apparently went off without incident, and the Klan writer noted that the mayor had recently been defeated in his bid for reelection.[70] Opposition from local authorities was clearly something that Klan leaders had to consider as they attempted to build their movement. Recovered Klan documents that assessed the movement's strengths and weaknesses in Indiana counties include notes about whether local politicians and law-enforcement agents were either friendly or hostile toward the Klan.[71] More often than not, in the early 1920s local authorities either left the movement alone or embraced the Klan as a way of bolstering their own political power.

Making the Klan a "Civic Asset"

Even if political authorities were wary of the Klan because of its violent reputation, it was risky to oppose the movement—so risky that most were unwilling to do so. The Klan's leaders invested substantial time, effort, and resources in public relations work, and they presented the movement as a patriotic organization whose members were sworn to protect and defend the U.S. Constitution. The Klan claimed to represent the interests of native-born, white Protestants during a time in which ethnic and religious identities strongly influenced voting behavior and electoral outcomes. Any politician who needed votes from members of the cultural majority had to think twice before attempting to stand in the path of a mass movement seeking to purge "un-American influences" from government. Klan leaders understood that they could create their own political opportunities by doing good deeds in the communities in which they operated and, just as important, shining a spotlight on their charitable activities.

Community service was centrally featured in the Klan leaders' strategic plan for building their movement. One Klansman addressed his fellow leaders at the Grand Dragon's meeting in Asheville, North Carolina, commenting on how community service was not only in line with the values that Klan members should hold but could also provide the movement with cover, shielding them from enemy attacks. The Klansman added,

> That we may hold the respect and confidence of the Christian people of
> every community, it behooves every executive, as well as every Klansman,

to make the Knights of the Ku Klux Klan the big civic asset in every Klanton in America. Be not unmindful of the fact that public opinion will be crystallized by your actions and your activities.[72]

In the pages of the *Imperial Night-Hawk,* readers were repeatedly reminded of the importance of community service. North Carolina's Grand Dragon scolded the Klan faithful, pointedly asking,

> What are you doing besides meeting once in a while? Are you taking a proper part in local affairs? Are you supporting public schools and seeing to it that the children of your communities are getting a proper education? Are you seeing to it that officers of the law are doing their duties? In other words, are you real citizens of your community, or are you just jellyfish, existing without interest in anything excepting that small portion of the universe that lies within yourselves? There is no vice so reprehensible as selfishness combined with laziness.[73]

Based on the content of the *Imperial Night-Hawk,* it appears that many Klan members across the country did seek to make the Klan a civic asset in their local communities. It is also clear that Klan members were eager to publicize news of their charitable activities. Many Klan chapters announced plans to provide funding for new hospitals. One article announced that the Klan broke ground for a new hospital in El Dorado, Arkansas, and noted that the hospital will care for patients "without regard to race, color or creed." Klansmen pledged to give the state of Oklahoma a great Protestant hospital. Klan leaders clearly deduced that charity directed toward sick children would go a long way toward creating a favorable impression of their movement. Klan members in Jacksonville, Florida, announced a significant contribution to the "Baby Milk Fund." One article noted that Klansmen in Wellsburg, West Virginia, were heavily involved in charitable work and had recently helped a needy family by sending a sick child to a health resort when her doctor advised that a change in climate was necessary to save her life. During "Klan Day" at the Texas State Fair, the Klan donated a "Hope Cottage" that would be built "to care for homeless and friendless babies."[74]

Many other articles describe the Klan's efforts to provide aid to widows, orphans, and families who were down on their luck. In Okmulgee, Oklahoma, Klansmen gave a new home to a woman whose husband had died, "leaving her in destitute circumstances." Not only that, they claimed to have found employment for her eldest son. Numerous stories describe how Klan members distributed gifts, food, and money to needy families at Christmastime. One story reports that Klansmen in Indianapolis "distributed five hundred baskets of Christmas cheer to the worthy poor of that city. The baskets contained every article of food necessary to make a complete Christmas dinner, articles of clothing where needed, and toys, candy and fruit for the children." In Blackwell, Oklahoma, Klansmen delivered baskets of food, toys, and clothing while dressed as Santa Claus.[75]

The Klan's writing also indicates that the men of the Ku Klux Klan perceived that Women of the Ku Klux Klan could be particularly valuable to the broader movement by taking on a disproportionate share of charitable work. Soon after announcing the founding of the Women's Ku Klux Klan, one article instructs, "The women of the Ku Klux Klan, while fighting for the same principles as the Knights of the Ku Klux Klan, will also be active in other lines of work peculiar to women's organizations, such as social welfare work, the prevention of juvenile delinquency, etc." Several other articles noted charitable activities carried out by the WKKK members, such as providing Christmas gift baskets for "all the deserving poor of Lisbon, Ohio." Klan writers also, on several occasions, made a point of demonstrating that race and ethnicity did not define who was or was not deserving of Klan aid. One article describes how the Klan gave money to a Polish widow with five children and added that the Klan "makes no distinction as to race, creed or color" when it comes to distributing aid. The article reports that the woman was astounded to learn that the gift had been provided by the Ku Klux Klan because she had been told by the Klan's enemies that the organization was opposed to foreigners and to her religion.[76]

Consistent with the movement's advocacy on behalf of public education, the Klan sought to publicize its contributions in support of education. Klansmen offered a scholarship to a twenty-six-year-old high school graduate so that he could attend the University of North Carolina. In Arkansas, Klan members paid $1,250 to purchase a park adjoining a public school, and they presented the park to the local school board for public use. The *Imperial Night-Hawk* also reports that the Klan donated $4,000 to the school fund in Cashville, Virginia, for construction of a public high school. In Asbury Park, New Jersey, the Klan offered to pay tuition at the Naturalization Night School for any "foreigner who wishes to be taught to speak and write in English." Klansmen, it seems, even aimed to be useful at the college level, as the *Imperial Night-Hawk* describes how members who were enrolled at the University of Kansas were organizing a "Fiery Cross Club" on campus. The club would "help new students by assisting in finding good rooms and in helping those who must earn a part or all of their way through school to find jobs."[77]

Conclusion

The emergence of the Ku Klux Klan did not require a change in the supply of organizational resources nor did it require a favorable shift in the structure of political opportunities. Resources possessed by Klan constituents were in abundant supply long before the movement was founded, and the native-born, white Protestants who would eventually join the organization had little to fear in terms of government repression before or after the time in which the movement took root. In this sense, the Ku Klux Klan cannot be explained by either resource-mobilization theory or by political-opportunity theory. This does not mean that resources and political opportunities are irrelevant when explaining the movement's growth and trajectory. Power devaluation and effective framing provided the incentives to utilize preexisting organizational resources and to exploit preexisting political opportunities. The resources that were available to the movement made it possible for the leaders to develop many innovative strategies for building the movement, offering selective incentives to entice individuals to participate.

The Klan did use violence to intimidate opponents and, in some cases, to impress potential supporters by demonstrating a commitment to enforce a moral code that was embraced by potential members. However, Klan leaders also sought to keep the violence under control to prevent government repression and to avoid a backlash from the general public that could damage its recruiting efforts. The Klan's charitable activities also could go a long way toward preventing such a backlash. By focusing on the Klan's charitable work, I do not mean to suggest that the movement was, as its leaders claimed, a wonderful civic asset for the communities in which it operated. Nor do I wish to be too cynical by suggesting that the charitable work only reflected the members' desire to create favorable publicity that would protect it from government repression. The truth is somewhere in between. Many members of the Ku Klux Klan truly believed in the value of doing good works for others and for the community, yet at the same time, Klan leaders emphasized the importance of charitable activity because they understood that favorable publicity that comes from community service would make it increasingly difficult for political representatives and community leaders to oppose their movement. Favorable publicity could also be useful in recruiting new members among those who came to view the movement as a civic asset.

8

Klan Activism across the Country

The time is coming when the Americans of the West, South, and Middle West must Americanize the East and it can't be done by putting the supreme power in the hands of a foreign-made section of the country.
— Judge Chas. J. Orbinson of Indiana, speaking at the first annual meeting of Grand Dragon Knights of the Ku Klux Klan in Asheville, North Carolina, in 1923

Changes in the structure of American society in the early 1900s provided fertile recruiting ground for the Ku Klux Klan. Many native-born, white Protestants were experiencing power devaluation in economic, political, and status-based exchange relationships, and the Klan's leaders constructed collective-action frames that struck a chord with those whom they wished to recruit. However, the Klan's framing was not embraced by all Americans and was, in many cases, strongly rejected. As I argued earlier, the resonance of the Klan's message should have depended, to a great extent, on geographic location. The Klan's opposition to deskilling of manufacturing jobs, for example, should have been most warmly received in locations where changes in manufacturing production were occurring, not in locations where large-scale manufacturing was already firmly entrenched or in locations that continued to be dominated by agricultural production. Similarly, the Klan's support for public education—more specifically its plan to use federal tax dollars to fully fund the public schools—should have been embraced in states where the vast majority of families enrolled their children in public schools. The Klan's proposals should have received a chillier reception where high proportions of families paid tuition in private schools and would likely resent the burden of paying higher taxes to support schools not attended by their own children.

In preceding chapters I have described structural changes taking place in the early 1900s and have shown how the Klan's framing should have been appealing to many individuals at this particular historical moment, especially in locations where significant numbers of native-born, white Protestant Americans were experiencing power devaluation. In this chapter I take a more quantitative approach, assessing state-level variation in Klan activity when the movement was at its peak in 1923 and 1924. The analysis shows that the Klan tended to stage more events in states where smaller proportions of residents were immigrants or Catholics. These relationships are only revealed after controlling for other state features that are related to economic, political, and status-based power devaluation of the Klan's constituency. The findings support my argument about how the Klan gained strength by interpreting economic, political, and social changes by appealing to and by constructing a common cultural identity.

Multivariate Analysis of Klan Activity

Engaging in a quantitative analysis of the Klan's strength is easier said than done. A highly secretive organization whose members wore sheets and hoods to conceal their identities in public, the Klan, not surprisingly, left few membership records behind. In earlier research, I used membership figures taken from recovered Klan documents to analyze county-level variation in Klan strength within the state of Indiana.[1] However, my goal in this book is to examine the movement's mobilization at the national level, rather than restricting the analysis to a single state.

Several scholars have referred to state-level estimates of Klan membership made by historian Kenneth Jackson to comment on regional variation in the movement's strength. However, Jackson's estimates are not ideal when it comes to a systematic quantitative analysis. Jackson makes it clear that his figures represent only personal estimates based on claims made by Klan leaders and based on Jackson's reading of scholarly accounts of the movement.[2] The estimates lack precision. For example, five states have an estimated membership of 25,000, and seven states are estimated to have had 5,000 members. The time period is also problematic. Jackson made estimates of the number of people joining the Klan from 1915 to 1944, but the Klan reached its peak in 1924 and membership declined rapidly beginning in 1925. The types of people who joined the Klan in the 1940s were likely quite different from those who joined in the 1920s, and they were drawn to the organization for reasons other than those that I have identified in this book. In my quantitative analysis, therefore, I return to the data that I presented in the opening chapter. The content of the *Imperial Night-Hawk* provides a unique opportunity to examine state-level variation in Klan activism in the early 1920s.

State-Level Variation in Klan Activity

The power-devaluation model, combined with the qualitative application of the theory in preceding chapters, can be used to identify varying state attributes that predict varying levels of Klan activism across the forty-eight states in the early 1920s. Multivariate analysis is required to assess the predictive power of the theory. For example, bivariate analysis reveals that more Klan activity tended to occur in states where a high percentage of farmland was devoted to corn production ($r = .453$), a finding that is consistent with my earlier research on county-level variation in Klan membership in the state of Indiana.[3] That relationship could be spurious, however, and may simply reflect the fact that corn-growing states also tended to be the more populous states ($r = .478$), and more events occurred in states with large populations ($r = .646$). My analysis is further complicated by the nature of the dependent variable, which is the total number of events or activities in each state as reported in the *Imperial Night-Hawk*. There is good reason to expect that the likelihood of any event occurring in a state (and being reported) was heavily influenced by the number of prior events occurring in the state. The events, in other words, are not statistically independent. A parade or initiation ceremony taking place in Alabama, for example, might spur additional activity within the state because the event captured public attention, attracted new members and resources, and thus provided incentives and the means to engage in more activity.

Because the dependent variable is a cumulative total of discrete events, and because there is good reason to expect that the events occurring in a state are not independent of one another, ordinary least squares regression is likely to produce biased estimates. Cases such as this are usually dealt with using techniques designed for event history analysis. However, because I am working with a relatively short time span (less than two years) and because I do not have complete information about the time that elapsed between events, I estimate models using a continuation-ratio logit model. This method is closely related to discrete-time methods used in survival analysis but was developed for use with ordinal-dependent variables. The model can be used when the dependent variable represents a progression through stages. For example, before a sixth Klan event can be reported for the state of Missouri, it must be preceded by a fifth event, which must be preceded by a fourth event, and so on. Here, I will discuss the technique in a way that should make intuitive sense to readers who are not interested in the technical details. Readers may refer to a number of sources for a more thorough discussion of the methodology.[4]

The method simultaneously estimates a series of binary logistic models. In the first stage, states with no events are compared with all other states. In the second stage, states with no events are discarded, and the states with just one event are compared to states in which more than one event occurred. The process continues until all categories have been exhausted. Gaps between categories are ignored. For example, several states have 2 reported events but the next highest value is 7. The gap between 2 and 7 is treated as the progression through a single stage. The model includes a separate intercept for each stage and constrains the coefficients so that they are the same across all stages. The technique yields beta coefficients, which represent the estimated effect of a one-unit increase in the explanatory variables on the log odds of moving to the next stage in the rank ordering of Klan events, holding other variables constant, and taking the interdependence of Klan events into account.

Independent Variables

I draw primarily on historical U.S. census data to construct measures of my independent variables. Because my units of analysis are states, rather than individuals or groups of individuals, I cannot directly measure the power-devaluation concept. However, when selecting independent variables, my aim is to identify state attributes that indicate that many individuals residing in the state would have been experiencing power devaluation and would also have been responsive to the Klan's framing. At this point, it is worth repeating my earlier argument that many factors that contributed to the Klan's growth were national in scope. An influx of immigrants could result in power devaluation for the native-born, white Protestants in Indiana, even (and perhaps especially) if those immigrants were settling in New York and not in Indiana. The Klan's rhetoric calls attention to sectional conflicts in which, for example, Catholic voters in the northeast advocated national policies and programs that were perceived to be detrimental to the interests of Protestants in the Midwest.

Political Context

Because the dependent variable represents a discrete count of events, it is essential to control for the population of the state. All else constant, we would expect that more events would take place in more populous states.

Therefore, I include the natural log of the states' total population in 1920 in all my analyses. Because the Klan represented itself as an organization devoted to promoting the interests of native-born, white, Protestant Americans, it is also important to account for racial, ethnic, and religious distributions in the states. I include a measure of the percent of the total population in the state that was nonwhite and a measure of the percent of white residents that were foreign-born in 1920. I use the religious census to calculate a measure of the percent of church adherents who were Catholic or Jewish in 1926.[5]

I also include measures of the percent increase in the number of nonwhite individuals in each state from 1910 to 1920, the percent increase in foreign-born residents from 1910 to 1920, and the percent increase in Catholic or Jewish adherents from 1916 to 1926. Ethnic competition theory proposes that intergroup conflict is most likely to occur when different ethnic groups are coming into closer contact and competing over scarce resources.[6] For the sake of this analysis it is important to make a conceptual distinction between episodes of intergroup conflict and mobilization of right-wing activism. Klan members did, at times, engage in direct conflict with African Americans, Catholics, and immigrants. Yet the movement's mobilization strategy involved interpreting economic, political, and status-based grievances in cultural terms, drawing upon shared values and worldviews held by many native-born, white Protestants. The effectiveness of this strategy should have depended to a great extent on how strongly the Klan's cultural framing resonated with high proportions of individuals residing in a state. I emphasize once again that the Klan's framing of national issues drew attention to sectional conflicts, with immigrants and Catholics concentrated in northeastern states embracing policies that, Klan leaders argued, were detrimental to the interests of Klan constituents in other regions of the country. I expect to find that states characterized by homogeneity, rather than heterogeneity, were most receptive to the Klan's framing and most likely to be sites for Klan activism.

Also relevant in regard to political-power devaluation is the percent increase in total votes cast for the president from 1916 to 1920. As discussed earlier, the effects of women's suffrage were not uniformly distributed across states. Voting rights had been extended to women prior to passage of the Nineteenth Amendment in many western states, and there was state-level variation in turnout among women who were newly eligible to vote. Klan leaders noted that new women voters were disproportionately located in northeastern states where the movement's enemies were concentrated. In response, they attempted to promote higher rates of voter turnout among women and men who were sympathetic to the Klan's agenda and sponsored the Women's Ku Klux Klan as a vehicle for promoting political participation among white, native-born, Protestant women. Because these incentives to promote higher turnout would have been stronger in states that did not gain new voters, I expected to find that the Klan was more active, holding other variables constant, in states that had the smallest increase in votes in 1920.

Also related to the political context, I include the percent of votes cast for either the Socialist or Farmer-Labor presidential candidate in 1920. The Klan, as discussed previously, rejected radical responses to the plight of farmers or unskilled laborers and viewed these campaigns as threatening to the interests of their own middle-class constituents. In preliminary analyses I included a dichotomous measure for states located in the South, but the variable was not statistically significant so I do not include it in my models.

Economic Context

The Klan's framing addressed economic grievances related to organization of manufacturing production. The main problems diagnosed by Klan leaders were rooted in the concentration of manufacturing production and the increasing reliance on unskilled labor. The demands of a wartime economy provided a rationale for economic concentration, and significant transformations in manufacturing production were enacted in the late 1910s. In 1914 the average number of wage earners per manufacturing establishment in the state of Indiana was 24.6. By 1919 that figure had jumped to 35.1. Similarly, the average number of wage earners per manufacturing establishment increased from 32.6 to 45.3 in Ohio during the same period. The change is particularly striking in the state of Michigan. In 1914 the average number of wage earners per establishment was 31.1. By 1919 the figure had risen to 56.7. Not all states experienced such significant changes in manufacturing production during this period, however. Many states whose economies were dominated by agricultural production were largely unaffected. In both North and South Dakota, for example, the average number of wage earners per establishment remained below 5 in 1919. In North Carolina the figure rose from 24.9 in 1914 to only 26.3 in 1919. Many northeastern states also experienced little change during this period because the concentration of manufacturing production had taken place at an earlier historical moment. In the state of Connecticut, for example, the average number of wage earners per establishment was already high in 1914 (55.1) and rose only to 60.1 by 1919. To capture these state-level differences in the concentration of manufacturing production, I include a measure of the percent increase in wage earners per manufacturing establishment from 1914 to 1919. The variable ranges from a high of 82.6 for the state of Michigan (followed by Oregon and Oklahoma, each with 74.2 percent increase) to a 17 percent decrease for the state of Arizona.

I have argued that the agricultural depression in the early 1920s also played a role in the Klan's mobilization. It is important to keep in mind, however, that Klan leaders' framing, as reflected in its national publication and also in regional papers such as Indiana's *Fiery Cross,* did not directly target farmers for recruitment. In fact, Klan leaders condemned radical responses to the farmers' plight and discouraged any solution to farmers' grievances that would benefit farmers at the expense of other Klan constituencies. As Klan leaders grappled with issues related to agriculture, they sought to draw support in rural locations by emphasizing common interests held by farmers and members of a broad middle class composed of shop owners, merchants, professionals, and skilled manufacturing workers. The Klan's framing was most likely unsatisfying in states such as South Dakota and North Dakota where agriculture dominated the economy and where state residents desperately sought direct relief for farmers' grievances. In such states, farmer-labor activism would have been more appealing than Klan activism.

Rather than endorsing policies that would benefit farmers as a group, the Klan instead aligned itself with progressive legislators in both the Republican and Democratic parties and drew on long-standing regional rivalries and resentments of tariff policies that benefited the industrial core at the expense of those residing outside of the core. The strength of the cotton economy, for example, had historically been largely dependent on the demand for cotton from abroad. Similarly, during the war years, local economies in corn-growing regions of the country were stimulated by an unusually high demand for pork and other meat products in European nations.[7] The effects of declining demand in Europe for U.S.-grown agricultural commodities after the war were exacerbated by restoration of high tariffs during the Harding administration in the early 1920s. Wheat farmers, on the other hand, were hoping that government subsidies rather than free-market dynamics would address their grievances.[8]

I include several variables that reflect state-level differences in agricultural conditions. First, I include a measure of the percent of the labor force in 1920 that was employed in agricultural occupations. The Klan's agenda would not have been attractive in many states where the economy was dominated by agricultural production because it neglected to directly address the grievances of farmers as a group. I also include a measure of the percent decrease in the estimated total value of twenty-two primary crops from 1919 to 1924, as reported in the U.S. census. Again, holding other factors constant, residents of states experiencing the sharpest declines in the value of farm commodities should have been unsatisfied with the Klan's approach to agricultural grievances—an approach that aimed to find common ground between farmers and the movement's other middle-class constituents. The Klan's framing should have been effective, however, in states with high levels of either corn production or cotton production. In such states, the Klan's identification with progressive and populist legislators and its leaders' attempt to identify common grievances of farmers and middle-class consumers should have facilitated recruiting. I include a measure of the acres devoted to cotton production as a percent of acres of improved farm land in the state. Similarly, I include a measure of acres devoted to corn production as a percent of total acres of improved farm land.

Status-Based Exchange Relations

When discussing status-based power devaluation, I gave particular attention to the Klan's advocacy on behalf of public schooling. The movement's support for public schooling and its opposition to parochial education should have been most warmly received in states where most residents enrolled their children in public schools and therefore stood to benefit from the Klan's agenda. I include a measure of the number of children enrolled in public elementary and secondary schools as a percentage of total elementary and secondary school enrollment in 1920. I also noted that the Klan's framing conveyed concerns about how other groups were catching up to the Klan's white Protestant constituents in terms of their educational credentials. Long before the 1920s, student enrollment had been relatively high in many states where the Klan became active. The Klan's argument about public schools failing to fulfill their mission should have been more compelling in states that were not experiencing significant growth in enrollment in the years prior to the Klan's mobilization. To test this argument, I include a measure of the percent increase in the number of students enrolled in public schools from 1900 to 1920. Because some of this growth in enrollment was due to migration and fertility, I also control for the percent increase in the total population during the same time period.

The Klan's support for Prohibition legislation should have been most effective in states where most individuals endorsed the movement's stand on the issue. To some extent, varying support for Prohibition should be captured by our measures of religion and nativity since opposition to the sale of alcohol was strongest among native-born Protestants, and the Klan emphasized the extent to which Catholics and immigrants opposed Prohibition.

Although it is not possible to directly measure state-level differences in support for Prohibition, these differences were likely reflected in votes cast by delegates to the 1924 Democratic National Convention. A platform plank was introduced that, if it had been approved, would have committed the party to legalizing the sale of light wines and beer for home consumption.[9] As noted in chapter 6, Klan leaders instructed members to oppose any effort to amend the Volstead Act.[10] I calculate a measure of the percentage of each state's delegates that opposed the plank at the 1924 Democratic National Convention. In twenty states, opposition to the plank was unanimous; support for the plank exceeded 80 percent in six states.

Results

Results of the analysis are presented in Table 4. I begin by examining the effects of variables related to race, religion, and nativity (with a control for population size) when the other variables are excluded from the models. In spite of the fact that the Klan claimed to represent all native-born, white Protestants, these cultural identity variables by themselves explain very little state-level variation in Klan activity. In the first model, the log of population has a strong positive effect on the number of Klan events. Aside from that, only the percent foreign-born variable is statistically significant. The coefficient, as expected, is negative, which indicates that the Klan was most active in states where higher percentages of residents were native-born. When I include measures of percent change in Catholics, immigrants, and nonwhites, as can be seen in model 2, none of the variables are statistically significant with the exception of the control for population size.

At this point it is worth remembering that my units of analysis are states, rather than individuals. Obviously, race, religion, and nativity were important factors distinguishing Klan members from nonmembers because only white, native-born Protestants were eligible for membership. Individuals ineligible for membership had good reasons to oppose the Klan. Yet when the goal is to explain state-level variation in Klan activity, racial, ethnic, and religious distributions seem, at first glance, to have been irrelevant. My theoretical argument suggests, however, that these factors should have played a role in the Klan's mobilization but only when considered in light of other important transformations taking place in the early 1900s. The incentive for right-wing mobilization came from economic, political, and status-based power devaluation among those whom the Klan hoped to recruit. The Klan articulated its members' grievances by drawing on cultural identities rooted in race, nativity, and religion. What's more, Klan leaders called attention to the way in which Catholic and immigrant voters

Table 4. State-level variation in Klan events as reported in the *Imperial Night-Hawk*, 1923–24

Independent variable	Model 1	Model 2	Model 3	Model 4
Population, 1920 (logged)	1.324***	1.325***	2.262***	3.699***
	(.219)	(.223)	(.391)	(.590)
Percent Catholic or Jewish, 1926	.006	−.005		−.072*
	(.014)	(.016)		(.031)
Percent foreign-born, 1920	−.010*	−.089		−.181*
	(.043)	(.049)		(.076)
Percent nonwhite, 1920	−.003	−.008		−.067
	(.015)	(.015)		(.038)
Percent increase in Catholic or Jewish, 1916–26		.003		−.032*
		(.009)		(.013)
Percent increase in foreign-born, 1910–20		−.002		−.061*
		(.013)		(.025)
Percent increase in nonwhite, 1910–20		.004		−.004
		(.003)		(.004)
Percent increase in votes cast, 1916–20			−.027***	−.036***
			(.007)	(.009)
Percent voting Socialist or Farmer-Labor, 1920			−.097	−.154*
			(.056)	(.076)
Percent increase of workers per establishment, 1914–19			.045***	.072***
			(.013)	(.019)
Percent employed in agricultural occupations			−.210***	−.435***
			(.038)	(.071)
Percent decrease in farm commodity prices, 1919–24			−.035**	−.069***
			(.012)	(.016)
Percent acres devoted to cotton, 1920			.140***	.319***
			(.029)	(.065)
Percent acres devoted to corn, 1920			.221***	.281***
			(.050)	(.069)
Percent of enrolled students in public schools, 1920			.377***	.442***
			(.076)	(.103)
Percent increase in students enrolled in public schools, 1900–20			.002	−.015*
			(.004)	(.006)
Percent increase in total population, 1900–20			−.010	.025
			(.012)	(.015)
Percent of delegates supporting prohibition, 1924			.035***	.039**
			(.010)	(.014)
Log likelihood	−149.12	−148.12	−118.39	−99.95
Number of observations	889	889	889	889
Pseudo r square	.138	.146	.317	.423

*p < .05   **p < .01   ***p < .001

Continuation-ratio logit estimates. Standard errors are in parentheses.

were concentrated in northeastern states and how these conditions held implications for national level political conflicts.

In the third column of Table 4 (model 3), I present results when all variables except the cultural identity variables are included. Most of these variables are statistically significant predictors of Klan activity. As expected, increases in the number of wage earners per manufacturing establishment have a strong positive effect on the dependent variable. Coefficients for the percent employed in agricultural occupations and the percent decline in crop prices indicate that the Klan had some difficulty gaining strength in predominantly agricultural states and where declines in crop prices were steep. As discussed previously, the Klan opposed radical policies that would address farmers' grievances, and they condemned policies that would advance the interests of farmers at the expense of other constituents. However, the results indicate that the Klan was able to establish a strong foothold in states where cotton and corn were primary crops. The coefficients of each variable are positive and highly significant. The Klan's self-identification with progressive legislators helped the movement to effectively argue that farmers and middle-class consumers had a common interest in opposing policies such as the protective tariff that disproportionately benefited large manufacturing interests in northeastern states.

Regional political conflicts also seem to have played a role in terms of how women's suffrage factored into the Klan's mobilization. Klan leaders noted that the supply of new voters was not uniformly distributed across states and emphasized the importance of stimulating voter turnout among women who were sympathetic to their agenda. My results confirm that the Klan tended to stage more events in states that gained the fewest new voters in 1920. Klan mobilization does not seem to have been in response to localized threats posed by Socialists or by the farmer-labor movement. Instead, the Klan tended to be strongest where the political left was weakest, and weakest where the left was strongest. In the midst of a steep agricultural depression and during a time period in which manufacturing production was becoming increasingly centralized and reliant on unskilled labor, Klan leaders reacted against political mobilization that sought to secure benefits for farmers and unskilled laborers at the expense of the middle class. Farmers mobilizing in the Dakotas and in Minnesota threatened the interests of Klan constituents in states such as Indiana, Ohio, and Illinois. While the relationship falls just shy of statistical significance, the percent vote for left-wing presidential candidates in 1920 has a negative effect on Klan activity, underscoring once again the regional nature of the political conflict.

The results also show that Klan activity was much more likely to occur in states where high percentages of students were enrolled in public rather than private schools. The exponentiation of the beta coefficient produces an odds ratio that is useful for interpretation. Each 1 percent increase in public schooling multiplies the odds of proceeding to the next stage in the states' rank ordering of Klan activity by 1.5. All the attention that Klan leaders gave to the issue of public education seems to have paid off. The variable measuring the percent increase in enrollment from 1900 to 1920 is not statistically significant, yet the measure of support for Prohibition is statistically significant and has a positive effect on Klan activity.

Several interesting findings emerge when all of the variables are included in the model simultaneously (model 4). First, it is noteworthy that most of the cultural identity variables are significant predictors of Klan activity, but only after controlling for other structural changes that were taking place during the time period. The results clearly demonstrate that the Klan tended to thrive on homogeneity within the state rather than on high rates of contact with Catholics, immigrants, or African Americans. This does not mean that the Klan did not respond to local threats posed by Catholics or immigrants, but the results do show that the Klan was more active in states in which higher proportions of the population were native-born and Protestant. Variables measuring the percent of church adherents who were either Catholic or Jewish, and the percent of the white population that was foreign-born, are statistically significant and negatively related to Klan activity. The percent nonwhite is also negatively related to Klan activity, but the coefficient falls just short of statistical significance ($p = .075$). The Klan was also more likely to stage events and activities in states that were not experiencing growth in the number of Catholics or immigrants. This underscores the point that new Catholic and immigrant voters represented a source of political power devaluation in national politics, often pitting Catholics residing in the northeast against Protestants residing in other sections of the country. The measure of the percent increase in the nonwhite population is also negative, but not statistically significant.

It is noteworthy that the effects of the other variables become stronger after including the cultural identity variables as controls. The measure of left-wing voting and the measure of the increase in public school enrollment become statistically significant after controlling for distributions of nonwhites, Catholic and Jewish adherents, and immigrants. The magnitude of the coefficient for each of the other variables also increases. This should be expected in light of the way in which the Klan drew on race, religion, and nativity to interpret changes in the structure of American society that generated economic, political, and status-based power devaluation for many individuals who were eligible to join the Klan.

The results of my analysis demonstrate that the Klan did tend to be more active in states where large proportions of the population were experiencing power devaluation stemming from changes in the structure of American society in the early 1920s. Holding other variables constant, states that experienced an increase in wage earners per manufacturing establishment had more Klan activity. The Klan also was strong in states where agricultural production was oriented more toward cotton and corn production, making it possible for the Klan's leaders to incorporate agricultural grievances into their frames without alienating other core constituencies. Klan activity was also highest in states that gained the fewest new voters in the first national election in which women in all forty-eight states were eligible to vote.

The Klan was more active in states with high percentages of students enrolled in public, rather than private, schools. Interestingly, the Klan was also more active in states that had experienced the smallest growth in public school enrollment since 1900. I have argued that this was due to the way in which Klan leaders drew attention to the way in which other groups were catching up to the Klan's constituents in terms of their educational credentials. Klan leaders noted gains made by Catholics, immigrants, and nonwhites and spoke with alarm about the need to improve educational opportunities for native-born white Protestants. The fight over public education in the 1920s was being carried out at the national level, pitting state against state in a competition for federal funding. States that had experienced the smallest gains in enrollment should have been most receptive to the Klan's claims that public education for native-born, white Protestants needed additional support from the federal government. Finally, the results suggest that the Klan's endorsement of Prohibition at a time when Prohibition had become the law of the land also played a role in the Klan's mobilization.

9

The Klan's Last Gasp: Campaigning to Keep a Catholic out of the White House, 1925–1928

The Imperial Night-Hawk is not dead—in being superseded by The Kourier Magazine, *it simply enters a new stage of growth or development.*
—*Imperial Night-Hawk,* November 19, 1924

By 1924 the Ku Klux Klan had emerged as a powerful social movement claiming the allegiance of millions of members and adherents. Its growth was in part fueled by the way in which recruiters opportunistically offered the Klan as a remedy for problems in local communities. However, the Klan quickly became a national social movement whose reach extended into all of the nation's forty-eight states. How was the movement able to diffuse so broadly? The Klan articulated the grievances of many native-born, white Protestants, and those grievances were to a great extent rooted in national, rather than localized, conflicts. As the analysis in the preceding chapter shows, the Ku Klux Klan became most active in states where high proportions of native-born, white Protestants were being affected by economic changes, political changes, and social changes related to status hierarchies. Just as important, the analysis shows that the movement thrived on cultural homogeneity and tended to be most active in states in which native-born, white Protestants greatly outnumbered immigrants and Catholics. The Klan used racial, ethnic, and religious identities to draw battle lines, and that strategy would have implications for the movement's long-term trajectory and for its attempts to influence the political process.

One should be careful not to exaggerate or overemphasize the unity and cohesiveness of the movement. If it were possible to go back in time and select a random sample of twenty Klan members, I suspect that each individual selected would offer a different explanation for her or his participation. That is not unusual, as individual motives for participation often vary widely even within social movements that appear, from the outside, to have clear goals and a unity of purpose. Indeed, in order to build a powerful social movement with a large and resourceful membership, leaders must provide a variety of incentives for participation. A common path to movement participation involves simply being asked to participate by a close friend or a neighbor. Initial exposure to a movement often comes through social activities rather than through an individual's burning ideological commitment to a particular cause.[1]

Yet as framing theorists emphasize, attracting and maintaining the support of movement members and adherents involves interpretive and cognitive processes. After all, one need not join a social movement to engage in social activities. There needs to be something more to motivate ongoing participation and commitment. Movement leaders must provide a rationale for collective action. The frames that they construct must come into alignment with the beliefs, values, and worldviews held by active members and by those who are being targeted for recruitment.[2] This does not mean that all members and participants come to share an identical set of logical and coherent beliefs. It does mean that the movement's framing resonates on some level with participants and does not repel them by contradicting their core beliefs, values, and interests.

The geographic distribution of Klan activities strongly suggests that the Klan's fortunes were linked to the way in which the movement attached itself to ongoing sectional conflicts in the United States. Structural changes in the early 1900s, described in previous chapters, provided incentives for action, and Klan leaders responded by constructing narratives that linked constituents' grievances to cultural identities and to preexisting narratives that pitted the interests of northeastern industrialists against the interests of white Protestant Americans residing in the South, West, and Midwest. The statistical analyses in the preceding chapter identify varying state-level attributes underlying these sectional conflicts that facilitated and constrained the Klan's geographic diffusion in the early 1920s.

While the Klan's growth in the early 1920s was impressive by almost any standard, its rapid decline was equally impressive. Perhaps the movement's general health was tenuous even during the years of rapid expansion. The organization was continually plagued by internal factionalism, and the movement made plenty of enemies during its ascendance who vigorously resisted the Klan and all that it stood for. Until 1925, the movement survived factionalism and several scandals involving its leaders. For the most part, it successfully deflected attacks launched by opponents. The movement, after all, argued on behalf of the nation's dominant racial, ethnic, and religious groups. Challenging such a movement entailed risks for political and legal authorities. Soon after the 1924 elections, however, Klansmen and Klanswomen began to leave the organization like rats fleeing a sinking ship. Hiram Evans, sounding temporarily optimistic about a Klan revival in 1929, commented on how "there had been a steady loss in membership for about four years and reaching its crisis during last winter."[3] Despite Evans's efforts, the anticipated revival never materialized. The historian David Chalmers describes it: "In the mid-twenties the Invisible Empire exercised dominion over more than three million subjects. By 1928, no more than several hundred thousand remained."[4]

For some early observers, the collapse of the Klan seemed inevitable. The sociologist John Moffat Mecklin argued that the Klan's failure resulted from its "dearth of great unifying constructive ideals." David Chalmers concurred, commenting that "apart from a certain skill in merchandising, its leadership was as uninspiring as its program." Kenneth Jackson adds that the Klan's ultimate weakness "was its lack of a positive program and a corresponding reliance upon emotion rather than reason." Lipset and Raab proposed that a kind of "Gresham's law" seems to operate within organizations that rely on overt bigotry to attract supporters. "Bad leaders constantly drive out the more respectable, who find a remote partnership and a less gross approach more tolerable. The resultant poverty and inferior brand of leadership often has its own deteriorative consequences."[5]

There may be a grain of truth in these interpretations. The Klan's leadership could be justifiably criticized for both incompetence and hypocrisy. Yet on the whole, such explanations of the movement's decline are unsatisfying because they beg the question of why the movement did not collapse sooner than it did. Why was recruiting by these "inept" leaders so successful until the end of 1924? These interpretations of the movement fail to appreciate the ways in which Klan leaders, in spite of their many shortcomings, effectively articulated grievances of a broad constituency, convinced these same constituents of the Klan's political efficacy, and offered numerous selective incentives to entice participation. So why did the Klan collapse in the midtwenties? To address that question, I return to the power-devaluation model.

As discussed in chapter 3, the logic of the power-devaluation model can be extended to guide an analysis of the consequences of right-wing movements. In order to influence the political process, a movement must not only gain strength in numbers by recruiting participants but also form alliances with other groups. These alliances are typically needed to seize power or to win victories within democratic political institutions. Yet a movement's capacity to form alliances is constrained by the strategic framing utilized to attract members and supporters. A strategic response to power devaluation, as stipulated in the theory, involves connecting constituents' grievances to cultural identities. If power devaluation results from a decrease in demand for what individuals offer in exchange relationships or from an increase in the supply of what they offer in exchange, then devaluation can be countered by appealing to cultural identities to stimulate demand and using cultural attacks to restrict the supply of competitors. The process involves redrawing battle lines, capitalizing on in-group solidarity to restore constituents' purchasing power within economic, political, and status-based exchange relationships.

This process of constructing group boundaries can be crucial to mobilization. Individuals are unlikely to participate in collective action if they are unable to see themselves as part of a clearly defined group.[6] Yet boundary construction that helps a movement grow can generate problems as the movement seeks to form alliances with other groups. The very process that stimulates movement growth can generate a backlash among those who fall outside of the movement's constructed cultural boundaries.[7] This tension between the general goals of mobilization and alliance formation contributed to the Klan's demise.

The Klan's Relation to Party Politics

To counter the economic, political, and status-based power devaluation of its constituency, Klan leaders sought to organize a solid (and massive) voting bloc composed of native-born, white, Protestant Americans. While Klan leaders discussed the specific merits of many policies and political agendas, they repeatedly argued that policies and programs running contrary to their preferences were inspired by foreigners, Bolsheviks, or the Vatican. The Klan claimed to represent "100 percent Americanism" and sought to purge foreign influences from government. Such a strategy had broad appeal. The goal of forming a huge voting bloc of native-born, white Protestants certainly was attractive to many Americans in the early part of the twentieth century. It could be applied at the local level, pitting "100 percent American" voters against urban political machines.[8] At the same time, a voting bloc composed of members of the cultural majority could check the influence of large corporations and of the industrial proletariat at a time when class conflict threatened the interests of an unorganized middle class.[9]

As the movement gained steam, its leaders were careful not to tie their organization to a single national political party. This tactic, first of all, gave the movement leverage against those seeking political office. In a national campaign it could be dangerous to ignore a large voting bloc claiming to represent the cultural majority group, and gaining the movement's support could potentially determine electoral outcomes. Klan leaders hoped to have all major candidates competing to win the movement's endorsement by promoting policies favorable to the Klan constituency. The Klan's leadership wanted to keep their options open and repeatedly announced that the movement was not aligned with any political party.

This nonalliance strategy was also valuable as a recruiting tool. The Klan drew its members from Democratic as well as Republican voters. If the movement had aligned itself with a single political party, it would have substantially narrowed its pool of potential recruits. The Klan, in other words, did not force its members to permanently abandon party loyalties that, in many cases, are products of life-long socialization processes and come to represent an important piece of one's identity or sense of self.[10] When forced to choose between party loyalty and the Ku Klux Klan, a significant number of individuals would have chosen to remain loyal to their party. Just as important, the Klan's leaders could convincingly argue that neither of the dominant parties was serving their constituents' interests. Both parties had been infected by foreign influences, they argued, and would have to be rescued by an organization comprised of 100 percent Americans.

The problem with the Republican Party, from the Klan's perspective, was that it was too closely linked to big business. Until the 1920s, that often meant that the party backed liberal immigration policies, tariff protection for industry, and tight monetary policies.[11] Klan leaders distinguished between "old guard" or "stand-pat" Republicans, on the one hand, and progressive Republicans on the other. They spoke approvingly of the latter and with disdain toward the former. Yet the progressive wing of the Republican Party was becoming increasingly marginalized in the early 1920s. Indeed, Senator Robert LaFollette's frustration with the declining influence of progressives within the Party motivated his third-party presidential challenge in 1924.[12]

The problem with the Democrats, from the Klan's perspective, was that the party had become deeply factionalized and therefore ineffective as a vehicle for pressing the movement's agenda. Catholic and immigrant voters in the northeastern states were pouring into the Democratic camp, strengthening the hand of urban Democrats who promoted policies that were often at odds with those favored by southern and western Democrats.

Klansmen were outraged, for example, when a large contingent of north-eastern delegates to the 1924 Democratic National Convention showered William Jennings Bryan with boos and catcalls when he addressed the convention for the last time and urged fellow delegates to reject New York's Catholic governor, Al Smith, as the party's presidential nominee.[13]

The Klan identified with the goals of progressive legislators in both the Republican and Democratic parties, yet in both parties the progressive wings were too weak to set the agenda. As discussed in chapter 5, Klan leaders were wary of backing a third-party candidate but did express some initial interest in LaFollette. LaFollette had, throughout his long career, been a sharp critic of monopoly power and of political corruption. He had enjoyed strong support from middle-class progressives in Wisconsin. And not unlike the Klan leaders, LaFollette attempted to forge a common bond among farmers, manufacturing workers, and middle-class consumers. Campaigning on Labor Day, for example, he made the following pitch:

> Farmers, driven from the soil at the rate of more than one million a year under the present administration, can earn their bread only in competition with the wage earners. Such an enormous annual reduction in the number of producers on the farm inevitably means a decreased production of food, lower wages, stagnant business and widespread discontent.[14]

Although LaFollette was not hostile to the Socialist Party and accepted its endorsement of his presidential bid, his position on class-based politics was not too distant from that expressed by Klan leaders. He frequently emphasized his opposition to any group that favored a dictatorship of the proletariat, and he was friendly toward small business, defending the right of businessmen to keep a just return on their investment. LaFollette's critique was directed not against capitalism but against the domination of both economic and political arenas by an elite minority.[15]

The Klan's construction of group boundaries along racial, ethnic, and religious lines, however, prevented an alliance between the Klan and LaFollette. Even before he hit the campaign trail, LaFollette was asked to state his position in regard to the Ku Klux Klan. On August 8, 1924, he expressed his opposition to discrimination of any kind and forcefully declared his opposition to the goals of the Ku Klux Klan. These comments drew a quick response from Hiram Evans, who declared that "no paternalistic, Communistic, Bolshevistic appeal to the political passions of the masses should go unchallenged." Robert LaFollette, Evans declared, is "the arch enemy of the nation." After rejecting the movement's rejecter, Evans announced that the Knights of the Ku Klux Klan find themselves "now and ever ready to work with any group of America's people where purposes are to make this a freer, a more homogenous, and a more enlightened nation."[16]

The Klan's construction of group boundaries also prevented an alliance with the Democratic nominee, John W. Davis. A stalemate at the Democratic National Convention in 1924 blocked the nomination of Al Smith but also thwarted the ambitions of another strong contender for the nomination, progressive William Gibbs McAdoo. McAdoo was a native of Georgia and the son-in-law of former president Woodrow Wilson. He had also served as Wilson's treasury secretary. He kept his distance from Klansmen at the convention, but instructed his lieutenants to court the movement's leaders and members.[17] Balloting continued for several days with neither Smith nor McAdoo gaining enough votes to secure the nomination. Eventually, Davis emerged as a compromise candidate.

Initially, the Klansmen seemed willing to give Davis the benefit of a doubt. He had remained silent during a debate over a proposed (and failed) platform plank that condemned the Ku Klux Klan.[18] Movement leaders interpreted his silence as a positive sign. After the convention, in a lead article of the *Imperial Night-Hawk* titled "Democrats Make Wise Choice," a Klan writer declared, "In nominating John W. Davis for president, the Democratic party chose a man admirably fitted to lead the party and a man who can appeal to all elements of the country."[19] The Klansmen were also encouraged by the selection of Davis's running mate, Charles W. Bryan.

> The fact that he is the brother of the "Great Commoner" will also carry weight in many quarters even though it is claimed that the name, Bryan, is losing its influence. The great speech of William Jennings Bryan against naming the Klan in the platform of the Democratic party, and the subsequent nomination of his brother for vice-president, proves that the name of Bryan is still weighty in political circles.[20]

Like LaFollette, Davis was forced to take a stand in regard to the Klan. With his party badly splintered along religious and ethnic lines, there were few good options available to the candidate. If he embraced the Klan, he risked losing Catholic and immigrant voters who might turn instead to LaFollette. If he condemned the Klan, he would lose votes among native-born Protestants, particularly in western and southern states. Davis chose to condemn the Klan, banking on the South's loyalty to the Democratic Party and the possibility of picking up votes from urban centers and from northern black voters.[21] Only days after accepting the nomination, Davis launched his first of many attacks against the Ku Klux Klan. In Sea Girt, New Jersey, he told a cheering crowd,

If any organization, no matter what it chooses to be called, whether Ku Klux Klan or by any other name, raises the standard of racial and religious prejudice or attempts to make racial origins or religious beliefs the test of fitness for public office, it does violence to the spirit of American institutions and must be condemned.[22]

Of the three major presidential candidates, only Calvin Coolidge chose not to condemn the Klan. Instead, he offered vague statements about religious freedom. At the Republican Convention, a small group of delegates failed in their effort to condemn the Klan within the party platform. The platform that was accepted expressed the party's devotion to the U.S. Constitution and its commitment to protect civil, political, and religious liberties.[23] Klan leaders could easily interpret such statements as endorsements of their position, arguing that Catholicism violated the separation of church and state and infringed on religious liberty. In many locations, after being rejected by both LaFollette and Davis, Klansmen concluded that the enemy of an enemy is a friend and embraced Coolidge's candidacy. Indiana's weekly publication, the *Fiery Cross*, ran numerous articles attacking both LaFollette and Davis and endorsing Coolidge. In previous research my colleagues and I showed that variation in Klan strength across Indiana counties was strongly associated with an increase in Republican voting in the 1924 election.[24]

Klan leaders were more cautious in the pages of their national publication. Coolidge scored points with the Klan faithful when he signed a bill in 1924 that severely limited immigration, and immigration restriction was a very important issue for the Klan's followers. Yet Coolidge was still a far cry from the progressive candidate that Klansmen had been pining for. The Klan's national leadership understood that a strong endorsement of Coolidge could lead to mass defection in southern states where loyalty to the Democratic Party was deep and long-standing. These concerns were well founded. In spite of his condemnation of the Klan, Davis actually gained votes (compared to the Democratic vote in 1920) in ten out of eleven states of the former Confederacy. As election day approached, the *Imperial Night-Hawk* offered a few mild jabs at LaFollette and Davis and offered some cautious praise for Coolidge. The magazine repeated Hiram Evans's announcement about how the Klan is willing to work with any group whose goals are consistent with those held by the Klan. The announcement also warned, "We will permit no political party and no group of politicians to annex, own, disown, or disavow us. Where our conscience leads us, we will be found, regardless of whom we find in the different political camps."[25]

A Defining Moment

When the votes were in, the one candidate who would not condemn the Ku Klux Klan scored an overwhelming victory. Coolidge received 54 percent of the popular vote while his Democratic challenger, John W. Davis, received 28.8 percent. LaFollette came in a distant third with 16.5 percent of the vote. The outcome of the election turned out to be a defining movement in the Klan's trajectory. Throughout the nation, many Klan members and Klan-supported candidates had been elected to local- and state-level offices. The movement was less successful at the national level. After being rejected by two candidates, the Klan's leaders struggled to define the significance of Coolidge's victory. The Klan had promised to unite progressive voters, who at the national level were split between the two major parties, and to use the movement's influence to elect a 100 percent American president. When the dust settled, many things remained unchanged and Calvin Coolidge remained in the White House. The Klansmen could point to Coolidge's endorsement of the restrictive immigration bill that passed in 1924, and Coolidge, like the Klan, supported Prohibition. Certainly these issues were important to the Klansmen and Klanswomen. But the Republican president opposed many of the Klan's other goals, including one of its most prized objectives—a federal department of education.

Klan leaders were forced to make a tough decision in the election's aftermath. They could have admitted that many of the movement's primary goals had yet to be accomplished, and they could have issued a call to arms for an ongoing struggle. Publicly acknowledging the movement's impotence, however, would have been risky. Certainly, many Klan members had been drawn to the organization because they perceived it to be a powerful political force that could defeat any foe and meet any challenge. Another option was to declare victory, in hopes that a sense of accomplishment would encourage rank-and-file members to stay with the movement as it outlined a new agenda and new challenges to be surmounted. The Klan leadership went with the second option.

Symbolic of the Klan's new orientation, its weekly national newspaper, the *Imperial Night-Hawk,* was superseded by a monthly publication titled the *Kourier.* The change was announced in the *Imperial Night-Hawk*'s penultimate issue and noted that the *Kourier* "will carry material of a thought-provoking nature rather than news items of passing interest." Indeed, the *Kourier* no longer invested much energy in updating readers on Klan events taking place across the nation. In its first year of publication, aside from fifteen cities visited by Hiram Evans during a four-week speaking tour, the

Kourier mentioned events in only seventeen towns or cities. Instead, the new publication offered lengthy articles on topics such as "Jesus the Protestant" and "Christian Citizenship."[26] The *Kourier* even included a series of articles containing rich descriptions of the geography and history of various cities in the Holy Land.

Soon after the election, Hiram Evans used the pages of the *Kourier* to proclaim that the Klan's primary goals had been achieved.

> No incident during nineteen twenty-four so aptly displayed the solidarity of our organization and its influence for Americanism as did the elections in November. From Maine to California, from Kentucky to Minnesota, native-born Americans who have high standards of Americanism and personal rectitude of life were swept into office. Those who sought office through combinations of un-American influences were hopelessly defeated. While the Klan takes no credit for the elections, with singular pride we note that our people supported the best offered, and are happy in victory.[27]

After his "mission accomplished" declaration, Evans proposed a new direction for the movement. "In nineteen twenty-five," he proposed, "our manifest duty lies before us in another field. Our program calls for active support of Protestant Christianity."[28]

In the months after the election, Klan writers used the *Kourier* to provide evidence that the Coolidge victory was indeed a Klan victory. One article praised the president's inauguration speech and quoted Coolidge as saying that "we must remember that every object of our institutions, of society and government will fail, unless America be kept American." Under the heading "Said President Coolidge, So Says the Klan," the *Kourier* listed a page of quotations from the president that were designed to demonstrate that Coolidge was, in fact, the "100 percent American" president that the movement had promised to deliver.[29] Beneath the quotations, as if to remind readers of the Klan's potency, the magazine printed the results of the popular vote showing that Coolidge had soundly defeated his less-than-100-percent-American challengers.

The Klan's strategy seems to have contributed to a predictable outcome. The pages of the *Kourier* show the Klan leadership struggling to develop a new course of action for the movement—one that would stem the flow of defections. If the mission had been accomplished, members had to be convinced that their participation was still needed. In the lead article of the September 1925 issue, for example, the *Kourier*'s editor sought to identify a new "National Objective." He writes:

Figure 23. In spite of sharply declining membership, the Klan managed to turn out large numbers for a 1926 march in Washington, D.C. National Photo Company Collection. Library of Congress.

What we Americans need, is a National Objective. We are going somewhere—but where? This is being asked on all sides, and asked by earnest,
determined men. In the Klan, as a National unit, and in the local Klans
as neighborhood groups, it is being asked. The question will not down.
The answer must be forth-coming.[30]

Addressing the problem even more directly, the editor noted that
Klansmen are asking, "Why are we still keeping the Klan alive?" Klansmen,
the editor complained, seem "to think the one mission of the Klan having
been accomplished, there was no longer any need for the Klan." Throughout
the article, the editor repeated the importance of a national objective.
Numerous articles published in 1925 and 1926 reveal the same struggle
to justify the movement's continued existence. In February 1926, Hiram
Evans boasted of past accomplishments but reminded readers that there was
more important work ahead. "So the Klan will always move forward from
one battle to another, from one crusade to another; and so it will always
have before it not merely a single fight, not even merely a single crusade, but
several crusades and many fights."[31]

Interestingly, Klan leaders could be quite introspective when discussing
the declining membership in their organization. Hiram Evans wrote, "Our
Organization is in a dangerous state—success may cause relaxation, hence
we must spur ourselves to grow, develop and advance, lest we stagnate and
die." Evans put his finger on the cause of the movement's precarious condition when he noted that the Klan had risen to its highest heights when it
was playing defense. "Our battle cry has ever been 'Americans Guard Your
Own.' It has carried us to many victories, but, thank God, the time has
now passed when that must be our only rallying cry." Evans argued that to
continue, the movement would have to "change from the defensive to the
constructive side," but he continued to struggle in terms of defining the
movement's new goals.[32]

The Imperial Wizard's problems were compounded by several issues.
One of these was a major scandal involving D. C. Stephenson, the Grand
Dragon of Indiana. After the 1924 election, intense feuding between Evans
and Stephenson reemerged, causing a fair amount of dissension among
rank-and-file Klansmen. Even more damaging, however, was a heinous
crime committed by Stephenson on March 15, 1925, that would later capture the attention of the entire nation. Stephenson, who had been drinking,
arranged to have twenty-eight-year-old Madge Oberholtzer accompany him
on a train ride to Chicago. Stephenson brutally assaulted Oberholtzer, literally chewing off pieces of her flesh. The next day, when she was temporarily
left unguarded, the deeply distressed woman swallowed poison, causing

her to become gravely ill.[33] Now sober, and fearful of bad publicity, Stephenson promised to take Oberholtzer to the hospital if she would agree to marry him. She refused. Stephenson held her captive for several days in a loft apartment above his garage while he continued to push his marriage proposal. Finally, he returned her to her parents' home. Oberholtzer died within a few weeks, but not before she told her gruesome tale to the police and to the press.[34] After his conviction, Stephenson felt betrayed when Governor Ed Jackson, who was closely tied to the Klan, failed to offer a pardon for the former Klan leader. In response, Stephenson revealed information about his former Klan associates leading to successful prosecutions of Republican officeholders in Indiana.[35]

The Klan's national publication was largely silent on the topic. A couple of articles made veiled references to the scandal. It is clear that the Stephenson fiasco, combined with the sharp drop in membership preceding it, emboldened the Klan's opponents and provided incentives for political authorities to distance themselves from the organization. One Klan writer made note of a newspaper article charging that "evidence was gradually accumulating that 'Klan leaders are utterly devoid of principle or regard for the truth.'"[36] The Klansmen responded with the following argument:

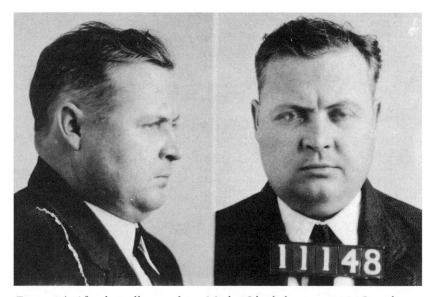

Figure 24. After brutally assaulting Madge Oberholtzer in 1925, Grand Dragon D. C. Stephenson was convicted of second-degree murder. Courtesy of Indiana State Archives, Commission on Public Records. All rights reserved.

It would seem by the gist of the article that if a Klan leader should happen to go adrift, one is immediately to conclude that the whole institution is born of the devil and the entire membership on a par with ordinary horse-thieves. Such logic would also infer that the Church of Christ
should be denounced when a single minister goes astray. Am I to repudi-
ate my country and my government because one or two United States
Senators are disloyal to a nation's ideals? God forbid! I am convinced that
there are traitors in every organization known to man. Even in Christ's
little band there was a Judas.[37]

An article published in the *Kourier* in May 1928 did address the issue directly, describing Stephenson as a former Indiana Grand Dragon who had
been "banished for gross misconduct, and later convicted of murder of a girl
and sentenced to the penitentiary for life." The article suggests that if there is
any truth in the stories that Stephenson was telling about the Klan—"tales
of murder, sudden death, lawlessness and political corruption"—they date
back to when Colonel Simmons, rather than Hiram Evans, was in charge of
the organization.[38]

Gearing Up for Another National Election

As the movement increasingly came under attack from outsiders, its leadership found that they had become snared in a trap of their own making.
They had declared victory in the aftermath of the 1924 elections, raising
questions about whether the movement had served its purpose and was
no longer needed. A declaration of "mission accomplished" led the Klan's
rank-and-file members to expect that solutions to their grievances would
be forthcoming. Economic conditions in agricultural districts did improve
in the mid-1920s, but such improvements led some of the Klan's supporters to conclude that participation in the movement was no longer urgent.
Yet many of the grievances confronting the Klan's constituency persisted,
which undoubtedly left many to wonder if the Klan's mission accomplished
declaration had been premature. The Klan, perhaps, was not as influential
and potent as its leaders claimed.

As the Klan moved into the second half of the decade, the pages of
the *Kourier* included many articles describing the unresolved grievances
confronting the Klan's constituency, such as lengthy essays about public
schools, descriptions of new threats posed by immigrants, and warnings of
efforts to repeal the Volstead Act. While appeals such as these were effective
in the early 1920s, they did not produce the intended results after 1924.
Undoubtedly, many who received the Klan's message wondered why the

problems identified by the Klan's leadership were not being addressed by their 100 percent American president.

The nomination of Al Smith as the Democratic presidential candidate provided the Klan with a new issue that could be used to resurrect a social movement that was in freefall. Beginning in 1927, the pages of the *Kourier* were filled with articles warning of the dangers of a Smith presidency. According to the Klansmen, a Catholic president, by definition, subordinated the United States to a foreign religious leader in the Vatican. Indeed, the Klan's writers seemed to be invigorated, sensing that they had now identified the national objective they had been seeking to revive the movement. However, if the movement did experience a brief resurgence from its fight against "The Happy Warrior," Al Smith, it was a minor resurgence and it was short-lived.

As the Klan's leaders took on Al Smith in the pages of the *Kourier,* they bemoaned the way in which aliens had wrested control of a great political party from the hands of real Americans. Hiram Evans sounded the alarm, warning Klan members that

> We sometimes forget how greatly the President is responsible for the administration of law, which, in the long run, depends upon him almost entirely. Except for the possible opposition of the Senate, which is seldom used and which would never be used under true alien ruler-ship, he appoints all important officers. He appoints all Federal judges, and within a few years could have alien tools on every Federal bench. He appoints all the prosecutors, and could have alien tools in those positions within a single term of office. He controls the administration of all Federal laws, through the Department of Justice, and could fill that with alien tools within a month. Through his power of patronage he has an immense power determining the local control of his party; he could throw that to aliens in almost every case. He has some power even over local elections; that, too, would go to aliens.[39]

Evans and other Klan writers spoke with nostalgia of former Democratic leaders who represented the interests of Americans living outside of the industrialized Northeast. The Kourier condemned the Democratic Party for turning away from paths blazed by the likes of Samuel Tilden, Grover Cleveland, William Jennings Bryan, and Woodrow Wilson.[40]

Hiram Evans lectured *Kourier* readers on the great tradition of the Democratic Party. According to Evans, John W. Davis turned his back on that tradition in 1924 and suffered a stinging defeat as a result. The Imperial

Wizard argued that the party had a chance to return to its historic principles in 1928 but instead nominated Al Smith. Of Smith, Evans declared,

> It is known positively that in his speech of acceptance of the nomination there will be further betrayal. He hopes to be able to convince manufacturers and business interests of the Eastern states that they will be as highly favored by him as by any Republican. To do this he will renounce the Democratic economic policies and the great Democratic principle of representing the common man.[41]

Another Klan writer added that upon receiving his party's nomination, Al Smith "completely submerged the principles, the desires and the purposes of the Southern and Western Democracies for the sole benefit of the Northeastern, city dwelling, unassimilated Democrats."[42]

Rhetoric such as this helped the Klan to become a powerful social movement. In the early 1920s, millions of American men and women, the majority of whom were native-born, white, and Protestant, felt that their interests were no longer being represented in national politics. The Klan promised to force the nation's leaders to hear their voices. A lot had changed, however, by 1928. The threat of an Al Smith presidency had pushed the Klan even further into the Republican camp. While movement leaders gave cautious praise to Calvin Coolidge, they virtually gushed with enthusiasm for Smith's Republican opponent, Herbert Hoover. In the September issue of the *Kourier,* Hiram Evans wrote a thirteen-page article titled "Hoover, the American," in which he described the many virtues of the Republican nominee. Hoover, according to the Imperial Wizard, represented a perfect contrast to Al Smith, "for there has never come before the American voters a man who so perfectly shows the character, principles and the attitude towards affairs which have for generations been universally regarded as the best product of Americanism, and none who has been more highly qualified for the duties of great office."[43]

In 1928 many Americans agreed with the Klan's characterizations of Smith. It would be another thirty-two years before a Catholic would be elected to the presidency. In November 1928, Herbert Hoover won in a landslide with over 58 percent of the popular vote. But aligning itself with the winner did little to boost the Klan's membership in the long run. Who needs a "100 percent American" social movement when a "100 percent American" president resides in the White House? As the nation fell into the grip of the Great Depression in the 1930s, little was heard from the Ku Klux Klan. The movement had cast its lot with the Republican Party and the party had no answer for the economic crisis.

Conclusion

Right-Wing Movements, Yesterday and Today

The purpose of the Klan is to capitalize love—to promote goodwill and the spirit of kindness. In opposing to the uttermost the wrongs and evils which are the root causes of the woes of humanity, the Klan may seem, to the uninitiated, to be narrowly sectarian, but this is not true; its policy is generous, its viewpoint broad and liberal, its tolerance unmeasured, but it strikes without mercy or compromise at the pernicious foreign influences which are undermining liberty and seeking to dominate American institutions.

—Imperial Night-Hawk, May 16, 1923

Beginning in 1915, the Ku Klux Klan organized to advance the interests of native-born, white, Protestant Americans and to restrict the rights and freedoms of individuals the organization chose to exclude by virtue of their racial, ethnic, or religious identities. The Klan's leaders and members expressed bigoted views while wearing sheets and hoods that concealed their identities. At times they intimidated or inflicted violence upon those they perceived to be enemies, and at all times they aimed to enforce conformity to behaviors and practices that they had determined to be "American." Yet at the same time, as the quotation at the beginning of this chapter illustrates, Klan leaders described their organization as liberal and tolerant and declared that the Klan's purpose was to spread love, goodwill, and kindness throughout the land. This type of contradiction is not uncommon in right-wing movements. Movement leaders stake a claim to moral authority while simultaneously attempting to persuade both insiders and outsiders that they are motivated by the purest of intentions. The Ku Klux Klan pledged to fix that which was wrong with America, and from the Klansmen's perspective, all Americans should hold their movement in highest regard. Those who opposed the Klan were by definition opposed to America.

In previous chapters I have used the power-devaluation model to analyze the growth and trajectory of the Ku Klux Klan from 1915 to 1928. Although I developed the theory with the case of the Klan in mind, it is intended to be a general theory of right-wing mobilization. It is fair to ask if we really need a new theory of right-wing mobilization. Couldn't we continue to analyze right-wing movements with theoretical tools that are already available? What does the power-devaluation model contribute that cannot be found in other theories? I address these questions and point to ways in which my theory might be particularly helpful in understanding right-wing mobilization in contemporary contexts.

In agreement with resource-mobilization theorists, the power-devaluation model draws attention to the importance of an organizational infrastructure for sustained mobilization. In chapter 7 I discussed in depth how the Ku Klux Klan capitalized on resources and organizational structures of fraternal lodges and Protestant congregations to facilitate the movement's growth. Without such resources at the disposal of its leaders, members, and constituents, the Klan would not have become a mass movement. However, when studying mobilization among relatively advantaged populations, it is necessary to ask what changed in the social environment that created the incentives to engage in collective action. As important as the organizational infrastructure was to the Klan's mobilization, these organizational resources were available long before the Klan's rise, and the lack of prior mobilization cannot be explained by a prior lack of resources.

In agreement with political opportunity theorists, the power-devaluation model calls attention to the way in which a favorable political context facilitates mobilization. Mobilization is unlikely to occur if individuals sense that the political environment is so oppressive that collective action will be fruitless. The Klan's leaders exploited a relatively open political opportunity structure as they organized to preserve, restore, and expand upon their constituents' privileges. Klan leaders learned early that as long as they kept the violence under control, or at least as long as they were able to successfully distract attention from violent acts committed by members, political and legal authorities would be reluctant to stand in the movement's path. Blocking the path of a large social movement representing members of the cultural majority would have been tantamount to political suicide for many political and legal authorities, particularly for those who primarily drew support from native-born, white, Protestant voters. This feature of the political context, while vital to the movement's growth, was relatively stable over time and therefore tells us little about why the Ku Klux Klan emerged at this particular moment in history.

Not unlike the so-called classical theories of social movements (such as collective-behavior theory, mass-society theory, or theories of status politics or status substitution), the power-devaluation model proposes that macro-level changes in the structure of society generate new forms of discontent that provide incentives for some groups to participate in collective action. To understand why groups organize to preserve or defend privileges, it is necessary to pay attention to what is changing in the social environment that poses a threat to those privileges. However, the power-devaluation model is very different from these classical theories in other important respects. The power-devaluation model contradicts mass-society theory by showing that movement participants are not disconnected from social bonds but instead tend to be embedded in dense social networks. The power-devaluation model also draws attention to rational motives for participation. My theory does not make unrealistic assumptions about the rationality and foresight of movement participants. Instead, it draws on a growing literature on social-movement framing processes to examine how social movement actors interpret changes in the structure of social relations, with the goal of winning and maintaining the support of a broad constituency.

Like theories of status politics or status substitution, I argue that participants in right-wing movements are motivated in part by a desire to preserve or restore status benefits. However, my model calls attention to ways in which economic, political, and status-based grievances often combine to provide incentives for collective action. My theory does not assume that status defense is only an issue for the lower middle class, and my model does not simply attribute collective action to individuals' anxiety, resentment, or frustration. Instead, movement members and supporters are typically engaged in cultural conflicts, and the stakes of these conflicts can be quite high for the combatants.

The power-devaluation model is similar in some respects to ethnic-competition theory and to other theoretical models that explain racial and ethnic conflict in terms of a threat to majority group interests. Yet right-wing mobilization does not always involve open conflict between racial or ethnic groups. As my analysis has shown, the Ku Klux Klan was most active in homogenous states, and its leaders more often advocated white separatism rather than open conflict. In some instances, the Klan was active in heterogeneous local contexts and responded to localized competition and threat. In many other instances, the Klan grew strong in local settings where Klan constituents were insulated from localized threats. The power-devaluation model provides specific guidelines for identifying changes in social structure that provide incentives for right-wing mobilization. In other words, it provides a means of identifying the nature of various threats to the interests of relatively advantaged groups. As the theory emphasizes, these threats do not automatically produce protest but must instead be interpreted or framed in ways that inspire individuals to act collectively in response to the threat.

I agree in agreement with Mary Jackman, I think that we too often neglect the nonconflictual ways in which dominant groups maintain an advantage over subordinate groups.[1] In a strange and interesting way, the Klansmen of the 1920s were early practitioners of "color-blind racism," as movement leaders repeatedly claimed innocence in terms of their harboring ill feelings toward out-group members or in terms of advocating discriminatory policies.[2] At the same time, they fought vigorously to hoard opportunities for native-born, white Protestants through the practice of "Klankraft," and made subtle and not-so-subtle use of stereotypes regarding African Americans and immigrant populations to rationalize their exclusionary practices.[3] Klansmen were not only deeply engaged in the "social construction of whiteness," their project involved the social construction of "native-born, Protestant whiteness."[4]

I began to think of Klan mobilization in terms of power devaluation long ago as an undergraduate student. At the time, I was thinking about the peaks and valleys in Klan strength throughout more than one hundred years of American history. The first Ku Klux Klan emerged in the aftermath of the Civil War and quickly spread throughout the South. It takes very little investigation to understand the driving force behind the first Ku Klux Klan: the movement was responding directly to new economic and political freedoms that had been granted to former slaves. The size of the pool of free labor and the size of the electorate had increased dramatically, and white men donned sheets and hoods and used violence and intimidation to protect their prior advantages. They justified their actions in terms of the natural superiority of the white race and by drawing on racial stereotypes that characterized African Americans as dangerous degenerates. The first Klan eventually collapsed in the 1870s, in part because of a crackdown from the federal government, but only as economic dominance over blacks in the South was being reestablished through a debt peonage system and political dominance was being reestablished through disfranchisement.

A third Ku Klux Klan emerged in the 1960s that was similar in many respects to the first one. It was largely confined to southern states, and its members reacted to gains made by the civil rights movement as the civil rights movement struggled, once again, to secure economic and political rights for African Americans. As in the 1860s, the Klan resorted to violence and intimidation and justified the response in terms of shared racial identity and appeals to negative stereotypes pertaining to African Americans. This Klan also collapsed partly as a result of federal intervention, but at a time when Klan constituents were discovering new paths to protect white privilege through institutionalized politics.[5] George Wallace articulated grievances of many white southerners in his 1968 third-party presidential bid, and Republican strategists took note of an opportunity to capitalize on white resentment. In a short time, a solid Democratic South was transformed into a solid Republican South.

When trying to understand the largest of the Klan's historical peaks, the one that took place in the 1920s, it seemed to me to be more than coincidence that each major rise in Klan strength coincided with the extension of suffrage to a previously excluded group and with significant transitions in the economic order that threatened the interests of many white Americans. These transitions provided incentives to band together to protect, and even expand on, preexisting privileges. Racial, ethnic, and religious identities provided a source of solidarity for those who were adversely affected by social transformations and provided a means to attract support from those who were not directly affected by the changes but shared a cultural bond. Catholics and immigrants, to a great extent, represented the largest threat to the Klan's constituency because they had a different stake in economic, political, and cultural conflicts of the time period. These conflicts could play out at the local level but were also national in scope and did not require localized competition to fuel the fire.

More than eighty years ago, the sociologist Guy B. Johnson offered his interpretation of the "New Ku Klux Movement" in the pages of the academic journal *Social Forces*. Johnson observed, "The notable thing in the whole program is the defensive characteristic: the Klan aims to *preserve*, to *protect*, to *prevent*, to *suppress*. In fact, the Ku Klux philosophy might best be expressed briefly as interference with anything that conflicts with the established order of American Society."[6] Such a philosophy would be most appealing to individuals who benefit from the established order and have something to lose if that order is transformed.

In 1925 another scholar, Frank Bohn, offered his interpretation of the Klan in the *American Journal of Sociology*. Bohn described the Klan as "the American Fascisti" and condemned the organization's tactics. However, he appears strikingly sympathetic when discussing the conditions that gave rise to the movement. Reflecting the prejudices of the day, Bohn suggested that the native stock in America was committing "race suicide." Pointing to low fertility rates among Americans of western European ancestry, he claimed that the "original population is being displaced at a speed which requires few citations of statistics to make the process evident." These types of concerns were also expressed by Klansmen of the era (and continue to be expressed by conservatives in contemporary times). Yet Bohn, in my view, misunderstood the link between demographic change and right-wing extremism. Not unlike other early analysts, Bohn viewed Klan mobilization primarily as a collective psychological phenomenon. The Klan, he argued, was an expression of pain and sorrow, as many Americans came to grips with the fact that the "old American and the old America are passing into history."[7] Bohn failed to consider the interpretation that I have offered in this book. Demographic shifts often produce changes in power relations. Power dynamics are influenced by shifts in the supply of, and the demand for, individuals possessing particular skills, traits, and values. Shifts in power relations, or threats to power relations, provide incentives for some individuals to act collectively, as Johnson put it, "*to preserve, to protect,* to *prevent,* to *suppress.*"[8]

The Ku Klux Klan has survived into the twenty-first century, but it is not poised to become a formidable political force and, unlike in the 1920s, it is far removed from the American mainstream. America's values have changed, and so has the Klan. Yet right-wing extremist movements continue to rise and at times thrive in the United States and in other countries throughout the world. These movements coexist with more mainstream conservative organizations that also seek to preserve advantages of their constituents. In the twentieth century, democratic expansion and economic transition provided a context that was conducive to Klan mobilization. In the twenty-first century, globalization and democratization provide opportunities for the formation of progressive coalitions seeking to promote human rights and a more equal distribution of wealth. These changes also provide new incentives for right-wing mobilization among those who experience economic, political, and status-based power devaluation. As vigilante groups patrol the border between the United States and Mexico, and as neo-Nazis boldly march through European cities spouting anti-Semitic rhetoric and threatening immigrant populations, it is my hope that the power-devaluation model will be used to identify the underlying causes of contemporary right-wing mobilization. With such knowledge, we may develop strategies for preventing the harm that right-wing extremism causes to individuals and to the social fabric of our communities.

Acknowledgments

In the mid-1990s, as a graduate student at the University of North Carolina, I wrote my doctoral dissertation on the rise of the Ku Klux Klan and its effect on the political left. I published a few articles based on my dissertation, but waited more than ten years to begin working on this book. Rather than revising my dissertation, I decided to start over. I held on to my general theoretical argument, the power-devaluation model, but gathered new data, performed new analyses, and rewrote virtually every word (saving a few choice sentences from the dissertation). Because I found that my theoretical argument stood the test of time, I do owe a debt of gratitude to those who provided mentorship as I worked on the dissertation.

I am particularly grateful to my primary adviser, Peter Bearman. Peter read numerous drafts of the dissertation, offered extensive comments, and spent countless hours meeting with me in his office. He helped me to bring my fuzzy ideas into focus, and he challenged me to think and to write on a deeper level. He also had a knack for knowing when I needed encouragement. I benefited from simply hanging around with a brilliant theorist for five years of my life.

François Nielsen was a valued friend and adviser during those years and was extraordinarily helpful. I thoroughly enjoyed arguing with Tony Oberschall about everything from social movements to golf, and I learned a lot from him along the way. Mike Savage served on my committee and provided helpful comments. Kathleen Schwartzman also served on my committee and gave much great advice. She had a strong impact on my thinking even before graduate school; I earned twelve credit hours taking Kathleen's difficult courses when I was an undergraduate student at the University of Arizona. While at Arizona I also took an amazing theory course taught by Liz Clemens; Liz later provided extraordinary feedback on my dissertation. I am also grateful to Judith Blau for her support and encouragement.

More recently, Edwin Amenta, David Cunningham, and Vinnie Roscigno each provided extensive and valued comments on earlier drafts of the book manuscript. Colleagues at Notre Dame, in particular Maureen Hallinan, Christian Smith, Dan Myers, David Sikkink, Maria Diaz, Jackie Smith, and Erika Summers-Effler, provided feedback on parts of the manuscript as did graduate students participating in a working research group that we call SPAM (Study of Politics and Movements). Liz Martinez offered valuable assistance, helping me to organize the coding project for content analysis of the *Imperial Night-Hawk* and assisting me as I tracked down photographs for the book. Stephen Armet, Josh Dinsman, Sarah Shafiq, Nicolas Somma, and Emma Yohanan also provided valuable research assistance.

I thank Maren L. Read of Ball State University library for helping me to obtain photographs. I thank Mark Lewis of the Library of Congress, Vickie Castell of the Indiana State Archives, and Christine Dunham for helping me to secure additional photographs. I especially appreciate the advice and assistance I have received from Jason Weidemann, my editor at the University of Minnesota Press.

On a personal note I express appreciation to family members who indirectly made this work possible. My parents, Catherine and Maurice McVeigh, inspired me with their intellectual curiosity and their passion for social justice. My sister Sheila showed me the value of striving for excellence, and my brother Kerry got me interested in politics (and introduced me to Chuck Berry and Little Richard). For more than fifteen years I have been inspired by the perseverance and kindness of my mother-in-law, Mariam (Bonga) Thomas. I am grateful for the love and support of my wife, Mim Thomas, and I dedicate this book to Mim and to our two amazing daughters, Bronwen and Meillyn.

Notes

1. The Klan as a National Movement

1. Lutholz, *Grand Dragon*, 85; Blee, *Women of the Ku Klux Klan*, 136.

2. *Imperial Night-Hawk,* July 11, 1923.

3. Chalmers, *Hooded Americanism,* 164.

4. *Fiery Cross,* July 6, 1923.

5. Coughlan, "Konklave in Kokomo," 109.

6. Ibid., 109.

7. See Greenapple, *D. C. Stephenson;* Moore, *Citizen Klansmen;* McVeigh, "Structural Incentives for Conservative Mobilization"; McVeigh, Myers, and Sikkink, "Corn, Klansmen, and Coolidge."

8. Blee, *Women of the Ku Klux Klan.*

9. Coughlan, "Konklave in Kokomo"; Blee, *Women of the Ku Klux Klan.*

10. U.S. Department of Commerce, *Historical Census of the United States;* U.S. Department of Commerce, *Statistical Abstract of the United States* (1926).

11. Coughlan, "Konklave in Kokomo."

12. *Fiery Cross,* July 6, 1923.

13. Ibid.

14. Mecklin, *Ku Klux Klan,* 103.

15. McVeigh, "Power Devaluation."

16. *Imperial Night-Hawk,* April 2, 1924.

17. Blee, *Women of the Ku Klux Klan;* MacLean, *Behind the Mask of Chivalry;* Horowitz, ed., *Inside the Klavern;* Rhomberg, *No There There;* Moore, *Citizen Klansmen.*

18. McVeigh, "Structural Incentives for Conservative Mobilization."

19. Olzak, *Dynamics of Ethnic Competition.*

20. Blalock, *Toward a Theory of Minority Group Relations.*

21. Jackman, *Velvet Glove;* Gaventa, *Power and Powerlessness.*

22. Lipsitz, *Possessive Investment in Whiteness,* 2.

23. Blee, *Inside Organized Racism;* McVeigh, "Structured Ignorance and Organized Racism"; McVeigh and Sikkink, "Organized Racism and the Stranger"; Adams and Roscigno, "White Supremacists."

24. MacLean, *Behind the Mask of Chivalry;* Rhomberg, *No There There;* Blee, *Women of the Ku Klux Klan.*

25. *Imperial Night-Hawk,* March 28, 1923.

26. The *Imperial Night-Hawk* changed its name to the *Kourier* in December 1924. At that time, it changed its format and also became a monthly publication. I do not include the *Kourier* in the analysis because it was published during a time in which the Klan's membership was in steep decline and when the movement had shifted its goals and strategies. I discuss the Klan's decline in more depth in chapter 8.

27. E.g., *Imperial Night-Hawk,* March 5, 1924.

28. *Imperial Night-Hawk,* June 4, 1924.

29. Valelly, *Radicalism in the States.*

30. E.g., Blee, *Women of the Ku Klux Klan;* MacLean, *Behind the Mask of Chivalry;* Rhomberg, *No There There.*

2. The Rebirth of a Klan Nation, 1915–1924

1. MacLean, *Behind the Mask of Chivalry,* 4.

2. Alexander, *The Ku Klux Klan in the Southwest,* 3.

3. Jackson, *Ku Klux Klan in the City,* 6, 7.

4. MacLean, *Behind the Mask of Chivalry,* 14.

5. Jackson, *Ku Klux Klan in the City,* 4.

6. Chalmers, *Hooded Americanism,* 30.

7. Bullard, ed., *Ku Klux Klan;* Lay, *Hooded Knights on the Niagra,* 7.

8. Jackson, *Ku Klux Klan in the City,* 7–8.

9. Alexander, *Ku Klux Klan in the Southwest,* 7.

10. Jackson, *Ku Klux Klan in the City,* 10.

11. Alexander, *Ku Klux Klan in the Southwest;* Tucker, *Dragon and the Cross,* 70.

12. Jackson, *Ku Klux Klan in the City,* 10.

13. Ibid.

14. Ibid., 11.

15. Fogelson and Rubenstein, eds., *Hearings on the Ku Klux Klan,* 69.

16. Ibid., 69–70.

17. Ibid., 73.

18. Ibid., 138.

19. Jackson, *Ku Klux Klan in the City,* 12.

20. Ibid.

21. Chalmers, *Hooded Americanism,* 164.

22. Jackson, *Ku Klux Klan in the City,* 16.

23. Ibid.

24. Chalmers, *Hooded Americanism,* 108.

25. *Imperial Night-Hawk,* August 29, 1923.

26. Blee, *Women of the Ku Klux Klan,* 27.

27. MacLean, *Behind the Mask of Chivalry,* 117.

28. Blee, *Women of the Ku Klux Klan.*

29. Jackson, *Ku Klux Klan in the City,* 74.

30. Chalmers, *Hooded Americanism,* 74.

31. Jackson, *Ku Klux Klan in the City,* 204, 207.

32. Chalmers, *Hooded Americanism,* 88.

33. Jackson, *Ku Klux Klan in the City.*

34. Chalmers, *Hooded Americanism,* 51, 53.

35. Ibid., 276.

36. Jackson, *Ku Klux Klan in the City,* 146, 154.

37. Greenapple, *D. C. Stephenson.*

38. McVeigh, Myers, and Sikkink, "Corn, Klansmen, and Coolidge."

39. *Kourier,* February 1925.

40. MacLean, *Behind the Mask of Chivalry,* 55–56.

41. Goldberg, *Grassroots Resistance.* See also Jackson, *Ku Klux Klan in the City;* MacLean, *Behind the Mask of Chivalry;* Horowitz, ed., *Inside the Klavern;* Rhomberg, *No There There.*

42. MacLean, *Behind the Mask of Chivalry;* Rhomberg, *No There There;* McVeigh, "Structural Incentives for Conservative Mobilization"; McVeigh, "Power Devaluation"; McVeigh, Myers, and Sikkink, "Corn, Klansmen, and Coolidge."

43. Mills, *White Collar.*

44. *Dawn,* October 21 and November 11, 1922.

45. E.g., see MacLean, *Behind the Mask of Chivalry;* Goldberg, *Grassroots Resistance;* Moore, *Citizen Klansmen;* Rhomberg, *No There There;* Jackson, *Ku Klux Klan in the City;* Cocoltchos, "Invisible Government"; Gerlach, *Blazing Crosses in Zion.*

46. See Clemens, *People's Lobby;* Valelly, *Radicalism in the States.*

47. MacLean, *Behind the Mask of Chivalry.*

48. *Imperial Night-Hawk,* November 21, 1923.

3. Power Devaluation

1. Smelser, *Theory of Collective Behavior.*

2. Kornhauser, *Politics of Mass Society;* Arendt, *Origins of Totalitarianism.*

3. Gurr, *Rogues, Rebels, and Reformers,* 82.

4. Ibid.; Merton, "Social Structure and Anomie."

5. McAdam, *Political Process and the Development of Black Insurgency.*

6. Oberschall, *Social Conflict and Social Movements;* Schwartz, *Radical Protest and Social Structure;* Tilly, *From Mobilization to Revolution;* McAdam, *Political Process and the Development of Black Insurgency;* Rule, *Theories of Civil Violence.*

7. McAdam, *Political Process and the Development of Black Insurgency;* also see Tilly, *From Mobilization to Revolution.*

8. Also see Oberschall, *Social Conflict and Social Movements;* Schwartz, *Radical Protest and Social Structure;* Tilly, *From Mobilization to Revolution;* Gamson, *Strategy of Social Protest.*

9. Oberschall, *Social Conflict and Social Movements.*

10. Olson, *Logic of Collective Action;* Fireman and Gamson, "Utilitarian Logic in the Resource Mobilization Perspective."

11. Oberschall, *Social Conflict and Social Movements;* McCarthy and Zald, *Trend of Social Movements in America;* McCarthy and Zald, "Resource Mobilization and Social Movements"; Jenkins, "Resource Mobilization Theory."

12. Tarrow, *Power in Movement,* 81.

13. Lipset and Raab, *Politics of Unreason;* Jackson, *Ku Klux Klan in the City;* Chalmers, *Hooded Americanism.*

14. Lipset and Raab, *Politics of Unreason;* Moore, *Citizen Klansmen;* Jackson, *Ku Klux Klan in the City;* Chalmers, *Hooded Americanism.*

15. Mecklin, *Ku Klux Klan,* 32–33.

16. Hofstadter, *Age of Reform,* 293–94.

17. Blee, *Women of the Ku Klux Klan;* MacLean, *Behind the Mask of Chivalry;* Rhomberg, *No There There;* Horowitz, ed., *Inside the Klavern.*

18. Grant, *Passing of the Great Race.*

19. Blee, *Women of the Ku Klux Klan;* MacLean, *Behind the Mask of Chivalry;* Rhomberg, *No There There;* Horowitz, ed., *Inside the Klavern.*

20. Moore, *Citizen Klansmen,* 189.

21. Gaventa, *Power and Powerlessness;* Jackman, *Velvet Glove.*

22. Blau, *Exchange and Power in Social Life;* Emerson, "Power-Dependence Relations."

23. Simmel, *Sociology of Georg Simmel,* 31.

24. Simmel, *Conflict and the Web of Group-Affiliations.*

25. Beisel, *Imperiled Innocents.*

26. Weber, "Class, Status, Party."

27. Beisel, *Imperiled Innocents.*

28. Bourdieu, "Forms of Capital."

29. See Granovetter, "Threshold Models of Collective Behavior"; Marwell, Oliver, and Prahl, "Social Networks and Collective Action"; Blee, *Inside Organized Racism.*

30. Snow, Rochford, Worden, and Benford, "Frame Alignment Processes,"; Goffman, *Frame Analysis.*

31. McAdam, *Political Process and the Development of Black Insurgency,* 34.

32. Snow, Cress, Downey, and Jones, "Disrupting the 'Quotidian'"; also see Snow, Soule, and Cress, "Identifying the Precipitants of Homeless Protest"; Useem, "Breakdown Theories of Collective Action"; Walsh, "Resource Mobilization and Citizen Protest."

33. Snow and Benford, "Ideology, Frame Resonance, and Participant Mobilization."

34. Also see Gamson, *Strategy of Social Protest.*

35. Snow and Benford, "Ideology, Frame Resonance, and Participant Mobilization."

36. McVeigh, "Structured Ignorance and Organized Racism."

37. Gamson, *Strategy of Social Protest.*

38. See Swidler, "Culture in Action."

39. McCarthy and Zald, *Trend of Social Movements in America;* Jenkins, "Resource Mobilization Theory"; Klandermans, *Social Psychology of Protest,* 150.

40. Tarrow, *Power in Movement,* 85.

41. See McAdam, McCarthy, and Zald, eds., *Comparative Perspectives on Social Movements.*

42. Amenta, Bernstein, and Dunleavy, "Stolen Thunder?"

43. Przeworski, *Capitalism and Social Democracy.*

4. Responding to Economic Change

1. E.g., *Imperial Night-Hawk,* November 14, 1923.

2. Lynd and Lynd, *Middletown.*

3. Ibid., 481.

4. Ibid., 22.

5. Ibid., 57, 74.

6. Link and McCormick, *Progressivism,* 67.

7. Ibid., 49.

8. Griffen, Wallace, and Rubin, "Capitalist Resistance to the Organization of Labor"; Weinstein, *Decline of Socialism in America;* National Industrial Conference Board, *Collective Bargaining through Employee Representation.*

9. Griffen, Wallace, and Rubin, "Capitalist Resistance to the Organization of Labor"; Clawson, *Bureaucracy and the Labor Process;* Edwards, *Contested Terrain;* Haydu, "Factory Politics in Britain and the United States."

10. Clawson, *Bureaucracy and the Labor Process.*

11. Stark, "Class Struggle and the Transformation of the Labor Process."

12. Griffin, Wallace, and Rubin, "Capitalist Resistance to the Organization of Labor."

13. Stark, "Class Struggle and the Transformation of the Labor Process."

14. U.S. Department of Commerce, *Statistical Abstract of the United States* (1925).

15. Tolnay, "Great Migration and Changes in the Northern Black Family," 1215.

16. Lee, Miller, Brainerd, and Easterlin, *Population Redistribution and Economic Growth in the United States;* McAdam, *Political Process and the Development of Black Insurgency,* 74.

17. For data before 1928, two or more stores compose a chain.

18. U.S. Department of Commerce, *Historical Statistics of the United States.*

19. Ryant, "The South and the Movement against Chain Stores."

20. Quoted in ibid., 209.

21. McMath, *American Populism.*

22. Redding, "Failed Populism," 341.

23. Valelly, *Radicalism in the States.*

24. Brustein, "Political Geography of Belgian Fascism"; Weber, *Varieties of Fascism,* 125; Schepens, "Fascists and Nationalists in Belgium," 507; Etienne, *Le Mouvement Rexiste Jusqu' en 1940,* 90–95.

25. Brustein and Markovsky, "Rational Fascist," 187; Noakes, *Nazi Party in Lower Saxony,* 114–19; MacLean, *Behind the Mask of Chivalry.*

26. Cardoza, *Agrarian Elites and Italian Fascism,* 338–39.

27. MacLean, *Behind the Mask of Chivalry;* Chalmers, *Hooded Americanism.*

28. *Imperial Night-Hawk,* April 4 and May 30, 1923.

29. Klan leaders did become critical of Mussolini, however, when he made peace with the pope. They also spoke in opposition to Italian fascist groups in the United States because these organizations pledged loyalty to Italy rather than to the United States.

30. MacLean, *Behind the Mask of Chivalry,* 160.

31. *Dawn,* November 10, 1923.

32. MacLean, *Behind the Mask of Chivalry;* Clemens, *People's Lobby;* Glenn, *Unequal Freedom.*

33. *Dawn,* November 10, 1923.

34. Ibid.

35. E.g., see Bonacich, "Theory of Ethnic Antagonism"; Bonacich, "Advanced Capitalism and Black/White Race Relations."

36. Tolnay and Beck, *Festival of Violence.*

37. *Imperial Night-Hawk,* May 30, 1923.

38. Ibid., May 30, 1923.

39. Ibid., May 30, 1923, and October 15, 1924.

40. Ibid., January 23, 1924.

41. *Dawn,* November 10, 1923.

42. *Imperial Night-Hawk,* August 29, 1923, and October 8, 1924.

43. *Fiery Cross,* September 28, 1923.

44. *Imperial Night-Hawk,* June 11, 1924.

45. Ibid., October 8, 1924.

46. Bonacich, "Theory of Ethnic Antagonism," and "Advanced Capitalism and Black/White Race Relations"; Wilson, *Declining Significance of Race.*

47. Alexander, *Ku Klux Klan in the Southwest,* 80; Chalmers, *Hooded Americanism;* Jackson, *Ku Klux Klan in the City;* MacLean, *Behind the Mask of Chivalry;* Blee, *Women of the Ku Klux Klan.*

48. *Imperial Night-Hawk,* January 23, 1924.

49. *Dawn,* November 10, 1923.

50. *Imperial Night-Hawk,* May 16, 1923.

51. Tolnay and Beck, *Festival of Violence;* Bonacich, "Advanced Capitalism and Black/White Race Relations"; Olzak, "Political Context of Competition."

52. *Imperial Night-Hawk,* May 30, 1923.

53. Ibid., May 23, 1923.

54. Ibid., March 28, 1923; Jackman, *Velvet Glove.*

55. *Imperial Night-Hawk,* April 18, 1923.

56. Ibid., June 20, 1923.

57. Ibid., August 6, 1924.

58. See MacLean, *Behind the Mask of Chivalry.*

59. *Imperial Night-Hawk,* July 23, 1924.

60. *Dawn,* January 13, 1923.

61. MacLean, *Behind the Mask of Chivalry;* Moore, *Citizen Klansmen.*

62. Blee, *Women of the Ku Klux Klan.*

63. Blee, Review of *Behind the Mask of Chivalry.*

64. MacLean, *Behind the Mask of Chivalry;* Blee, *Women of the Ku Klux Klan.*

65. MacLean, *Behind the Mask of Chivalry;* Blee, *Women of the Ku Klux Klan.*

66. *Kourier,* April 1925.

67. *Imperial Night-Hawk,* June 13, 1923.

68. *Kourier,* April 1925.

69. *Imperial Night-Hawk,* May 14, 1924.

70. Ibid., October 1, 1924.

71. Ibid., May 28, 1924.

72. Ibid.

73. Ibid., May 16, 1923.

74. Ibid., December 12 and 26, 1923.

75. Ibid., October 10 and December 12, 1923, July 16, 1924; *Fiery Cross,* February 29, 1924, and December 14, 1923.

76. See McVeigh, Myers, and Sikkink, "Corn, Klansmen, and Coolidge."

77. *Imperial Night-Hawk,* October 8 and November 5, 1924.

78. E.g., *Fiery Cross,* October 26, November 9, and December 28, 1923; May 2 and October 17, 1924.

79. *Imperial Night-Hawk,* November 14, 1923.

80. *Fiery Cross,* November 9, 1923.

81. Ibid.

82. *Imperial Night-Hawk,* November 14, 1923.

83. Ibid., November 7, 1923.

84. Blee, *Women of the Ku Klux Klan;* MacLean, *Behind the Mask of Chivalry.*

85. MacLean, *Behind the Mask of Chivalry,* 78.

86. *Imperial Night-Hawk,* February 6, 1924.

87. Ibid., June 11, 1924.

88. Ibid., September 17, 1924.

89. Jackson, *Ku Klux Klan in the City,* 104, 109, 174.

90. Chalmers, *Hooded Americanism,* 180.

5. National Politics and Mobilizing "100 Percent American" Voters

1. E.g., see Lipset and Raab, *Politics of Unreason;* Hofstadter, *Age of Reform;* Chalmers, *Hooded Americanism.*

2. Mecklin, *Ku Klux Klan;* Alexander, *Ku Klux Klan in the Southwest;* Lipset and Raab, *Politics of Unreason;* Hofstadter, *Age of Reform;* Chalmers, *Hooded Americanism;* Jackson, *Ku Klux Klan in the City.*

3. Chalmers, *Hooded Americanism,* 114–15; also see Lipset and Raab, *Politics of Unreason,* 123.

4. Horowitz, ed., *Inside the Klavern;* Rhomberg, *No There There;* Blee, *Women of the Ku Klux Klan;* Moore, *Citizen Klansmen;* Johnston, *Radical Middle Class.*

5. Sanders, *Roots of Reform,* 15–16.

6. Schwartzman, *Social Origins of Democratic Collapse;* Moore, *Social Origins of Dictatorship and Democracy.*

7. Schwartz, *Radical Protest and Social Structure;* Redding, "Failed Populism," 342.

8. McMath, *American Populism,* 206; Redding, "Failed Populism."

9. Link and McCormick, *Progressivism.*

10. Burner, *Politics of Provincialism,* 103, 106.

11. Quoted in ibid., 160–61.

12. *Fiery Cross,* July 4, 1924.

13. Sanders, *Roots of Reform,* 351.

14. Clemens, *People's Lobby;* Valelly, *Radicalism in the States.*

15. MacLean, *Behind the Mask of Chivalry;* Glenn, *Unequal Freedom.*

16. McGuiness, *National Party Conventions.*

17. Valelly, *Radicalism in the States.*

18. Weinstein, *Decline of Socialism in America.*

19. Ibid.

20. Valelly, *Radicalism in the States.*

21. Ibid.

22. LaFollette and LaFollette, *Robert M. LaFollette.*

23. Gieske, *Minnesota Farmer-Laborism.*

24. Valelly, *Radicalism in the States.*

25. LaFollette and LaFollette, *Robert M. LaFollette,* 1115.

26. Ibid., 1118.

27. Quadagno, *Transformation of Old Age Security.*

28. Clemens, *People's Lobby,* 31.

29. Link and McCormick, *Progressivism,* 85.

30. Clemens, *People's Lobby,* 182.

31. Rhomberg, *No There There,* 32.

32. Ibid.

33. *Imperial Night-Hawk,* September 19 and November 21, 1923.

34. Ibid., September 10, 1924.

35. Ibid., September 17, 1924.

36. Ibid.

37. Ibid., September 19, 1923.

38. MacLean, *Behind the Mask of Chivalry.*

39. *Imperial Night-Hawk,* October 1, 1924.

40. Ibid., March 28, 1923.

41. Ibid., September 3 and October 8, 1924.

42. Blee, *Women of the Ku Klux Klan,* 88.

43. Grob, ed., *First Annual Meeting of Grand Dragon Knights,* 98.

44. *Imperial Night-Hawk,* June 4, 1924.

45. Ibid., May 30, 1923.

46. Ibid., May 30, 1923, and October 8, 1924.

47. Ibid., May 30, 1923.

48. Ibid., October 15, 1924.

49. McVeigh, Myers, and Sikkink, "Corn, Klansmen, and Coolidge"; Thornbrough, "Segregation in Indiana during the Klan Era."

50. *Imperial Night-Hawk,* April 25, 1923.

51. Ibid., May 9, 1923.

52. Kimeldorf, *Battling for American Labor,* 2.

53. *Imperial Night-Hawk,* April 25, 1923.

54. Ibid., June 20, 1923.

55. Ibid.

56. Ibid., November 21, 1923, and October 15, 1924.

57. Ibid., April 25, May 30, and December 19, 1923.

58. Ibid., March 28, 1923.

59. At the time, D. C. Stephenson was promoting a plan for the Klan to purchase Valparaiso and run it as the Klan's institution of higher learning.

60. *Imperial Night-Hawk,* November 21, 1923.

61. *Dawn,* October 21, 1922.

62. *Imperial Night-Hawk,* August 29, 1923.

63. Ibid., September 19, 1923.

64. Ibid., September 12 and December 16, 1923.

65. Ibid., November 28, 1923.

66. Ibid., October 22, 1924.

67. Ibid., September 24, 1924.

68. Ibid., October 8, 1924.

69. Ibid., October 3, 1923.

70. Blee, *Women of the Ku Klux Klan.*

71. *Imperial Night-Hawk,* October 3, 1923.

72. *Kourier,* April 1925.

73. Ibid., April 1925.

74. *Imperial Night-Hawk,* September 17, 1924.

6. Fights over Schools and Booze

1. Chalmers, *Hooded Americanism,* 295.

2. Jackson, *Ku Klux Klan in the City,* 255.

3. Hofstadter, *Age of Reform,* 292; Lipset and Raab, *Politics of Unreason,* 118.

4. E.g., see Alexander, *Ku Klux Klan in the Southwest;* Jenkins, *Steel Valley Klan.*

5. See Blee, *Women of the Ku Klux Klan;* MacLean, *Behind the Mask of Chivalry;* Rhomberg, *No There There;* Johnston, *Radical Middle Class;* McVeigh, "Structural Incentives for Conservative Mobilization"; McVeigh, Myers, and Sikkink, "Corn, Klansmen, and Coolidge."

6. See Blee, *Women of the Ku Klux Klan;* MacLean, *Behind the Mask of Chivalry;* Chalmers, *Hooded Americanism.*

7. Beisel, *Imperiled Innocents;* Bourdieu, "The Forms of Capital."

8. *Imperial Night-Hawk,* July 18 and 25, 1923.

9. Tyack, James, and Benavot, eds., *Law and the Shaping of Public Education,* 180.

10. Beisel, *Imperiled Innocents.*

11. Dumenil, "Insatiable Maw of Bureaucracy."

12. U.S. Department of Commerce, *Statistical Abstract of the United States* (1926).

13. U.S. Department of Education, *120 Years of American Education.*

14. McAdam, *Political Process and the Development of Black Insurgency.*

15. Lieberson, *Piece of the Pie,* 136; Tolnay and Beck, *Festival of Violence.*

16. Lieberson, *Piece of the Pie,* 136.

17. Walch, *Parish School,* 60.

18. Bureau of Education, *Directory of Catholic Colleges and Schools,* 246, 478.

19. Tyack, James, and Benavot, eds., *Law and the Shaping of Public Education,* 162.

20. Ibid., 163–64.

21. Walch, *Parish School,* 68–69.

22. Veverka, *"For God and Country."*

23. Walch, *Parish School.*

24. Ibid.

25. Veverka, *"For God and Country."*

26. Quoted in ibid., 83.

27. Labaree, "Curriculum, Credentials, and the Middle Class," 50.

28. Lynd and Lynd, *Middletown,* 187.

29. Labaree, "Curriculum, Credentials, and the Middle Class."

30. U.S. Department of Education, *120 Years of American Education.*

31. *Imperial Night-Hawk,* May 23, 1923.

32. Ibid., September 24, 1924.

33. Tyack, *One Best System;* Dumenil, "Insatiable Maw of Bureaucracy."

34. *Imperial Night-Hawk,* September 24, 1924.

35. Ibid., May 28, 1924.

36. Ibid., May 9 and 30, 1923.

37. Ibid., October 1, 1924.

38. Ibid., September 12, 1923.

39. Ibid., October 10, 1923.

40. Ibid., July 25, 1923.

41. *New York Times,* February 20, 1921; Dumenil, "Insatiable Maw of Bureaucracy," 499.

42. Tyack, *One Best System;* Dumenil, "Insatiable Maw of Bureaucracy," 506.

43. *Imperial Night-Hawk,* May 14 and 28, 1924.

44. Ibid., February 14 and May 14, 1924.

45. Ibid., November 14, 1923.

46. Ibid., March 12, 1924.

47. Ibid., September 10, 1924.

48. Ibid., September 12, 1923, and September 24, 1924.

49. Ibid., May 16, 1923.

50. Ibid.

51. Ibid., July 11, 1923.

52. Ibid., July 18, 1923.

53 Snow, Rochford, Worden, and Benford, "Frame Alignment Processes, Micromobilization, and Movement Participation."

54. McVeigh, Myers, and Sikkink, "Corn, Klansmen, and Coolidge."

55. Grob, ed. *First Annual Meeting of Grand Dragon Knights,* 68.

56. E.g., see Blee, *Women of the Ku Klux Klan;* MacLean, *Behind the Mask of Chivalry.*

57. Jackson, *Ku Klux Klan in the City,* 145, 146; Chalmers, *Hooded Americanism,* 166.

58. E.g., see Rumbarger, *Profits, Power, and Prohibition.*

59. Beisel, *Imperiled Innocents.*

60. *Imperial Night-Hawk,* July 4, 1923.

61. Rumbarger, *Profits, Power, and Prohibition,* 190.

62. *Imperial Night-Hawk,* July 11, 1923.

63. Ibid., August 27, 1924.

7. How to Recruit a Klansman

1. Snow and Benford, "Ideology, Frame Resonance, and Participant Mobilization"; McVeigh, "Structured Ignorance and Organized Racism."

2. Klandermans, *Social Psychology of Protest.*

3. E.g., see Granovetter, "Threshold Models of Collective Behavior"; Marwell, Oliver, and Prahl, "Social Networks and Collective Action."

4. Olson, *Logic of Collective Action.*

5. Klandermans and Oegema, "Potentials, Networks, Motivations, and Barriers," 520; Fireman and Gamson, "Utilitarian Logic in the Resource Mobilization Perspective," 8–44.

6. McCarthy and Zald, *Trend of Social Movements in America;* McCarthy and Zald, "Resource Mobilization and Social Movements"; Oberschall, *Social Conflict and Social Movements.*

7. *Imperial Night-Hawk,* July 25, 1923.

8. Jackson, *Ku Klux Klan in the City,* 171, 179; Chalmers, *Hooded Americanism,* 251.

9. Clemens, *People's Lobby;* Chalmers, *Hooded Americanism,* 251.

10. Clemens, *People's Lobby.*

11. Polletta, *Freedom Is an Endless Meeting.*

12. MacLean, *Behind the Mask of Chivalry,* 160.

13. *Imperial Night-Hawk,* September 3, 1924.

14. E.g., see Clawson, "Fraternal Orders and Class Formation."

15. MacLean, *Behind the Mask of Chivalry,* 108.

16. Chalmers, *Hooded Americanism; Imperial Night-Hawk,* October 24, 1923.

17. See *Imperial Night-Hawk,* June 6 and 13, and July 18, 1923; September 10, 1924.

18. Ibid., June 11, 1924.

19. Ibid.

20. Ibid., April 2, 1924.

21. Ibid., October 24, 1923, and March 19, 1924.

22. Jackson, *Ku Klux Klan in the City,* 10.

23. *Imperial Night-Hawk,* April 25, 1923.

24. Ibid., May 23 and June 6, 1923.

25. Ibid., May 2 and June 13, 1923.

26. Ibid., December 12, 1923.

27. Ibid., June 4, 1923.

28. Ibid., May 2 and 23, and October 24, 1923; January 16, 1924.

29. Ibid., July 11, August 1, and September 26, 1923; June 4, 1924.

30. Ibid., May 23 and 30, 1923; March 19, 1924.

31. Ibid., November 14, 1923.

32. Ibid., July 11 and 25, 1923.

33. Ibid., September 19, 1923.

34. Ibid., June 13, 1923; January 30 and May 14, 1924.

35. Ibid., August 8 and October 3, 1923.

36. Ibid., July 18, September 26, and October 17, 1923.

37. Ibid., April 25 and May 30, 1923; February 21 and 27, 1924.

38. Ibid., August 8, 1923.

39. Ibid., June 4, 1924.

40. Ibid., December 12, 1923.

41. Ibid., July 4 and August 8, 1923; December 5, 1924.

42. Ibid., August 15, 1923.

43. Ibid., June 4, 1924.

44. Blee, *Women of the Ku Klux Klan.*

45. *Imperial Night-Hawk,* January 2 and March 12, 1924.

46. Ibid., January 16, April 2, and May 14, 1924.

47. Ibid., June 4, 1924.

48. Jenkins, "Resource Mobilization Theory and the Study of Social Movements"; Smith, McCarthy, McPhail, and Augustin, "From Protest to Agenda-Building."

49. *Imperial Night-Hawk,* March 28, 1923.

50. Ibid., July 18, 1923.

51. Ibid., July 11 and 25, 1923.

52. Ibid., May 9 and December 19, 1923.

53. Ibid., August 1 and 8, 1923.

54. Ibid., May 30 and August 29, 1923; January 30, 1924.

55. Ibid., May 16, July 25, and August 22, 1923.

56. Ibid., July 16, 1923.

57. See Blee, *Women of the Ku Klux Klan.*

58. *Imperial Night-Hawk,* May 16, 1923.

59. Chalmers, *Hooded Americanism.*

60. Valelly, *Radicalism in the States;* Alexander, *Ku Klux Klan in the Southwest.*

61. Chalmers, *Hooded Americanism.*

62. Blee, *Women of the Ku Klux Klan;* MacLean, *Behind the Mask of Chivalry.*

63. *Imperial Night-Hawk,* April 4, 1923.

64. Grob, ed., *First Annual Meeting of Grand Dragon Knights,* 13.

65. MacLean, *Behind the Mask of Chivalry,* 159.

66. Jackson, *Ku Klux Klan in the City,* 190.

67. MacLean, *Behind the Mask of Chivalry.*

68. *Imperial Night-Hawk,* October 17, 1923.

69. Blee, *Women of the Ku Klux Klan.*

70. *Imperial Night-Hawk,* October 10 and November 21, 1923.

71. Greenapple, *D. C. Stephenson.*

72. Grob, *First Annual Meeting of Grand Dragon Knights,* 4.

73. *Imperial Night-Hawk,* May 23, 1923.

74. Ibid., June 27, July 4 and 25, September 19, and November 28, 1923.

75. Ibid., September 19, 1923; January 2 and 9, 1924.

76. Ibid., June 20 and December 26, 1923; August 6, 1924.

77. Ibid., July 25 and September 26, 1923; January 30 and October 1, 1924.

8. Klan Activism across the Country

1. McVeigh, "Structural Incentives for Conservative Mobilization"; McVeigh, Myers, and Sikkink, "Corn, Klansmen, and Coolidge."

2. Jackson, *Ku Klux Klan in the City,* 237.

3. McVeigh, Myers, and Sikkink, "Corn, Klansmen, and Coolidge."

4. Allison, *Logistic Regression Using the SAS System,* 159; Agresti, *Categorical Data Analysis;* Allison, *Event History Analysis,* 81; Fienberg, *Analysis of Cross-Classified Categorical Data;* McVeigh, Welch, and Bjarnason, "Hate Crime Reporting as a Successful Social Movement Outcome."

5. U.S. Department of Commerce, *Statistical Abstract of the United States* (1926).

6. Olzak, *Dynamics of Ethnic Competition and Conflict.*

7. McVeigh, Myers, and Sikkink, "Corn, Klansmen, and Coolidge."

8. Valelly, *Radicalism in the States.*

9. McVeigh, "Power Devaluation."

10. *Imperial Night-Hawk,* July 11, 1923.

9. The Klan's Last Gasp

1. Blee, *Inside Organized Racism.*

2. Snow, Rochford, Worden, and Benford, "Frame Alignment Processes."

3. *Kourier,* November 1929.

4. Chalmers, *Hooded Americanism,* 291.

5. Mecklin, *Ku Klux Klan,* 32–33; Chalmers, *Hooded Americanism,* 296; Jackson, *Ku Klux Klan in the City,* 254; Lipset and Raab, *Politics of Unreason,* 143.

6. Gamson, *Talking Politics.*

7. McVeigh, Myers, and Sikkink, "Corn, Klansmen, and Coolidge."

8. Rhomberg, *No There There.*

9. MacLean, *Behind the Mask of Chivalry.*

10. Campbell, Converse, Miller, and Stokes, *American Voter.*

11. Valelly, *Radicalism in the States.*

12. LaFollette and LaFollette, *Robert M. LaFollette.*

13. Bain, *Convention Decisions and Voting Records;* Chalmers, *Hooded Americanism.*

14. Burgchardt, *Robert M. LaFollette Sr.,* 214.

15. Ibid.

16. *New York Times,* August 9, 11, and 23, 1924.

17. Judah and Smith, *The Unchosen,* 204.

18. McVeigh, "Power Devaluation."

19. *Imperial Night-Hawk,* July 16, 1924.

20. Ibid.

21. Chalmers, *Hooded Americanism,* 213–14.

22. Ibid., 213.

23. Ibid.

24. McVeigh, Myers, and Sikkink, "Corn, Klansmen, and Coolidge."

25. E.g., *Imperial Night-Hawk,* October 15, 1924.

26. *Imperial Night-Hawk,* November 12, 1924; *Kourier,* February and March 1925.

27. *Kourier,* February 1925.

28. Ibid.

29. Ibid., February and April 1925.

30. Ibid., September 1925.

31. Ibid., September 1925 and February 1926.

32. Ibid., November 1926.

33. Chalmers, *Hooded Americanism.*

34. Greenapple, *D. C. Stephenson.*

35. Chalmers, *Hooded Americanism.*

36. *Kourier,* December 1925.

37. Ibid.

38. Ibid., May 1928.

39. Ibid., May 1927.

40. Ibid., July and September 1928.

41. Ibid., August 1928.

42. Ibid., September 1928.

43. Ibid.

Conclusion

1. Jackman, *Velvet Glove.*

2. E.g., see Bonilla-Silva, *Racism without Racists.*

3. See Tilly, *Durable Inequality,* for an extended discussion of the role of "opportunity hoarding" in the reproduction of inequality.

4. Frankenberg, *White Women, Race Matters.*

5. Cunningham, *There's Something Happening Here.*

6. Johnson, "Sociological Interpretation of the New Ku Klux Movement," 441.

7. Bohn, "The Ku Klux Klan Interpreted," 405, 407.

8. Johnson, "Sociological Interpretation of the New Ku Klux Movement," 441.

Works Cited

Adams, Josh, and Vincent J. Roscigno. "White Supremacists, Interpretational Framing, and the World Wide Web." *Social Forces* 84 (2005): 759–78.

Agresti, Alan. *Categorical Data Analysis*. Hoboken, N.J.: John Wiley and Sons, 2002.

Alexander, Charles C. *The Ku Klux Klan in the Southwest*. Norman: University of Oklahoma Press, 1995.

Allison, Paul. *Event History Analysis: Regression for Longitudinal Event Data*. Newbury Park, Calif.: Sage, 1984.

———. *Logistic Regression Using the SAS System: Theory and Application*. Cary, N.C.: SAS Institute, 1997.

Amenta, Edwin, Mary Bernstein, and Kathleen Dunleavy. 1994. "Stolen Thunder? Huey Long's 'Share Our Wealth,' Political Mediation, and the Second New Deal." *American Sociological Review* 59 (1994): 678–702.

Arendt, Hannah. *The Origins of Totalitarianism*. New York: Harcourt, Brace, 1951.

Bain, Richard. *Convention Decisions and Voting Records*. Washington, D.C.: The Brookings Institution, 1960.

Beisel, Nicola. *Imperiled Innocents: Anthony Comstock and Family Reproduction in Victorian America*. Princeton, N.J.: Princeton University Press, 1997.

Blalock, Hubert M. *Toward a Theory of Minority Group Relations*. New York: John Wiley, 1967.

Blau, Peter M. *Exchange and Power in Social Life*. New York: Wiley, 1964.

Blee, Kathleen. *Inside Organized Racism: Women in the Hate Movement*. Berkeley: University of California Press, 2002.

———. Review of *Behind the Mask of Chivalry: The Making of the Second Ku Klux Klan*, by Nancy MacLean. *Contemporary Sociology* 24 (1995): 346–47.

————. *Women of the Ku Klux Klan: Racism and Gender in the 1920s.* Berkeley: University of California Press, 1991.

Bohn, Frank. "The Ku Klux Klan Interpreted." *American Journal of Sociology* 30 (1925): 385–407.

Bonacich, Edna. "Advanced Capitalism and Black/White Race Relations in the United States: A Split Labor Market Interpretation." *American Sociological Review* 41 (1976): 34–51.

————. "A Theory of Ethnic Antagonism: The Split Labor Market." *American Sociological Review* 37 (1972): 547–59.

Bonilla-Silva, Eduardo. *Racism without Racists: Color-blind Racism and the Persistence of Racial Inequality in the United States.* Lanham, Md.: Rowman and Littlefield, 2006.

Bourdieu, Pierre. "The Forms of Capital." In *Handbook of Theory and Research for the Sociology of Education,* ed. J. G. Richardson, 241–58. New York: Greenwood, 1986.

Brustein, William. "The Political Geography of Belgian Fascism: The Case of Rexism." *American Sociological Review* 55 (1988): 69–80.

Brustein, William, and Barry Markovsky. "The Rational Fascist: Interwar Fascist Party Membership in Italy and Germany." *Journal of Political and Military Sociology* 17 (1989): 177–202.

Bullard, Sarah, ed. *The Ku Klux Klan: A History of Racism and Violence.* Montgomery, Ala.: Southern Poverty Law Center, 1991.

Burgchardt, Carl. *Robert M. LaFollette Sr.: The Voice of Conscience.* New York: Greenwood Press, 1992.

Burner, David. *The Politics of Provincialism: The Democratic Party in Transition, 1918–1932.* New York: Knopf, 1968.

Campbell, Angus, Philip Converse, Warren Miller, and Donald Stokes. *The American Voter.* New York: John Wiley and Sons, 1960.

Cardoza, Anthony L. *Agrarian Elites and Italian Fascism: The Province of Bologna, 1901–1926.* Princeton, N.J.: Princeton University Press, 1982.

Chalmers, David. *Hooded Americanism: The History of the Ku Klux Klan.* 3rd ed. Durham, N.C.: Duke University Press, 1987.

Clawson, Dan. *Bureaucracy and the Labor Process: The Transformation of U.S. Industry, 1860–1920.* New York: Monthly Review Press, 1980.

Clawson, Mary Ann. "Fraternal Orders and Class Formation in Nineteenth-century United States." *Comparative Studies in Society and History* 27 (1985): 672–95.

Clemens, Elisabeth S. *The People's Lobby: Organizational Innovation and the Rise of Interest Group Politics, 1890–1925.* Chicago: University of Chicago Press, 1997.

Cocoltchos, Christopher. "The Invisible Government and the Visible Community:

The Ku Klux Klan in Orange County, California during the 1920s." Doctoral dissertation, University of California at Los Angeles, 1979.

Coughlan, Robert. "Konklave in Kokomo." In *The Aspirin Age, 1919–1941,* ed. Isabel Leighton, 105–29. New York: Simon and Schuster, 1949.

Cunningham, David. *There's Something Happening Here: The New Left, the Klan, and FBI Counterintelligence.* Berkeley: University of California Press, 2004.

Dumenil, Lynn. "'The Insatiable Maw of Bureaucracy': Antistatism and Education Reform in the 1920s." *Journal of American History* 77 (1990): 499–524.

Edwards, Richard. *Contested Terrain: The Transformation of the Workplace in the Twentieth Century.* New York: Basic Books, 1979.

Emerson, Richard. "Power-Dependence Relations." *American Sociological Review* 27 (1962): 31–41.

Etienne, J. M. *Le Mouvement Rexiste Jusqu'en 1940.* Paris: Colin, 1968.

Fienberg, Stephan. *The Analysis of Cross-Classified Categorical Data.* Cambridge, Mass.: MIT Press, 1980.

Fireman, Bruce, and William Gamson. "Utilitarian Logic in the Resource Mobilization Perspective." In *The Dynamics of Social Movements,* ed. Mayer Zald and John McCarthy, 8–44. New York: Winthrop, 1979.

Fogelson, Robert M., and Richard E. Rubenstein, eds. *Hearings on the Ku Klux Klan, 1921.* New York: Arno Press and the New York Times, 1969.

Frankenberg, Ruth. *White Women, Race Matters: The Social Construction of Whiteness.* Minneapolis: University of Minnesota Press, 1993.

Gamson, William. *The Strategy of Social Protest.* Homewood, Ill.: Dorsey Press, 1975.

———. *Talking Politics.* Cambridge: Cambridge University Press, 1992.

Gaventa, John. *Power and Powerlessness: Quiescence and Rebellion in an Appalachian Valley.* Urbana: University of Illinois Press, 1982.

Gerlach, Larry. *Blazing Crosses in Zion: The Ku Klux Klan in Utah.* Logan: Utah State University Press, 1982.

Gieske, Millard. *Minnesota Farmer-Laborism: The Third Party Alternative.* Minneapolis: University of Minnesota Press, 1979.

Glenn, Evelyn Nakano. *Unequal Freedom: How Race and Gender Shaped American Citizenship and Labor.* Cambridge: Harvard University Press, 2004.

Goffman, Erving. *Frame Analysis.* Cambridge: Harvard University Press, 1974.

Goldberg, Robert Alan. *Grassroots Resistance: Social Movements in Twentieth Century America.* Belmont, Calif.: Wadsworth, 1991.

Granovetter, Mark. "Threshold Models of Collective Behavior." *American Journal of Sociology* 83 (1978): 1420–43.

Grant, Madison. *The Passing of the Great Race.* New York: Charles Scribner's Sons, 1916.

Greenapple, H. R. *D. C. Stephenson. Irvington 0492: The Demise of the Grand Dragon of the Indiana Ku Klux Klan.* Plainfield, Ind.: SGS Publications, 1989.

Griffen, Larry, Michael Wallace, and Beth Rubin. "Capitalist Resistance to the Organization of Labor before the New Deal: Why? How? Success?" *American Sociological Review* 51 (1986): 147–67.

Grob, Gerald N., ed. *First Annual Meeting of Grand Dragon Knights of the Ku Klux Klan.* New York: Arno Press, 1977.

Gurr, Ted Robert. *Rogues, Rebels, and Reformers: A Political History of Urban Crime and Conflict.* Beverly Hills, Calif.: Sage, 1976.

Haydu, Jeffrey. "Factory Politics in Britain and the United States: Engineers and Machinists, 1914–1919." *Comparative Studies in Society and History* 27 (1985): 57–85.

Hofstadter, Richard. *The Age of Reform: From Bryan to F.D.R.* New York: Knopf, 1955.

Horowitz, David, ed. *Inside the Klavern: The Secret History of a Ku Klux Klan of the 1920s.* Carbondale: Southern Illinois University Press, 1999.

Jackman, Mary. *The Velvet Glove: Paternalism and Conflict in Gender, Class, and Race Relations.* Berkeley: University of California Press, 1994.

Jackson, Kenneth. *The Ku Klux Klan in the City, 1915–1930.* New York: Oxford University Press, 1967.

Jenkins, J. Craig. "Resource Mobilization Theory and the Study of Social Movements." *Annual Review of Sociology* 9 (1983): 527–53.

Jenkins, William D. *Steel Valley Klan: The Ku Klux Klan in Ohio's Mahoning Valley.* Kent, Ohio: Kent State University Press, 1990.

Johnson, Guy B. "A Sociological Interpretation of the New Ku Klux Movement." *Journal of Social Forces* 1 (1923): 440–45.

Johnston, Robert. *The Radical Middle Class: Populist Democracy and the Question of Capitalism in Progressive Era Portland, Oregon.* Princeton, N.J.: Princeton University Press, 2003.

Judah, Charles, and George Winston Smith. *The Unchosen.* New York: Coward and McCann, 1962.

Kimeldorf, Howard. *Battling for American Labor: Wobblies, Craft Workers and the Making of the Union Movement.* Berkeley: University of California Press, 1999.

Klandermans, Bert. *The Social Psychology of Protest.* Cambridge, Mass.: Blackwell, 1997.

Klandermans, Bert, and Dirk Oegema. "Potentials, Networks, Motivations, and Barriers: Steps toward Participation in Social Movements." *American Sociological Review* 52 (1987): 519–31.

Kornhauser, William. *The Politics of Mass Society.* Glencoe, Ill.: The Free Press, 1959.

Labaree, David F. "Curriculum, Credentials, and the Middle Class: A Case Study of a Nineteenth Century High School." *Sociology of Education* 59 (1986): 42–57.

LaFollette, Belle Case, and Fola LaFollette. *Robert M. LaFollette, June 14, 1855–June 18, 1925.* New York: Macmillan, 1953.

Lay, Shawn. *Hooded Knights on the Niagra: The Ku Klux Klan in Buffalo, New York.* New York: New York University Press, 1992.

Lee, Evertetts, Ann Ratner Miller, Carol P. Brainerd, and Richard A. Easterlin. *Population Redistribution and Economic Growth in the United States, 1870–1950. Volume 1, Methodological Considerations and Reference Tables.* Philadelphia: American Philosophical Society, 1957.

Lieberson, Stanley. *A Piece of the Pie: Blacks and White Immigrants since 1880.* Berkeley: University of California Press, 1980.

Link, Arthur, and Richard McCormick. *Progressivism.* Arlington Heights, Ill.: Harlan Davidson, 1983.

Lipset, Seymour Martin, and Earl Raab. *The Politics of Unreason: Right-wing Extremism in America, 1790–1970.* New York: Harper and Row, 1970.

Lipsitz, George. *The Possessive Investment in Whiteness: How White People Profit from Identity Politics.* Philadelphia: Temple University Press, 1998.

Lutholtz, William M. *Grand Dragon: D. C. Stephenson and the Ku Klux Klan in Indiana.* West Lafayette, Ind.: Purdue University Press, 1991.

Lynd, Robert, and Helen Lynd. *Middletown: A Study in Contemporary American Culture.* New York: Harcourt, Brace, 1929/1956.

MacLean, Nancy. *Behind the Mask of Chivalry: The Making of the Second Ku Klux Klan.* New York: Oxford University Press, 1994.

Marwell, Gerald, Pamela Oliver, and Ralph Prahl. "Social Networks and Collective Action: A Theory of the Critical Mass III." *American Journal of Sociology* 94 (1988): 502–34.

McAdam, Doug. *Political Process and the Development of Black Insurgency, 1930–1970.* 2nd ed. Chicago: University of Chicago Press, 1999.

McAdam, Doug, John McCarthy, and Mayer Zald, eds. *Comparative Perspectives on Social Movements: Political Opportunities, Mobilizing Structures, and Cultural Framings.* New York: Cambridge University Press, 1996.

McCarthy, John, and Mayer Zald. *The Trend of Social Movements in America: Professionalization and Resource Mobilization.* Morristown, N.J.: General Learning Press, 1973.

McCarthy, John, and Mayer Zald. "Resource Mobilization and Social Movements: A Partial Theory." *American Journal of Sociology* 82 (1977): 1212–41.

McGuiness, Colleen. *National Party Conventions, 1831–1988.* Washington, D.C.: Congressional Quarterly, 1991.

McMath, Robert. *American Populism: A Social History, 1877–1898*. New York: Hill and Wang, 1993.

McVeigh, Rory. "Power Devaluation, The Ku Klux Klan, and the Democratic National Convention of 1924." *Sociological Forum* 16 (2001): 1–31.

———. "Structural Incentives for Conservative Mobilization: Power Devaluation and the Rise of the Ku Klux Klan, 1915–1925." *Social Forces* 77 (1999): 1461–96.

———. "Structured Ignorance and Organized Racism in the United States." *Social Forces* 82 (2004): 895–936.

McVeigh, Rory, Daniel J. Myers, and David Sikkink. "Corn, Klansmen, and Coolidge: Structure and Framing in Social Movements." *Social Forces* 83 (2004): 653–90.

McVeigh, Rory, and David Sikkink. "Organized Racism and the Stranger." *Sociological Forum* 20 (2005): 497–522.

McVeigh, Rory, Michael Welch, and Thoroddur Bjarnason. "Hate Crime Reporting as a Successful Social Movement Outcome." *American Sociological Review* 68 (2003): 843–67.

Mecklin, John Moffat. *The Ku Klux Klan: A Study of the American Mind*. New York: Harcourt, Brace, 1924.

Merton, Robert. "Social Structure and Anomie." *American Sociological Review* 3 (1938): 672–82.

Mills, C. Wright. *White Collar: The American Middle Classes*. New York: Oxford University Press, 1956.

Moore, Barrington. *Social Origins of Dictatorship and Democracy: Lord and Peasant in the Making of the Modern World*. Boston: Beacon Press, 1966.

Moore, Leonard. *Citizen Klansmen: The Ku Klux Klan in Indiana, 1921–1925*. Chapel Hill: University of North Carolina Press, 1991.

National Industrial Conference Board. *Collective Bargaining through Employee Representation*. New York: NICB, 1933.

Noakes, Jeremy. *The Nazi Party in Lower Saxony, 1921–1933*. London: Oxford University Press, 1971.

Oberschall, Anthony. *Social Conflict and Social Movements*. Englewood Cliffs, N.J.: Prentice-Hall, 1973.

Olson, Mancur. *The Logic of Collective Action: Public Goods and the Theory of Groups*. Cambridge: Harvard University Press, 1965.

Olzak, Susan. *The Dynamics of Ethnic Competition and Conflict*. Palo Alto, Calif.: Stanford University Press, 1992.

———. "The Political Context of Competition: Lynching and Urban Racial Violence, 1882–1914." *Social Forces* 69 (1990): 395–421.

Patillo-McCoy, Mary. "Church Culture as a Strategy of Action in the Black Community." *American Sociological Review* 63 (1988): 767–84.

Polletta, Francesca. *Freedom Is an Endless Meeting: Democracy in American Social Movements.* Chicago: University of Chicago Press, 2002.

Przeworski, Adam. *Capitalism and Social Democracy.* Cambridge: Cambridge University Press, 1985.

Quadagno, Jill. *The Transformation of Old Age Security: Class and Politics in the American Welfare State.* Chicago: University of Chicago Press, 1988.

Redding, Kent. "Failed Populism: Movement-Party Disjuncture in North Carolina, 1890–1900." *American Sociological Review* 57 (1992): 340–52.

Rhomberg, Chris. *No There There: Race, Class, and Political Community in Oakland.* Berkeley: University of California Press, 2004.

Rule, James. *Theories of Civil Violence.* Berkeley: University of California Press, 1988.

Rumbarger, John J. *Profits, Power, and Prohibition: Alcohol Reform and the Industrializing of America, 1800–1930.* Albany: State University of New York Press, 1989.

Ryant, Carl G. The South and the Movement against Chain Stores. *The Journal of Southern History* 39 (1973): 207–22.

Sanders, Elizabeth. *Roots of Reform: Farmers, Workers, and the American State, 1877–1917.* Chicago: University of Chicago Press, 1999.

Schepens, Luc. "Fascists and Nationalists in Belgium, 1919–1940." In *Who Were the Fascists?,* ed. Stein Ugelvik Larsen, Bernt Hagtvet, and Jan Petter Myklebust, 501–16. Oslo, Norway: Universitetsforlaget, 1980.

Schwartz, Michael. *Radical Protest and Social Structure: The Southern Farmers' Alliance and Cotton Tenancy, 1880–1890.* New York: Academic Press, 1976.

Schwartzman, Kathleen. *The Social Origins of Democratic Collapse: The First Portuguese Republic in the Global Economy.* Lawrence: University of Kansas Press, 1989.

Simmel, Georg. *Conflict and the Web of Group-Affiliations.* New York: Free Press, 1955.

———. *The Sociology of Georg Simmel.* Translated and edited by Oscar Louis Wolff, Hans Schiebelhuth, and Karl Wolfskehl. New York: Free Press, 1950.

Smelser, Neil. *Theory of Collective Behavior.* New York: Free Press, 1962.

Smith, Jackie, John McCarthy, Clark McPhail, and Boguslaw Augustin. "From Protest to Agenda-Building: Description Bias in Media Coverage of Protest Events in Washington D.C." *Social Forces* 79 (2001): 1397–1423.

Snow, David A., and Robert Benford. "Ideology, Frame Resonance, and Participant Mobilization." In *From Structure to Action: Social Movement Participation across Cultures,* ed. Bert Klandermans, Hanspeter Kreisi, and Sidney Tarrow, 197–217. Greenwich, CT: JAI Press, 1988.

Snow, David A., E. Burke Rochford Jr., Steven Worden, and Robert Benford. "Frame Alignment Processes, Micromobilization, and Movement Participation." *American Sociological Review* 51 (1986): 454–81.

Snow, David A., Daniel M. Cress, Liam Downey, and Andrew W. Jones. "Disrupting the 'Quotidian': Reconceptualizing the Relation between Breakdown and the Emergence of Collective Action." *Mobilization* 3 (1998): 1–22.

Snow, David A., Sarah A. Soule, and Daniel Cress. "Identifying the Precipitants of Homeless Protest Across 17 U.S. Cities, 1980 to 1990." *Social Forces* 83 (2005): 1183–1210.

Stark, David. "Class Struggle and the Transformation of the Labor Process." *Theory and Society* 9 (1980): 89–130.

Swidler, Ann. "Culture in Action: Symbols and Strategies." *American Sociological Review* 51 (1986): 273–86.

Tarrow, Sidney. *Power in Movement: Social Movements, Collective Action and Politics.* New York: Cambridge University Press, 1994.

Thornbrough, Emma Lou. "Segregation in Indiana during the Klan Era of the 1920s." *Mississippi Valley Historical Review* 47 (1961): 594–618.

Tilly, Charles. *Durable Inequality.* Berkeley: University of California Press, 1998.

———. *From Mobilization to Revolution.* Reading, Mass.: Addison-Wesley, 1978.

Tolnay, Stewart. "The Great Migration and Changes in the Northern Black Family, 1940–1990." *Social Forces* 75 (1997): 1213–38.

Tolnay, Stewart, and E. M. Beck. *A Festival of Violence: An Analysis of Southern Lynching, 1882–1930.* Urbana: University of Illinois Press, 1995.

Tucker, Richard. *The Dragon and the Cross: The Rise and Fall of the Ku Klux Klan in Middle America.* Hampden, Conn.: Archon Books, 1991.

Tyack, David. *The One Best System: A History of American Urban Education.* Cambridge: Harvard University Press, 1974.

Tyack, David, Thomas James, and Aaron Benavot, eds. *Law and the Shaping of Public Education, 1785–1954.* Madison: University of Wisconsin Press, 1987.

U.S. Bureau of Education. *Directory of Catholic Colleges and Schools.* Washington, D.C.: National Catholic Welfare Conference, 1926.

U.S. Department of Commerce. *Historical Census of the United States.* Washington, D.C.: Government Printing Office, 1920.

———. *Historical Statistics of the United States: Colonial Times to 1970.* Washington, D.C.: Government Printing Office, 1975.

———. *Statistical Abstract of the United States.* Washington, D.C.: Government Printing Office, 1924, 1925, 1926.

U.S. Department of Education. *120 Years of American Education: A Statistical Por-*

trait. Edited by Thomas D. Snyder. Washington, D.C.: National Center for Education Statistics, 1993.

Useem, Bert. "Breakdown Theories of Collective Action." *Annual Review of Sociology* 24 (1998): 215–38.

Valelly, Richard. *Radicalism in the States: The Minnesota Farmer-Labor Party and the American Political Economy.* Chicago: University of Chicago Press, 1989.

Veverka, Fayette Breaux. *"For God and Country:" Catholic Schooling in the 1920s.* New York: Garland, 1988.

Walch, Timothy. *Parish School: American Catholic Parochial Education from Colonial Times to the Present.* New York: Crossroad, 1996.

Walsh, Edward J. "Resource Mobilization and Citizen Protest in Communities around Three Mile Island." *Social Problems* 29 (1981): 1–21.

Weber, Eugen. *Varieties of Fascism.* Princeton, N.J.: Princeton University Press, 1964.

Weber, Max. "Class, Status, Party." In *From Max Weber: Essays in Sociology,* ed. H. H. Gerth and C. Wright Mills, 180–95. New York: Oxford University Press, 1946.

Weinstein, James. *The Decline of Socialism in America, 1912–1925.* New York: Monthly Review Press, 1967.

Wilson, William Julius. *The Declining Significance of Race: Blacks and Changing American Institutions.* 2nd ed. Chicago: University of Chicago Press, 1980.

Index

AAPA. *See* Association Against the Prohibition Amendment

activism: across country, 167–79, 218–19n; cities with no reported activity, 14; and collective action, 167; cultural identity variables, 178; economic context, 172–74; geographic diffusion 7, 10–18, 181; independent variables, 170; multivariate analysis, 168–69; political context, 170–72; and power devaluation, 167–71, 174–76, 178–79; state-level variation, 169–70, 176, status-based exchange relations, 174–75; and women voters, 179

AFL. *See* American Federation of Labor

African American migration: and economic change, 57–58, 69–73, 92

African Americans. *See* blacks

African Blood Brotherhood, 72

agricultural depression: and economic change, 59–62, 77–79, 80, 89, 139, 173, 174, 177, 179

Akron, Ohio. Klan in, 15, 145

Alabama: Klan in, 13, 15, 19, 21, 129, 144, 148, 150, 169

Altoona, Pennsylvania: Klan in, 15, 147

American Federation of Labor (AFL), 7, 54, 91, 94, 96, 104

Americanism, 3, 21, 25–27, 62, 68–69, 82–84, 103–6, 105, 109–10, 115, 121, 126–27, 128–29, 143, 147, 159, 167, 183–84, 188–89, 193–95, 196

American Journal of Sociology 200

American Legion, 144

American Railroad Union, 93

anarchism, 63, 104–6

Anderson, Indiana: Klan in, 53

Anglo-Saxons, 2, 36, 37, 70

anti-Semitism, 210

antivice movement, 42

Arizona: Klan in, 16, 102, 172–73

Arkansas: Klan in, 15, 148, 154–55, 164, 165

Armageddon (film), 159

Asbury Park, New Jersey, 165

Asheville, North Carolina: Klan in, 112, 115, 161, 163–64, 167

Ashmore, J. W., 154

assimilation, 66, 69, 91, 119, 121, 195

Association Against the Prohibition Amendment (AAPA), 137

Athens, Georgia: Klan in, 6, 10, 29, 83, 143–44

Atlanta, Georgia: first national convention, 1922, 24, 26; Klan in, 1, 13, 15, 20–21, 25–26; national headquarters, 13, 21, 157–58. *See also* Imperial Palace

Atlantic City, New Jersey, 15, 144

"Back to the Constitution" (Stephenson), 2

Baptist Church, 147, 148

Beck, E. M., 70–71

Beisel, Nicola, 41, 42, 114, 136

Belgium, 62

Benford, Robert, 44, 135, 140

Berger, Victor, 94

bigotry, 5–6, 9–10, 85, 101–2, 113, 182. *See also* racism; white supremacy

Birmingham, Alabama: Klan in, 15, 150

Birth of a Nation, The (film), 20–21, 159

blacks: disenfranchisement of, 103; and education, 126–27, 129, 134; as enemy of Klan, 5–6, 9; stereotypes regarding, 20, 199–200; and unskilled labor, 73, 104. *See also* civil rights movement

Blackwell, Oklahoma, 165; Klan in, 165

Blau, Peter M., 40

Blee, Kathleen, 3, 6, 73, 154

bloc recruitment, 34, 37, 141

Bohn, Frank, 200–201

Bolsheviks, 72, 90, 104–6, 183, 185

Borah, William Edgar, 78, 80

Boston, Massachusetts: Klan in, 142

boycotts and boycotting: of businesses, 3, 160; of Catholic merchants, 3; and economic change, 79–84; and vocational klannishness, 79, 82–84, 106

Brothers, Elmer D., 107

Bryan, Charles W., 186

Bryan, William Jennings, 77, 89, 90–91, 184–85, 186, 194

Buckhead, Georgia, 157

Budd Dairy Company (Columbus, Ohio), 84

Buffalo, New York: Klan in, 16, 84

Bureau of Publication and Education (Klan), 158

burning crosses. *See* fiery crosses

buy American (slogan), 45

California: Klan in, 10, 15, 18, 88, 98–99, 104, 152, 153–54, 158, 162, 189

Canton, Ohio: Klan in, 94

capital: cultural, 114, 133, 136; and labor, 30, 50

capitalism: and deskilling of labor, 51–59; and economic change, 51–59; industrial, 30, 58, 65, 73, 76, 111

Carnegie, Pennsylvania: Klan in, 12, 142

Cashville, Virginia: Klan in, 165

Casper, Wyoming: Klan in, 147

Catholicism: as incompatible with democracy, 3; as infringement on religious liberty, 187; lectures about, 145; opposition to, 105; and parochial schools, 125, 131; politics of, 101; and public schools, 120, 131; vs. republican virtue, 101; and societal problems, 3; as threat to values, 133. *See also* parochial schools

Catholics: as enemy of Klan, 3, 4, 5–6, 9, 32, 200

census. *See* U.S. census

Chalmers, David, 36, 84, 88, 113, 144, 182

Chattanooga, Tennessee: Klan in, 146

Chicago: Klan in, 191

Christianity, 21, 145, 146, 147, 189

Christianson, Parly Parker, 95

churches. *See* Baptist Church; Catholicism; Methodist Church; Protestant churches

civil rights movement, 32–33, 34, 141, 200

Civil War, 53, 89, 199

Clansman, The (Dixon), 20

Clarke, Edward Young, 21, 23–24

Clarksburg, West Virginia: Klan in, 151–52

classical theories, 34, 36–38, 43, 50, 198. *See also specific theory or movement*

Clemens, Elisabeth (Liz) S., 92, 97–98, 143, 204

Cleveland, Grover, 194

Cleveland, Ohio: Klan in, 15, 27

cognitive liberation: in political process model, 43

collective action: and activism, 167; and communication networks, 160; and economic change, 63; and education, 113–16, 126; and political

mobilization, 86, 100, 181, 183; and power devaluation, 33–35, 38, 43–48, 49, 160; and recruitment, 140–41, 155, 158; and right-wing mobilization, 197–98, 199, 201; and social movements, 8, 31, 33–35, 38, 43–48, 49, 198

collective-behavior theory, 33–34, 198

collective grievances. *See* grievances

collective psychology, 8, 30–31, 201

college students: as members, 102, 165

Colorado: Klan in, 16, 99, 101, 107–8, 149

Columbus, Ohio, 84; Klan in, 15, 18, 84

communication networks: and recruitment, 141, 156–60

communism, 62, 63, 67, 72, 94–96, 104–6, 105, 185

Connecticut: Klan in, 14, 17

Convention of the Conference on Political Action, 96

conventions and conferences (Klan), 24, 26, 67, 101–2, 103, 109, 112, 115

Coolidge, Calvin, 27, 187–89, 195

Coraopolis, Pennsylvania, 148

Coughlan, Robert, 2–3

Crookston. *See* Klan movement

cultural capital, 114, 133, 136

cultural identities, 45, 48, 50, 66, 168, 175, 177–78, 181, 183, 200

cultural solidarity. *See* solidarity

Dallas, Texas: Klan in, 15, 25

Danville, Arkansas: Klan in, 154

Darwin, Charles, 131

Davis, John W., 27, 186–87, 188, 194

Dawn (Klan publication), 30

Dayton, Washington: Klan in, 153

Debs, Eugene, 93–96

Delaware: Klan in, 17

Delaware County, Indiana: Klan in, 51

demand, stimulation of: and economic change, 59, 62–69, 76–82, 85; and education, 129–33; and political mobilization, 87, 99, 106–9, 110–11, 183; and power devaluation, 38, 39–42, 39–45, 44–45, 48, 140, 183; and power dynamics, 201. See also supply restriction

democracy, 3, 90, 97–98, 108, 130

Democratic National Conventions, 27, 90, 175, 184–86

Democratic Party, 89–91, 103, 186–87, 194

democratization: and globalization, 201

Denver, Colorado: Klan in, 99

devaluation. See power devaluation

deviance and deviant action, 33–34

Dial, Nathaniel B., 81, 90

discontent, 33–35, 61, 63, 185, 198. See also grievances

disenfranchisement/disfranchisement, 92, 103, 109, 199

Dixon, Thomas: Clansman, 20

Du Bois, W. E. B., 72–73

Dumenil, Lynn, 128

Durham, North Carolina: Klan in, 152, 158

economic change: and activism, 172–74; and African American migration, 57–58, 69–73, 92; and boycotting strategy, 79, 82–84; and capitalism, 51–59; and collective action, 63; and elite, 63; and labor force, 51–59, 73–76; and power devaluation, 49–50, 58–59, 62–63, 66, 68, 74, 85; redefining mar-

kets along cultural lines, 49–85, 209–12n; and vocational klannishness, 79, 82–84, 106. See also agricultural depression; demand, stimulation of; grievances; supply restriction

education: and blacks, 126–27, 129, 134; and collective action, 113–16, 126; college enrollment, 123–24; framing of, 126, 129, 130; high school graduates, 122–23, 165; and middle class, 122; and power devaluation, 113–16, 122–24, 127–29, 133–38, 174; and stimulation of demand, 129–33; and supply restriction, 124–29. See also illiteracy; parochial schools; public schools

El Dorado, Arkansas: Klan in, 164

Elgin, Oregon: Klan in, 158

elite: as dominant group, 185; and economic changes, 63; industrial, 53, 64–65, 136; as Klan members, 29, 47; and laborers, 98; vs. masses, 41; and prohibition, 137

Elks, 144

Emergency Tariff Act of 1921, 60–61

Emerson, Richard, 40

emigrants, 127

ethnic competition theory, 8–9, 171, 198–99

Evans, Hiram Wesley, Imperial Wizard: appears on cover of Time, 27, 28; on black immigrants, 70; on Catholicism, 101–2; on Democratic Party, 194–95; on economic transitions, 63–64; on education and schools, 112, 113, 115, 125–26, 131, 133; financial growth of Klan under direction of, 19, 25, 157–58; on growth of Klan in Indiana, 1–2;

as guest pastor, 148; on immigration restriction, 65–67; on industrial capitalism, 30; Intelligence Bureau under direct control of, 160; on Klan, 27, 29, 143, 182, 185–86, 187, 188–89, 191; vs. LaFollette, 185–86; leads coup against Simmons, 24; named Imperial Wizard, 1922, 24; and national elections, 27–29; on paternalism, 103; on presidential election, 194–95; vs. Stephenson, 27, 156–57, 191; as Texas resident, 13; on unskilled labor in rural areas, 65; on violence, 161, 162

Evansville, Indiana: Klan in, 159
evolution, theory of, 131
Exalted Cyclops, 103, 146
exchange markets: and power devaluation, 39–43, 134, 139, 174

factionalism, 24, 40, 91, 95, 142, 157, 181–82, 184
families: and labor force participation, 73–76
Farmer-Labor Party, 14, 26, 94–96, 172–73, 176, 177
Farmers' Alliance, 89
fascism, 62–63, 87
Federal Reserve Bank, 81
Ferguson, Jim, 25
Fiery Cross (Klan newspaper), 1, 68, 73, 78, 79, 81, 135, 173, 187
Fiery Cross Club (University of Kansas), 165
fiery crosses, 2, 148–53
Florida: Klan in, 16, 147, 164
Fordney-McCumber Tariff Act of 1922, 60–61
Foster, William Z., 96
frame alignment theory, 43, 181

frame extension, 135
framing: of economic grievances, 62–66, 76, 77, 85–87, 172, 179; of education, 126, 129, 130; and social movements, 39, 43–45, 48, 63, 79, 100, 113–15, 126, 134, 140, 155, 158, 167, 198, 199. *See also* recruitment
Frank, Leo, 20, 21
fraternal organizations: as model for recruitment, 19, 21, 29–30, 37, 88, 140–45, 149, 197. *See also* specific organization(s)
Freemasons, 19
Fresno, California: Klan in, 154, 162
fusionists, 89

Gainesville, Georgia, 152
Gaventa, John, 9
geographic diffusion: of activism, 7, 10–18, 181
Georgia: Kan in, 1, 6, 10, 11, 13, 15, 20, 21, 25–26, 29, 83–84, 143–44, 152, 157, 186
Gifford, Fred L.: Grand Dragon of Oregon, 26
globalization: and democratization, 201
Goffman, Erving, 43
Goldberg, Robert Alan, 29
Grange, The, 89
Grant, Madison: *Passing of the Great Race,* 37
Gravelly, Arkansas: Klan in, 154
Great Depression, 51, 195
Gresham's law, 182
grievances: collective, 33–38, 44, 47, 66, 142, 156; and economic change, 62–66, 76, 77, 85–87, 172, 179; national, articulated by Klan, 7; and power devaluation, 33–35;

and recruitment, 30; and social
movements, 33–35, 38. *See also* agricultural depression; discontent
Griffith, D. W.: *Birth of a Nation*
(film), 20–21, 159
group identity, 9
Gurr, Ted Robert, 33–34

Hamilton County, Kentucky: Klan
in, 151
Harding, Warren, 60, 173
Hardwick, Thomas W., 26
heterogeneity, 171, 198–99. *See also*
homogeneity
Hillquit, Morris, 94
Hofstadter, Richard, 36, 113
home rule, 20. *See also* martial law
homogeneity, 8, 84, 140, 171,
178, 180, 186, 198. *See also*
heterogeneity
hooded empire, 26
hoods, 2–3, 9, 147, 161, 168, 196, 199.
See also masks
Hoover, Herbert, 195
Hot Springs, Arkansas: Klan in, 148
Howard County, Indiana: Klan in,
3–4
Howell, Michigan: Klan in, 12

Idaho: Klan in, 17, 78
identity. *See* cultural identities; group
identity
Illinois: Klan in, 1, 2, 7, 13, 15, 30,
159, 177, 191
illiteracy, 5, 65, 75, 115–16, 119,
125–26, 127
immigrants and immigration: as
enemy of Klan, 5–6, 9, 200; and
racial and ethnic conflict, 10;
stereotypes regarding, 199; and
unskilled laborers, 65

immigration restriction, 65–67, 76, 91,
101, 106, 110, 127–29, 134, 187
Imperial Night-Hawk (Klan national
newspaper), 5–6, 19, 25, 30, 32,
49, 196, 204; and activism, 10–13,
169; on economic change, 63, 67,
69–70, 72, 74–75, 77–78, 83–84;
on education, 112, 115, 128; events
reported in (table), 15–17; finances
published in, 25; and geographical
variation in activities, 10–13,
169; mailing address, 84; mission
and purpose of, 11; name change,
260n26; on politics, 86, 100, 104,
107, 108, 180, 186–88; and Prohibition, 134, 136; and recruitment,
139, 142, 144–51, 153–54, 157–59,
162–65
Imperial Palace (Atlanta, Georgia), 11,
24, 144, 157
Indiana: Klan in, 1–13, 15, 18, 27,
51–53, 68, 73, 78, 79, 81, 93,
102–3, 132, 135, 144–45, 150,
152–56, 159, 162–65, 167–70, 173,
177, 187, 191–93
Indianapolis, Indiana: Klan in, 15, 18,
27, 153, 162, 164–65
industrial capitalism. *See* capitalism
industrial elite. *See* elite
industrialism and industrialists, 30,
36, 54, 55, 58, 66, 67, 69, 84–85,
181
industrialization, 53, 54, 122
Industrial Revolution, 53
Industrial Workers of the World
(IWW), 26, 104–5
Inglewood, California: Klan in, 162
initiation (naturalization) ceremonies,
12, 149–50, 152, 159, 165, 169
institutionalized group identity, 9
Intelligence Bureau (Klan), 160

intimidation, 23, 62, 71, 166, 196, 199–200, 234

intolerance, 23, 131, 161

Invisible Empire, 2, 6, 27, 78, 82–83, 84, 97, 109, 113, 144, 182

Iowa: Klan in, 16

IWW. *See* Industrial Workers of the World

Jackman, Mary, 9, 71, 199

Jackson, Ed, 192

Jackson, Kenneth, 20, 36, 113, 168, 182

Jacksonville, Florida: Klan in, 16, 147, 164

Jefferson, Thomas, 161–62

Jeffersonian ideals, 64

Jews: as enemy of Klan, 9, 32, 57, 82–84, 106, 153, 171, 176, 178

job market. *See* labor force

Johnson, Guy B., 200–201

Judaism, 105

Kansas: Klan in, 15, 78, 137–38, 147, 165

Kansas City, Missouri: Klan in, 15, 67, 103, 150

Kentucky: Klan in, 1, 16, 147–48, 151, 152, 189

Kirksville, Missouri: Klan in, 153

Kiwanis, 144

Klankraft, 199

Klan Kreed, 148

Klan nation. *See* Ku Klux Klan: as national movement

Klan Oath, 104–5

Klansman's Creed, 30, 50, 82

Klanswomen, 2, 3, 10, 13, 25, 36–37, 93, 115, 141, 142, 152, 154, 158–60, 182, 188. *See also* Women's Ku Klux Klan

Klanswomen's Creed, 74–75

Klaverns (Klan meeting halls), 149, 154

Kleagles, recruiters, 21

Klonvocations, 24, 67, 103. *See also* conventions and conferences

Kloran, 19–20, 23

Knights of Columbus, 153–54

Knights of Pythias, 19, 145

Knights of the Ku Klux Klan, 11, 19, 22, 71, 74, 107, 113, 146–47, 158–59, 163–64, 165, 167, 185–86

Kokomo, Indiana: Klan in, 1–4, 9, 51, 79

Kourier (Klan magazine), 73–74, 180, 188–89, 193–95, 206n26

Ku Klux Klan: cities with no reported activity, 14; as civic asset, 163–65; first annual meeting of state Grand Dragons, 161; first annual national convention Atlanta, 24, 26; as military organization, 143; as national movement, 1–18, 21–23, 205–6nn; organizational framework for, 19; revival of, 19–31, 206–7nn; self-preservation of, 82. *See also* hooded empire; Invisible Empire; Knights of the Ku Klux Klan; Women's Ku Klux Klan

Ku Klux Klan, The (Mecklin), 5, 36, 182

Labaree, David F., 122

labor: and capital, 30, 50

laborers: and elite, 98; vs. industrialists, 30

labor force: deskilling of and capitalism, 51–59; and economic change, 51–59; as members of Klan, 29–30; traditional families, participation in, 73–76

labor radicalism: Klan hostile toward, 30
LaFollette, Robert, 27, 78, 81, 95–97, 184–88
Lanier University, 19, 23
Law Enforcement Committee (Klan), 143–44
left, the. *See* political left
Lenoir City, Tennessee, 152
Library of Congress, 204; *Kloran* in, 20, 23
Link, Arthur, 53–54, 98
Lipset, Seymour Martin, 36, 113, 182
Lipsitz, George, 9
Lisbon, Ohio: Klan in, 165
Logtown, Mississippi: Klan in, 18
Loogootie, Indiana: Klan in, 144–45
Lorain, Ohio: Klan in, 158
Los Angeles: Klan in, 162
Louisiana: Klan in, 16, 103, 153, 158, 160
Lynd, Robert and Helen: *Middletown,* 51–53, 122

MacLean, Nancy, 6, 83, 143–44
Mahoney, William, 95–96
Maine: Klan in, 14, 17, 27, 189
Marion, Indiana: Klan in, 150
martial law, 26, 160. *See also* home rule
Marxism, 93, 114
Maryland: Klan in, 16
masks, 26. *See also* hoods
Mason-Dixon Line, 103
Masons, 21, 29–30, 115, 143, 144–45
Massachusetts: Klan in, 14, 17, 92, 142
mass society theory, 33–34, 198
Mayfield, Earle B., 25, 81
McAdam, Doug, 34, 43
McAdoo, William Gibbs, 186

McCormick, Richard, 53–54, 98
Mecklin, John Moffat: *The Ku Klux Klan,* 5, 36, 182
members and membership: attributes of, 29–31; college students, 102, 165; economic motives and benefits of, 30; elite underrepresented, 29; fees and costs, 21, 142; industrial proletariat underrepresented, 29; middle class, 5, 6, 29–30; and rural communities, 13, 19, 36, 62, 66, 68, 72, 77–78, 87–89, 113, 173; socioeconomic diversity of, 29. *See also* recruitment
Methodist Church, 139, 144–45, 147, 148
Michigan: Klan in, 1, 12, 15, 129
microeconomics, 39, 44–45, 66, 87, 100, 140
middle class: and education, 122; Klan as hysteria of, 5; as Klan members, 5, 6, 29–30; and republican ideology of Klan, 6, 30
Middletown (Lynd), 51–53, 122
Milwaukee, Wisconsin: Klan in, 159
Minnesota: Klan in, 14, 17, 94–95, 148, 177, 189
Mississippi: Klan in, 16, 18
Missouri: Klan in, 15, 67, 103, 150, 153, 169
Modesto, California: Klan in, 18, 158
Monroe, Louisiana, 103; Klan in, 103
Montana: Klan in, 17, 96
Moore, Barrington, 89
Moore, Leonard, 36, 37
Morgantown, West Virginia: Klan in, 159
Muncie, Indiana: Klan in, 51–53, 122, 155–56
Mussolini, Benito, 63, 210n29

National Education Association (NEA), 125
"National Objective," 189, 191
National Unity League, 84
nativism and nativity, 3–5, 9, 13, 14, 29–30, 36, 37, 50–51, 57–59, 85, 109–11, 113, 121, 132–33, 141–42, 166–68, 170–72, 174–76, 178–80, 199, 201
naturalization ceremonies. *See* initiation (naturalization) ceremonies
Nazi Party, 62, 201
NEA. *See* National Education Association
Nebraska: Klan in, 17, 91
Nevada: Klan in, 17
New Castle, Indiana: Klan in, 132; Klanswomen in, 93
New Hampshire: Klan in, 14, 17
New Jersey: Klan in, 13, 15, 142, 144, 148, 154, 165, 186–87
New Mexico: Klan in, 17, 102
New Philadelphia, Ohio: Klan in, 154
New York (city and state): Klan in, 13–14, 16, 27, 84, 96, 133, 170, 185
New York Times, 3, 128
New York World, 21–22, 23, 161
Nineteenth Amendment, 91, 99, 109, 171
Non-Partisan League, 94
Nordic colonizers, 37
Norris, George, 91
North Carolina: Klan in, 13, 17, 112, 115, 152, 158, 159, 161, 163–64, 165, 167
North Dakota: Klan in, 14, 17, 173, 177
nouveaux riche, 42

Oakland, California: Klan in, 10, 15, 88, 98–99

Oberholtzer, Madge, 191–92
Oberschall, Anthony, 34, 141, 203
Odd Fellows, 19, 29–30, 142–43, 144–45
Ohio: Klan in, 1, 2, 7, 15, 18, 27, 84, 94, 115, 133, 135, 139, 145, 147–48, 154, 158, 163, 165, 177
Oklahoma: Klan in, 15, 26, 145, 160, 164, 165
Olson, Mancur, 141
"Onward Christian Soldiers" (anthem), 143, 149
Orbinson, Charles J., Judge, 167
Oregon: Klan in, 5, 16, 25, 26, 99, 115, 129, 148, 158

parochial schools, 116–34, 174. *See also* education; public schools
Passing of the Great Race, The (Grant), 37
paternalism, 54, 69–73, 103, 109, 185
patriotism, 2, 45, 64, 101, 104, 109, 114, 121, 130, 134
Pawnee, Texas: Klan in, 153
Peddy, George, 25
Pekin, Illinois: Klan in, 159
Pekin Daily Times (Klan-owned town newspaper), 159
Pennsylvania: Klan in, 7, 12, 14, 15, 125, 142, 147, 148, 161
People's Party, 89. *See also* populism
Perth Amboy, New Jersey: Klan in, 142
Phagan, Mary: rape and murder of, 20
Pierce, Walter, 26, 115, 148
Pisgah, Alabama: Klan in, 144
political left, 62, 92–97, 103–6, 160, 177, 203
political opportunity theory, 8, 35, 37, 43, 45–46, 160–63, 166, 197

political process model, 43, 145–46

politics: and activism, 170–72; attacking the left, 103–6; and candidate support and endorsements, 4, 25–29; of Catholicism, 10; challenge from the left, 92–97; and collective action, 86, 100, 181, 183; and expansion of suffrage, 91–92; exploiting openings, 160–63; involvement and participation in, 7, 25–29, 86–111, 180–95; and justice, 1; machine politics, 97–99; members elected to U.S. Senate, 25; and mobilization, 86–111, 212–14n; and national elections, 27–29, 180–95, 219–20n; and power devaluation, 45–47, 85, 87, 97, 99–100, 106, 182–83; and recruitment, 31, 160–63; relation to party politics, 183–87; during revival period, 25–29; role of Klan in, 2; and stimulation of demand, 87, 99, 106–9, 110–11, 183; and supply restriction, 99–103. *See also* political left; right-wing movements; specific political movements and parties

populism, 6, 20, 77–78, 79, 85, 87, 89, 90–91, 93–94, 161–62, 174

Portland, Oregon: Klan in, 16, 17, 26, 99

Portuguese Republic: collapse of, 89

power devaluation, 8, 18, 31, 197–99, 201, 203, 207–9n; and activism, 167–71, 174–76, 178–79; and classical theory, 36–38; and collective action, 33–35, 38, 43–48, 49, 160; and economic change, 49–50, 58–59, 62–63, 66, 68, 74, 85; and education, 113–16, 122–24, 127–29, 133–38, 174; and exchange markets, 39–43, 134, 139, 174; and grievances, 33–35; interpretive processes, 42–45; multiple sources of, 41–42; organizational resources, 45–47; and political mobilization, 45–47, 85, 87, 97, 99–100, 106, 182–83; and purchasing power, 39–45; and recruitment, 139–40, 160, 166; and resource mobilization theory, 197; and right-wing mobilization, 8–9, 31, 32–48, 49, 87, 139–40, 182–83, 197; and social change, 36, 43–44, 46; and social movements, 8, 32–48; and solidarity, 45; sources of, 41–42, 133–38; status-based, 7, 122–24, 133–38

power-devaluation model, 207–9n; and ethnic-competition theory, 198–99; and geographic diffusion of activism, 18; political, 97, 99, 106, 182–83; and right-wing mobilization, 8, 31, 32–33, 38–39, 182–83; and social movements, 8, 38–39, 47–48; status-based, 174–75; three key components, 39

power dynamics, 201

Princeton, Kentucky: Klan in, 147–48

Princeton University, 154

Progressive party, 27, 77–78, 90, 91, 95, 96, 134, 184, 185

progressivism, 6, 32–33, 54, 76, 87, 93, 128, 174, 188

Prohibition, 23–24, 78, 114, 134–41, 174–79, 188

proletariat, 29–30, 65, 99, 122, 129, 183, 185

Propagation Department (Klan), 21, 23–24

Protestant churches: reciprocal ties between Klan, 3, 145–49; and recruitment, 21, 140–49

protests: collective, 33; social, 33–34

psychology, collective, 8, 30–31, 201

public schools: defense of, 115–21; high school graduates, 122–23, 165; and power devaluation, 122–24, 174; role of in society, 121; and stimulation of demand, 129–33; student enrollment in, 118, 176, 179; and supply restriction, 124–29; total expenditures per pupil, 117. *See also* education; parochial schools

Pueblo, Colorado: Klan in, 149

purchasing power, 7, 61, 100, 122–23, 128, 183; and power devaluation, 39–45

Raab, Earl, 36, 113, 182

race: and construction off boundaries, 3–4; as cultural construct, 9; and group identity, 9

race suicide, 201

racism, 9–10, 113, 199. *See also* bigotry; white supremacy

radicalism, 5, 30, 74, 96–97, 109

Raleigh, North Carolina: Klan in, 159

Reconstruction-era, 19–20, 152, 160

Reconstruction Klan Prescript (1867), 19

recruitment, 139–66, 216–18n; bloc, 34, 37, 141; ceremonies, parades, and social gatherings, 149–50; and civic assets, 163–65; and collective action, 140–41, 155, 158;

communication networks, 141, 156–60; and framing, 5, 6, 31, 43–45, 48–50, 124, 135, 140, 155, 158, 160, 166–68, 170, 171, 173, 174, 181, 183, 198; and grievances, 30; and Klan as civic asset, 163–65; opportunistic strategy of, 29; organizational models, 140–45; and political opportunities, 31, 160–63; and power devaluation, 139–40, 160, 166; reciprocal ties with Protestant churches, 21, 140–49. *See also* members and membership

religion: and construction off boundaries, 3–4; intolerance, 23, 131. *See also* Catholicism; *specific churches*

republican ideology, 6, 30, 64, 67, 82, 92–93, 101, 106, 124–25

Republican National Conventions, 27, 28, 95, 187

Republican Party, 27, 54, 89–90, 95, 103, 184, 195

resource mobilization theory, 8, 34–35, 37, 43, 45–46, 141, 145–46, 157, 166, 197

Rexists (Belgium), 62

Rhode Island: Klan in, 14, 17, 92

Rhomberg, Chris, 88, 98

right wing movements, 1911–201, 220n; and collective action, 197–98, 199, 201; consequences of, 47–48; economic incentives, 8; and extremism, 201; political incentives, 8, 182–83; and power devaluation, 8–9, 31, 32–48, 49, 87, 139–40, 182–83, 197; and social movements, 31, 32–48; and social theory, 9; and status-based interests, 8

Rochford, E. Burke, Jr., 135
Roman Catholic Church, 66, 106–7
Roosevelt, Theodore, 78
Russian revolution, 94, 103–4
Ryant, Carl G., 58–59

San Antonio, Texas: Klan in, 155
Sanders, Elizabeth, 88, 91
Santa Monica, California: Klan in, 152
schools. *See* parochial schools; public
    schools
Schwartzman, Kathleen, 89
Scottish Rites Masons, 115
Sea Girt, New Jersey, 186–87
Seattle, Washington: Klan in, 151
secularism, 104, 131
self-determination, 2
Sherwood, Tennessee, 162–63; Klan
    in, 162–63
Shreveport, Louisiana, 153, 158
Shriner's Circus, 145
Shuler, Allen C., 147
Silver Party, 89
Simmel, Georg, 40–41
Simmons, William Joseph, Colonel:
    coup against and banishment from
    Klan, 24–25, 156–57; as founder
    and Imperial Wizard of second
    Klan, 1915, 19–21, 193; fraternal
    organizations experience, 143;
    Kloran, 19–20; on movement's
    opponents, 23; testifies before con-
    gressional hearing, 22–23, 161
Sims, Walter A., 26
slavery, 64–65, 69–70, 89, 199
Smelser, Neil, 33
Smith, Al, 133, 185, 186, 194–95
Smith-Towner Bill, 128
Snow, David, 43, 44, 135, 140
social atomization, 36

social change, 8, 9, 31–36, 43–44, 46,
    63, 168, 180; and power devalua-
    tion, 36, 43–44, 46
social equality, 72
Social Forces (journal), 200
socialism, 62, 90, 94, 105
Socialist party, 26, 62, 91, 93–96, 160,
    172, 176, 177, 185
social movement theory: and collective
    action, 8, 31, 33–35, 38, 43–48,
    49, 198; and deviance, 33–34; and
    framing of, 39, 43–45, 48, 63, 79,
    100, 113–15, 126, 134, 140, 155,
    158, 167, 198, 199; and grievances,
    33–35, 38; historical development
    of, 33; and political rebellion,
    33–34; and power devaluation, 8,
    32–48; and right-wing mobiliza-
    tion, 31, 32–48; and social policy,
    9. *See also* political opportunity
    theory; resource mobilization
    theory
social protest, 33–34
sociologists, 5, 32
solidarity: cultural, 66, 68, 82, 85;
    and identity, 200; in-group, 34, 48,
    183; and national elections, 189;
    and power devaluation, 45
South Bend, Indiana: Klan in, 12, 15,
    102
South Carolina: Klan in, 16, 71, 90,
    91, 107, 137
South Dakota: Klan in, 14, 17, 173,
    177
Southern Publicity Association (Clarke
    and Tyler), 21
Sovietism, 105, 106
SPAM (Study of Politics and Move-
    ments), 204
Stephenson, D. C.: appointed Grand

Dragon of Indiana, 2; "Back to the Constitution," 2; convicted of murder, 191–92; on currency and credit, 4; vs. Evans, 27, 156–57, 191; on farmers' grievances, 79; and Indiana politics, 27; leads coup against Simmons, 24; on world war, 4–5

Sterling-Reed Bill, 75, 128–29

Stigler, Oklahoma: Klan in, 145

stimulation of demand. *See* demand, stimulation of

Stockton, California: Klan in, 153–54

Study of Politics and Movements (SPAM), 204

suffrage, 40, 74, 91–92, 99, 109, 139, 171, 177, 200

Sunday, Billy, 148

supply restriction: and economic change, 66–69; and education, 124–29; and national political mobilization, 99–103. *See also* demand, stimulation of

Tammany Hall, 90–91

Tarrow, Sidney, 35, 47

Tennessee: Klan in, 16, 146, 152, 162–63

Terre Haute, Indiana: Klan in, 152

Texas: Klan in, 13, 15, 24, 25, 69, 102, 135, 136, 153, 155, 159, 164

theory of evolution, 131

Tilden, Samuel, 194

Time magazine: Evans on cover, 27, 28

Tolerance (National Unity League), 84

Tolnay, Stewart, 70, 71

Towner-Sterling Bill, 128

Trade with a Klansman (TWK), 3–4

"Traitor Within, A" (Klan film), 156

Trenton, New Jersey: Klan in, 15, 154

Trotsky, Leon, 104

Tullahoma, Tennessee, 152

TWK. *See* Trade with a Klansman

Tyack, David, 120

Tyler, Elizabeth, 21, 23–24

universalism, 105

University of Kansas, 165

University of North Carolina, 165, 203

University of Notre Dame, 102

urbanization, 117

U.S. census, 4, 13, 55, 57–58, 116, 119, 170–71, 173–74

U.S. Constitution, 2, 4, 5, 102, 105, 107, 115, 121, 163, 187

U.S. Dept. of Commerce, 14, 56, 57, 60, 61, 118

U.S. Federal Trade Commission, 58

U.S. House: Committee investigation and hearing (1922), 22–23, 24, 161

U.S. Senate, 25, 80–81, 94–95, 194

Utah: Klan in, 17, 95

Valparaiso University, 107

Vatican, 126, 183, 194

Vermont: Klan in, 14, 17

vigilantism, 10, 51, 135, 136, 161, 201

violence, 9, 21–22, 26, 62–63, 69–72, 114, 142, 160–63, 166, 187, 196–97, 199–200

Virginia: Klan in, 13, 16, 165

vocational klannishness: and economic change, 79, 82–84, 106

Volstead Act, 135–36, 137, 175, 193

Walker, Clifford, 26

Wallace, George, 200

Walton, Jack, 26, 160

Washington (state): Klan in, 16, 95, 151, 153

Washington, Booker T., 103

Washington, D.C.: Klan in, 158, 190

Watson, Thomas E., 20

Weber, Max, 41

Wellsville, Ohio: Klan in, 139, 147–48

West Virginia: Klan in, 16, 147, 148, 151–52, 159, 164

Wheeler, Burton, 96

white separatism, 9, 10, 147, 198

white supremacy, 6, 8–9, 10, 70, 72–73, 85, 113, 142, 147, 160–61. *See also* bigotry; racism

Wichita Falls, Kansas, 15, 147

Wilson, Woodrow, 54, 60, 90–91, 186, 194

Wisconsin: Klan in, 17, 27, 78, 95, 159, 185

WKKK. *See* Women's Ku Klux Klan

Wobblies. *See* Industrial Workers of the World

women. *See* suffrage; Klanswomen; Women's Ku Klux Klan

Women's Ku Klux Klan (WKKK), 3, 6, 25, 73–74, 109, 152, 165, 171–72. *See also* Klanswomen

women's rights, 73, 109

Woodmen of the World, 19

Woodward, James G., 26

Worden, Steven, 135

workers. *See* labor force

World War I, 4, 54, 55, 79, 84–85, 93, 94, 121, 125, 127

Wyoming: Klan in, 17, 95, 147, 158

xenophobia, 6, 113

Yell County, Arkansas: Klan in, 154

Youngstown, Ohio: Klan in, 15, 163

RORY MCVEIGH is associate professor of sociology at the University of Notre Dame.

Social Movements, Protest, and Contention

Series Editor: Bert Klandermans, Free University, Amsterdam

Associate Editors: Ron R. Aminzade, University of Minnesota
David S. Meyer, University of California, Irvine
Verta A. Taylor, University of California, Santa Barbara

Volume 32   Rory McVeigh, *The Rise of the Ku Klux Klan: Right-Wing Movements and National Politics*

Volume 31   Tina Fetner, *How the Religious Right Shaped Lesbian and Gay Activism*

Volume 30   Jo Reger, Rachel L. Einwohner, and Daniel J. Myers, editors, *Identity Work in Social Movements*

Volume 29   Paul D. Almeida, *Waves of Protest: Popular Struggle in El Salvador, 1925–2005*

Volume 28   Heidi J. Swarts, *Organizing Urban America: Secular and Faith-based Progressive Movements*

Volume 27   Ethel C. Brooks, *Unraveling the Garment Industry: Transnational Organizing and Women's Work*

Volume 26   Donatella della Porta, Massimiliano Andretta, Lorenzo Mosca, and Herbert Reiter, *Globalization from Below: Transnational Activists and Protest Networks*

Volume 25   Ruud Koopmans, Paul Statham, Marco Giugni, and Florence Passy, *Contested Citizenship: Immigration and Cultural Diversity in Europe*

Volume 24   David Croteau, William Hoynes, and Charlotte Ryan, editors, *Rhyming Hope and History: Activists, Academics, and Social Movement Scholarship*

Volume 23   David S. Meyer, Valerie Jenness, and Helen Ingram, editors, *Routing the Opposition: Social Movements, Public Policy, and Democracy*

Volume 22   Kurt Schock, *Unarmed Insurrections: People Power Movements in Nondemocracies*

Volume 21   Christian Davenport, Hank Johnston, and Carol Mueller, editors, *Repression and Mobilization*

Volume 20   Nicole C. Raeburn, *Changing Corporate America from Inside Out: Lesbian and Gay Workplace Rights*

Volume 19   Vincent J. Roscigno and William F. Danaher, *The Voice of Southern Labor: Radio, Music, and Textile Strikes, 1929–1934*

Volume 18   Maryjane Osa, *Solidarity and Contention: Networks of Polish Opposition*

Volume 17   Mary Margaret Fonow, *Union Women: Forging Feminism in the United Steelworkers of America*

Volume 16   Bert Klandermans and Suzanne Staggenborg, editors, *Methods of Social Movement Research*

Volume 15   Sharon Kurtz, *Workplace Justice: Organizing Multi-Identity Movements*

Volume 14   Sanjeev Khagram, James V. Riker, and Kathryn Sikkink, editors, *Restructuring World Politics: Transnational Social Movements, Networks, and Norms*

Volume 13   Sheldon Stryker, Timothy J. Owens, and Robert W. White, editors, *Self, Identity, and Social Movements*

Volume 12   Byron A. Miller, *Geography and Social Movements: Comparing Antinuclear Activism in the Boston Area*

Volume 11   Mona N. Younis, *Liberation and Democratization: The South African and Palestinian National Movements*

Volume 10   Marco Giugni, Doug McAdam, and Charles Tilly, editors, *How Social Movements Matter*

Volume 9   Cynthia Irvin, *Militant Nationalism: Between Movement and Party in Ireland and the Basque Country*

Volume 8   Raka Ray, *Fields of Protest: Women's Movements in India*

Volume 7   Michael P. Hanagan, Leslie Page Moch, and Wayne te Brake, editors, *Challenging Authority: The Historical Study of Contentious Politics*

Volume 6   Donatella della Porta and Herbert Reiter, editors, *Policing Protest: The Control of Mass Demonstrations in Western Democracies*

Volume 5   Hanspeter Kriesi, Ruud Koopmans, Jan Willem Dyvendak, and Marco G. Giugni, editors, *New Social Movements in Western Europe: A Comparative Analysis*

Volume 4   Hank Johnston and Bert Klandermans, editors, *Social Movements and Culture*

Volume 3   J. Craig Jenkins and Bert Klandermans, editors, *The Politics of Social Protest: Comparative Perspectives on States and Social Movements*

Volume 2   John Foran, editor, *A Century of Revolution: Social Movements in Iran*

Volume 1   Andrew Szasz, *EcoPopulism: Toxic Waste and the Movement for Environmental Justice*